To the Diamond Mountains

ASIA/PACIFIC/PERSPECTIVES
Series Editor: Mark Selden

Crime, Punishment, and Policing in China
  edited by Børge Bakken
Woman, Man, Bangkok: Love, Sex, and Popular Culture in Thailand
  by Scot Barmé
Making the Foreign Serve China: Managing Foreigners in the People's Republic
  by Anne-Marie Brady
Marketing Dictatorship: Propaganda and Thought Work in China
  by Anne-Marie Brady
Collaborative Nationalism: The Politics of Friendship on China's Mongolian Frontier
  by Uradyn E. Bulag
The Mongols at China's Edge: History and the Politics of National Unity
  by Uradyn E. Bulag
Transforming Asian Socialism: China and Vietnam Compared
  edited by Anita Chan, Benedict J. Tria Kerkvliet, and Jonathan Unger
China's Great Proletarian Cultural Revolution: Master Narratives and Post-Mao Counternarratives
  edited by Woei Lien Chong
North China at War: The Social Ecology of Revolution, 1937–1945
  edited by Feng Chongyi and David S. G. Goodman
Little Friends: Children's Film and Media Culture in China
  by Stephanie Hemelryk Donald
Gender in Motion: Divisions of Labor and Cultural Change in Late Imperial and Modern China
  edited by Bryna Goodman and Wendy Larson
Social and Political Change in Revolutionary China: The Taihang Base Area in the War of Resistance to Japan, 1937–1945
  by David S. G. Goodman
Islands of Discontent: Okinawan Responses to Japanese and American Power
  edited by Laura Hein and Mark Selden
Women in Early Imperial China, Second Edition
  by Bret Hinsch
Civil Justice in China: Past and Present
  by Philip C. C. Huang
Local Democracy and Development: The Kerala People's Campaign for Decentralized Planning
  by T. M. Thomas Isaac with Richard W. Franke

To the Diamond Mountains

A Hundred-Year Journey through China and Korea

Tessa Morris-Suzuki

ROWMAN & LITTLEFIELD PUBLISHERS, INC.
Lanham • Boulder • New York • Toronto • Plymouth, UK

Published by Rowman & Littlefield Publishers, Inc.
A wholly owned subsidary of The Rowman & Littlefield Publishing Group, Inc.
4501 Forbes Boulevard, Suite 200, Lanham, Maryland 20706
http://www.rowmanlittlefield.com

Estover Road, Plymouth PL6 7PY, United Kingdom

British Library Cataloguing in Publication Information Available

Library of Congress Cataloging-in-Publication Data

Morris-Suzuki, Tessa.
   To the Diamond Mountains : a hundred-year journey through China and Korea /
Tessa Morris-Suzuki.
      p. cm. — (Asia/Pacific/perspectives)
   Includes bibliographical references.
   ISBN 978-1-4422-0503-1 (cloth : alk. paper) — ISBN 978-1-4422-0505-5 (electronic)
   1. China—Description and travel. 2. Diamond Mountains (Korea)—Description and
travel. 3. Korea (North)—Description and travel. 4. Korea (South)—Description and
travel. 5. Morris-Suzuki, Tessa—Travel—China. 6. Morris-Suzuki, Tessa—Travel—
Korea. 7. Kemp, E. G. (Emily Georgiana), b. 1860—Travel. 8. China—Social life and
customs. 9. Korea (North)—Social life and customs. 10. Korea (South)—Social life
and customs. I. Title.
   DS712.M673 2010
   915.104'6—dc22
                                                                    2010023685

Printed in the United States of America

To my three sisters

Contents

Illustrations

Acknowledgments

The kindness and support of many people made this journey possible. I cannot possibly name all those to whom I owe a debt of gratitude, but my particularly deep thanks go to my traveling companions Emma Campbell and Sandy Morris, and also to Ochiai Katsuto who joined us for part of the route. I am deeply grateful to the companies who arranged our travel and to the guides who helped us in China and Korea, and to Sissi Chen and others at China Highlights Tours, who assisted us in arranging our visit to the Thousand Peaks.

My first introduction to Emily Kemp came about through the kind offices of Barbara and Sally Burdon, in whose wonderful Asia Bookroom (surely one of the world's most delightful bookshops) I found *The Face of Manchuria, Korea and Chinese Turkestan*. My profound thanks also go to Leonid Petrov of the University of Sydney, for his support and advice throughout the writing of this book; to Kim Yeonghwan of the Peace Museum, Seoul, for his help and encouragement; to Jeong Ho-Seok of the University of Tokyo for his helpful advice; and to Mayumi Shinozaki and other staff members of the National Library of Australia for their assistance in finding obscure materials.

A Note on Romanization

The process of romanizing Korean words and names in a book that deals with both past and present, and both North and South Korea, is a complex one. In this text, I have chosen to follow the system of romanization and capitalization recommended by the government of the Republic of Korea (South Korea), except in the case of North Korean place names and specifically North Korean terms, where I use the standard form of romanization applied in the Democratic People's Republic of Korea (North Korea). Personal names are romanized using the form preferred by the persons themselves. The original romanization is retained in works cited in the endnotes. Chinese words and names are romanized using the Hanyu Pinyin system.

East Asian names are given in the normal East Asian order: family name first. In some cases, certain minor personal details of people encountered on the journey have been altered to protect privacy.

Emily Kemp's route through Manchuria and Korea

Prologue
May Day on the Yalu River

Walking the Dog

With red flag billowing bravely from its stern, our boat moves away from the Chinese shore and out into the wide, opaque waters of the Yalu River, which marks the border between China and North Korea. The passengers crowd the boat's rail, and my two traveling companions and I join them, eagerly straining our eyes toward the pale outlines of the North Korean side. A jagged range of hills rises against the sky, blue-gray at first, but tinged with russet as our boat draws nearer. They are bare hills, empty of trees, their bleak slopes marked only by the terraces of dry fields.

"Look," cries one of the passengers, "a soldier!"

I can just pick out the diminutive figure with weapon slung over one shoulder, wobbling by bicycle down a track on the opposite bank. Little by little, as the shore approaches, other people appear, and then houses. White-washed farm cottages cluster tightly in a valley that runs down to the water's edge. Each building has an identical gray-tiled roof with its ridge picked out in white paint, square windows, and a door leading out into a walled court-yard: a cottage from a child's drawing.

Villagers move like ants across the distant fields, tilling the earth with ox-drawn ploughs. A woman and a little girl crouch on a strip of shingle by the water's edge, gathering something—plants or shellfish, perhaps. It is May Day. On the Chinese side of the Yalu, the road is jammed solid with traffic, as China's new generation of car owners heads for scenic picnic spots along the river. But there are neither motor vehicles nor any obvious signs of celebrations to be seen in the village on the Korean side.

As we come closer, the woman and child on the shingle look up briefly before returning to their tasks. A man is walking his dog along a path by the river, and when we sweep past, the dog pulls at its leash as though wanting to race our boat. Some of the passengers on the boat have turned their binoculars and cameras toward the dog and its owner. How does it feel, I wonder, when your daily walk with the dog is turned into an exotic spectacle to be viewed, photographed, and filmed by foreign tourists?

Now we are very close to the opposite shore, which rises sheer above our boat. On the top of the cliff a couple of boys appear, hands raised above their heads. Are they waving or throwing stones? The deep waters of the Yalu River are international, and our boat can approach as close to shore as its skipper dares. But the land ahead is the Democratic People's Republic of Korea (DPRK): the most closed country on earth, the last and strangest fruit of Cold War isolationism. To run aground would mean disaster.

Only here, where every facet of ordinary life is so resolutely concealed from the outside world, could these mundane scenes—riding bicycles and walking the dog—provoke such consuming curiosity from observers.

Our boat swings back, further out into the current. On the North Korean side of the river, a huge, rusting factory comes into view. The crumbling buildings and gaunt chimney stacks look like ruins, but smoke still issues from some vent deep in its interior, as though from the very bowels of the earth itself. Little by little the factory's forbidding shape recedes as we head back toward the Chinese side, and the bare Korean mountains fade to misty blue.

The day after tomorrow we will, I hope, stand on the North Korean side of this river. But times are tense. The DPRK has just launched another long-range missile, raising the stakes in an already dangerous game of international brinkmanship. Recent nuclear tests and threats of violence against assorted enemies are signs of tensions within North Korea's secretive regime. Omens of change are in the air, but whether these portend new waves of repression or the possibility of reform, no one knows.

And we are still waiting to receive our North Korean visas.

They would, we were promised, be waiting for us here at the border-post of Dandong. "Just ring this number and ask for Mr. Sin," was the airy instruction I received before leaving home in Australia. But we have rung the

The Yalu River from Dandong (S. Morris)

number several times to be greeted by nothing but a saccharine burst of pop music and voice mail. Mr. Sin has his cell phone firmly turned off.

Meanwhile, as we wait for a response to our recorded messages, we stand at the rail of the boat, watching the hills on the southern side of the Yalu dissolve again into the distance.

Beyond those bare hills lies the wide, coastal plain of northwestern Korea; beyond the coastal plain lies the surreal city of Pyongyang; and far away to the southeast, just before the razor wire, landmines, and militarized wilderness that divide North from South, lie the Diamond Mountains . . .

The Mountains

The Flower Adornment Sutra of Mahayana Buddhism reveals that "in the midst of the ocean there is a place called Diamond Mountain. Since days of yore all the bodhisattvas have stopped there to dwell. . . . They reside there constantly expounding the Dharma."[1]

Chinese chronicles of the Tang Dynasty state that there are eight Diamond Mountains in this universe: "Seven lie far away in the midst of the sea, but one appears on the east sea coast of Korea."[2]

At the end of the fourteenth century, in a poem depicting the Diamond Mountains, the Korean scholar and statesman Kwon Geun wrote the following:

Snow settles on the myriad peaks,
sea clouds lift and the jade lotus emerges.
The mysterious light is clear and ripples across the vast ocean nearby,
clear air slithers and winds around the peaks forming gusts.
Protruding and precipitous mountain peaks approach the flight path of birds,
quiet and secluded valleys hide the hermits' footprints. Touring in the east one immediately wants to traverse the high peaks,
looking down on the chaotic state of Heaven and Earth I clear my heart.[3]

The 1974 North Korean revolutionary opera, *The Song of Kumgang-san Mountains* (Kumgang-san being the Korean name for the Diamond Mountains), proclaims as follows:

> Our world-famous Kumgang-san
> Will shed brilliant rays over our land of 3,000 leagues reunified.
> When brothers in the north and the south embrace each other,
> Kumgang-san will be a paradise for fifty million.
>
> O Marshall Kim Il-Sung, our sun,
> Fifty million Koreans wish you a long life and good health.
> We wish you, our leader, a long life and good health.[4]

Death before Dawn

In the summer of 2008, a middle-aged South Korean woman named Park Wang-ja traveled to the Diamond Mountains to spent a couple of days in the Mount Kumgang tourism resort, a project run jointly by the North Korean government and the giant South Korean Hyundai Corporation. Very early on the morning of July 11, while it was still dark, Park Wang-ja left her hotel room and walked through the cool of the fading night to the beach, to see the sun rise over the East Sea and cast its light on the mountain peaks. The beach was flat and the tide was far out. Park walked across the dark, shining sand. She walked and walked: past the fence surrounding the resort, across the rivulets of water that ran silently toward the sea, until she reached a clump of pines behind the beach.

There, a North Korean soldier suddenly appeared from the shadows and shouted at her to stand still. Seized by panic, Park turned and fled back in the direction from which she had come.

The soldier fired, and Park fell to the ground.

Slowly, cautiously, other soldiers appeared from among the trees and approached her body. One pushed her crumpled form with his boot to see if there was any sign of life, but there was no movement. Park Wang-ja was already dead.

The shooting of Park Wang-ja was the first sign of an emerging crisis that gripped Northeast Asia for more than a year, and the Diamond Mountains were at the heart of the crisis. The Hyundai Asan Mount Kumgang tourism resort had become the most visible symbol of the slow and painful process of Korean reunification. Since its opening in 1998, the resort, just a fifteen minute drive north of the dividing line between the two Koreas, had given almost two million South Koreans a first glimpse of the inside of their feared communist neighbor.[5]

The resort is also the site for reunions of families sundered by the division of the peninsula and the Korean War. In a specially constructed building, surrounded by breathtaking mountain peaks, ageing men and women—husbands and wives, sisters and brothers, and parents and children—who have not seen one another for more than half a century, and who had lived their lives in utterly different worlds—share a few fleeting hours together before being torn apart again and boarding their buses for tearful departures in opposite directions. When reunions began in 2000, some 125,000 people registered for the opportunity to meet close family members on the other side of the divide. Ten years on, just over sixteen thousand had had their wish fulfilled, while forty thousand had died still waiting in vain for their moment of reunion to arrive.[6]

After the shooting of Park Wang-ja the resort was closed down, and family reunions were suspended. Strange rumors started to circulate. Was her killing a tragic misadventure—a shot in the dark by a nervous soldier? Or was it part of some wider conspiracy by those who feared détente? Maybe North Korea's elusive leader Kim Jong-Il was ailing. Maybe he was dead. Perhaps there was a power struggle underway, in which the bullets fired amongst the pines at the foot of Diamond Mountains had been just a first salvo.

Over the months that followed, other joint North-South Korean projects were closed or curtailed, one by one. The DPRK tested a long-range missile, and then a nuclear weapon. The Six Party Talks on North Korea's nuclear program, which bring the countries of the region and the United States together, and were seen by some as the best hope for regional stability, ground to a stalemate. Two Korean American journalists who strayed over the border between China and North Korea were arrested. By the time I reached the Yalu River, the situation was grim, and there was even talk of possible war.

Strange how political conflict makes the past and future invisible. When we look at North Korea, we see only endless present—the eternal rule of the late Kim Il-Sung, who died in 1994 but remains officially president in perpetuity, and of his son Kim Jong-Il, that curious figure in his dung colored nylon tracksuit, who, as it turned out, did not die in 2008 but survived illness and operations to reappear in shrunken form on the stage of world history the following year. For most people around the globe, the image of North Korea is condensed into a few moments of film footage in which tanks, rockets, and phalanxes of goose-stepping soldiers process across the bleak expanse of Pyongyang's Kim Il-Sung square as though on an endless playback loop.

My interest in the Diamond Mountains began with the present. I knew the mountains as a place imbued with political and symbolic significance, lying on a dividing line that is probably the most dangerous border on earth. The ironically misnamed "Demilitarized Zone" is the world's last Cold War divide: a massively militarized four-kilometer-wide strip of land whose destiny will shape the future of the entire Northeast Asian region, and indeed of the world.

In the months before Park Wang-ja's shooting, however, I was busy reading accounts of Western travelers who journeyed through this region in the late nineteenth and early twentieth centuries, and as I did so, I gradually became aware of the layer upon layer of history that, like the sediment that builds continents, is sealed into the very rock of those mountains. Park Wang-ja's fateful journey was just the most recent of thousands of journeys—some triumphant, some tragic—that have brought monks, hermits, poets, artists, warriors, tourists, scientists, and revolutionaries to this range of precipitous cliffs and soaring, impossible rock forms. As I read, I began to glimpse millennia of history, within which the life of the DPRK (and also of South Korea in its present form) will someday be no more than a transitory moment; and I was reminded of the three-volume history of the Soviet Union that still sits in my bookcase, displaying—with absurd but defiant pathos—chapter headings such as "Important Dates in the History of the USSR from Ancient Times to the Seventeenth Century."

To journey through time and space to the Diamond Mountains, exploring the traces of multiple past journeys while carving out my own, might be a way of seeing North Korea and its surrounding region in an unfamiliar light. Beyond ideology lies the quiet persistence of human lives—the gathering of shellfish, the walking of dogs. Beyond the political present lie the centuries of past and future. By opening our eyes to the depths of the past, perhaps we may begin to see the outlines of a future for this region beyond its current sufferings and division.

I began to plan a journey—a pilgrimage through history—to the mountains.

There were many generations of earlier pilgrims waiting to guide me.

I could follow the path of the monk Dhyanabhadra, who in the fourteenth century walked from India across the expanse of China to the Diamond Mountains on the far eastern coast of Korea; I could take an easier itinerary in the steps of the great eighteenth-century Korean painters Kim Hong-do and Jeong Seon. I could take my lead from an eminent westerner like Lord Curzon (later viceroy of India) who came to Korea in the 1890s, and whose supercilious comments about East Asians were briefly replaced by a moment of breathless awe as he encountered the Diamond Mountains; or I could follow the path of American woman Helen Burwell Chapin, who shaved her head and dressed as a man in order to stay in the mountains' Buddhist temples in the 1930s.[7]

I could travel in the company of Norbert Weber, a learned German Benedictine monk who visited the mountains in 1925. Weber described the extraordinary cultural riches of the region but also wrote of "the rapid descent from exceptional cultural heights, the harsh consequences of two terrible assaults by the Japanese at the end of the 16th century (1592 to 1598), the misrule of the land, which was delivered up to the greed of the bureaucrats." All of this, he said, had "settled like a thick veil of mist over the once so celebrated Diamond Mountains, and concealed them more and more completely from the eyes of their own people as well as from the eyes of the outside world."[8] I have indeed learnt much from Weber's writings, and from the observations of other Korean, Japanese, European, and American writers and artists who watched the mist briefly lift, and then thicken again as the mountains were once again veiled from outside eyes by the division of the Korean Peninsula, the brutal conflict of the Korean War (some whose fiercest fighting occurred in this place), and the deepening isolation of the DPRK.

In the end, however, the guide I chose for my journey was a woman who came to the mountains almost exactly a century earlier than me—a down-to-earth Englishwoman from a family of Lancashire Baptist textile entrepreneurs. Emily Georgiana Kemp was an artist, writer, and erudite traveler, who developed a lifelong and passionate love for Northeast Asia, despite the fact that this was the site and source of her life's most terrible tragedy.

The "Far East" through which Kemp and other Western visitors journeyed was a space formed and reshaped by the rise and decline of empires. In 1903, a newly opened ferry service across Lake Baikal completed the last link in the greatest overland route in human history: the Trans-Siberian Railway, connecting Europe to easternmost Asia. But the jubilant celebration of the railway's completion had barely subsided when Russia and Japan were plunged into a war that resulted, in 1905, in the resounding defeat of Russia: the first modern military defeat of a European by an Asian power. In the end, the benefits brought by the Great Siberian Railway (as it was then called) were largely enjoyed by Japan, which, after its victory over Russia, controlled the railways that linked the Siberian trunk line to the rail networks of China and Korea.

Kemp and her traveling companion Mary MacDougall were among the earliest of Western travelers to use the Trans-Siberian Railway as a gateway to the realm then often called "the New Far East": a Far East constituted by Japanese empire building. The Japanese annexation of Korea ("Chosen" in Japanese) in 1910, the year of Kemp's visit, and Japan's deepening grip on Manchuria and later on other parts of eastern China, carved out a space not just for military dominance but also for travel and tourism—and the Japanese government was perhaps the first in the world to grasp the propaganda potential of tourism.

I have selected Kemp as a guide on this journey not only because she generally observed the landscape though which she passed with a calm, measured, and sympathetic eye but also because she saw Manchuria and Korea at a particularly critical turning point in their history: the moment when the Chinese empire was on the brink of extinction and Japan's dominance of East Asia was sealed by the acquisition of its most important colony. In the introduction to her travel account, *The Face of Manchuria, Korea and Russian Turkestan*, she wrote the following of the Chinese empire:

> The European and other Powers who have wrangled over the possibility of commercial and political advantages to be obtained from the Chinese Government (after the Boxer troubles) have withdrawn to a certain extent, but like snarling dogs dragged from their prey, they still keep their covetous eyes upon it, and both Russia and Japan continue steadily but silently to strengthen their hold on its borders. These borders are Manchuria and Korea, and it is in this direction that fresh developments must be expected.[9]

Kemp sensed that these borderlands were in the midst of profound change and that this change had the power to shake the world. For a new element had recently been added to the volatile mix: the advance of Japan into the region: "The latest step in advance is the annexation of Korea, the highroad into Manchuria."[10] These words were written on August 26, 1910; just four days earlier, Korea had become a Japanese colony.

A century on, the region where Kemp traveled is once again in the grip of momentous transformations. The rise of China is overturning the old certainties of regional and global power relations. As the world confronts economic crises, China, the last major self-proclaimed communist power, has ironically come to hold the key to the future of global capitalism. Just as Japan's ascendance aroused international anxieties in the first part of the twentieth century, in the early years of the twenty-first century China's assertiveness evokes a similar mixture of admiration and nervousness from regional neighbors, and from the wider world. Above all, though, a century after the annexation, it is the fate of the Korean Peninsula that lies in the balance: Korea, still divided by the world's last Cold War frontier, still technically at war in a military conflict that has lasted sixty years.

The shots that killed Park Wang-ja in the Diamond Mountains raised echoes that continue to reverberate through the region. Like the gradual cracking of snow that presages an avalanche, strange fissures are opening in Korea's still-frozen Cold War order. But to understand the implications of these cracks, we need to look beyond the present moment and beyond the Korean Peninsula itself, seeing contemporary politics in the broader context of Northeast Asia's past.

In the borderlands of Northeast Asia, the forces of China, Russia, Japan, and Korea mingle and contend in endlessly changing patterns. These countries of the region will help to determine the ultimate fate of the divided Korea, and their interactions in turn will be irrevocably shaped by the belated ending of Korea's Cold War. Following Kemp's century-old journey through the region once called the "New Far East" to the slopes of the Diamond Mountains, we can begin to see the deep forces that produced today's tensions and divisions, and so find new ways of imagining the possibilities that lie ahead.

When Emily Kemp traveled through Manchuria and Korea, the veil of mist that shrouded those mountains from outside eyes was temporarily dissipating. Kemp's better-known predecessor in East Asia, the famous woman traveler Isabella Bird, was among the first westerners to visit the mountain range, and her description of its "tiger haunted forest," fantastic temples, and intoxicating canyons helped to spread the fame of the Diamond Mountains to the English-speaking world.[11] By 1910, encroaching Japanese colonialism was remaking the image of the mountains in a new form. Scientific surveys of their natural wonders, architectural heritage, and mineral resources were underway. All these would be developed for the greater glory of the emerging Japanese empire.

Adventurous westerners were urged to visit the "new Korea" being re-made by Japanese hands: "an ancient land that is loosing its garments of old and donning the garb of youth." And the promised highlight of the itinerary through Japanese-dominated Manchuria and Korea, for Kemp and a stream of Western visitors that followed, was a visit to the Diamond Mountains (known as Kongō-san in Japanese) with their "torrential wa-terfalls, clear lakes and crystal streams; picturesque mountains and valleys covered with Alpine flowers; fantastic peaks shaped by nature's artful hand," which were soon being billed as "the future vacation land of the Far East."[12]

Kemp and MacDougall entered China from Siberia through the city of Harbin and headed south across the Manchurian plains by train, cross-ing the Yalu River from China to Korea at Dandong and continuing to Pyongyang, Seoul, and the port of Busan on the southern tip of the Korean Peninsula. They then doubled back by ship to Wonsan, a port on the east coast of what is now North Korea, before journeying in horseback south along the coast to the Diamond Mountains. Indefatigable travelers that they were, after retracing their steps through Manchuria and Siberia they set off on further adventures in "Russian Turkestan" (now Uzbekistan and Kazakhstan)—a section of their journey that I shall not attempt to follow. My hope is to cover their itinerary through Manchuria (today's north-eastern China) and the Korean Peninsula, as far as the point where Kemp and MacDougall walked among "the precipitous mountains of granite formation" with their forbidding rocks "like mammoth beasts in all sorts of shapes."[13]

A century after their visit, transport has been revolutionized in ways that these early twentieth-century travelers could never have imagined. Taxis and four-wheel drives have replaced sleighs and pack ponies. Hotels in Shenyang and Seoul and can be booked online. Jumbo jets whisk us between continents in a few hours. But politics has made some things much more dif-ficult. In fact, politics makes a precise reenactment of the journey impossible. The pathway that Kemp took through Northeast Asia is now blocked by the impassable barrier created by the division of Korea.

Even if Mr. Sin appears with our visas, a journey down the length of the Korean Peninsula is going to require some complex detours.

Back in our Dandong hotel room, I remove all the contents from my two suitcases and check through each item one by one. If the elusive Mr. Sin makes contact and we manage to cross the river, it will be necessary to ensure that there is nothing in our luggage to arouse the readily stimulated suspicions of North Korean officialdom.

I set aside a small pile of things to be left on the Chinese side of the border: papers from a conference I have just attended in South Korea (material from the South being prohibited in the North); the alternative guidebook to Pyongyang, which discusses such unmentionable places as prisons and the compounds of the party elite; and the dog-eared photocopy of Kemp's *The Face of Manchuria, Korea and Russian Turkestan*, which describes the Pyongyang of 1910 as one of the great centers of Christianity in Asia.

Finally, on top of the pile of things to leave behind, I place my folder full of poems, maps, photocopies of brush paintings and fading postcards, writings by Confucian scholars, Japanese colonizers, American Marxists, and others, all describing the wonders and perils of the Diamond Mountains, whose phantasmagoric landscape has recently occupied many of my waking moments and appeared in still more impossible forms on the margins of my dreams.

According to beliefs that predate the coming of Buddhism, the mountains are a place where heaven meets earth, and humans who stray too far into their heights encounter capricious shape-shifting spirits who force mortal intruders to confront their hidden desires and secret fears. In the remorseless world of reality, the dreams of enlightenment and revolutionary utopias glimpsed in the mountains have all too often shone with an evanescent light, only to vanish again, just as the crags of the Diamond Mountains themselves appear and disappear in the sea of mist that rises endlessly from the jagged shoreline below.

Before discarding my Diamond Mountain folder, I take out three maps, old and new, inscribed with varying romanizations of Chinese, Japanese, and Korean place names. Once more I try to trace the circuitous line of Kemp's journey. The route ahead seems clear until it approaches the mountains. But then the track peters out into a confusion of false turnings and indecipherable place names.

Maybe the Diamond Mountains, as in the days of the poet Kwon Geun, still provide a vantage point from which to perceive the chaotic state of heaven and earth; but maybe trickster spirits lurk in wait for those who climb their peaks.

There is a knock on the door, and there is my traveling companion Emma Campbell, pointing to the cell phone that she holds to her ear, and mouthing at me silently.

"I think it's Mr. Sin on the line," she says.

Notes

1. Quoted in Richard D. McBride II, *Domesticating the Dharma: Buddhist Cults and the Hwaŏm Synthesis in Silla Korea* (Honolulu: University of Hawaii Press, 2008), 132.

2. Quoted in Mantetsu Keijō Tetsudōkyoku, ed., *Chōsen Kongōsan: Man-Ni-Sen Hō* (Tokyo: Author, 1924), 2.

3. Kŭn Kwŏn, *Kugyok Yangch'onjip*, vol. 1, Kojŏn kugyŏk ch'ongsŏ 173 (Seoul: Minjok munhwa ch'ujin hoe, reprinted 1984), 42 (*hangŭl*) and 4b–5a (*hanmun*); translation of first lines quoted from Dane Alston, "Emperor and Emissary: The Hongwu Emperor, Kwŭn Kŏn and the Poetry of Late Fourteenth-Century Diplomacy," *Korean Studies* 32 (2008): 104–47.

4. *The Song of Kumgang-san Mountains*, libretto (Pyongyang, North Korea: Foreign Languages Publishing House, 1974), 45.

5. See, for example, "N. Korea Blasts South for Barring Mountain Tour," *Yonhap News*, November 20, 2009.

6. See ROK Ministry of Unification website, at http://www.unikorea.go.kr/eng/default.jsp?pgname=AFFhumanitarian_reunion.

7. See Elizabeth Huff, *Teacher and Founding Curator of the East Asiatic Library: From Urbana to Berkeley by Way of Beijing* (Berkeley: Regional Oral History Office, Bancroft Library, University of California, 1977), 22.

8. Norbert Weber, *In den Diamantbergen Koreas* (Oberbayern, Germany: Missionverlag St. Ottilen, 1927), 3.

9. E. G. Kemp, *The Face of Manchuria, Korea and Russian Turkestan* (New York: Duffield and Co., 1911), vii.

10. Kemp, *Face of Manchuria, Korea and Russian Turkestan*, xii.

11. Isabella Bird Bishop, *Korea and Her Neighbours* (New York: Fleming H. Revell Co., 1898), 133–49.

12. Advertisement by the Chosen Government Railways, in T. Philip Terry, *Terry's Guide to the Japanese Empire*, rev. ed. (Boston: Houghton Mifflin, 1928).

13. Kemp, *Face of Manchuria, Korea and Russian Turkestan*, 120.

CHAPTER ONE

On the Move
To Harbin and Hulan

Lying Down on the Clouds

Imagine Northeast Asia spread out below you, as though seen from far above the clouds, from the viewpoint of a satellite that silently circles the earth on some covert mission. To the west stretches the tawny expanse of the Gobi Desert, extending toward Central Asia like a vast, dry lake, with the land to the south of the desert rising in folds toward the Himalayas and the Karakorums. The brown steppes that stretch in a great swathe across the north give way further south to the rich green of southern China's rice fields. Beyond the plains of Manchuria in the northeast, the Korean Peninsula points down toward the southernmost islands of the Japanese archipelago.

In this landscape, only one border is unmistakably visible—and its contours appear only at night. That border is the dividing line between North and South Korea. As natural light fades from the land, the acid artificial light of cities appears, forming constellations and nebulae that cluster thickly across the Japanese islands, down the east coast of China, and over the expanse of South Korea. But the lights stop in a clear line that runs across the middle of the peninsula, snaking roughly along the course of the 38th parallel: the dividing line that bisects Korea. North of the line, the energy-starved land is a pool of blue darkness, with just a small star marking the capital, Pyongyang.[1]

Recent reports suggest that per capita income in North Korea is about one-twentieth of the level in the South. It is the widest wealth gap between

13

two neighboring countries to be found anywhere in the world—and these are not two but one divided country.

A hundred years ago, if anyone had been able to view Northeast Asia's landscape from this celestial perspective, the view they saw at night would have been completely different—a great expanse of darkness with perhaps just two or three faint specks of light marking Tokyo, Shanghai, and Hong Kong. But the daytime landscape has changed only slightly and gradually over the centuries and millennia—mountains fading from green to khaki as they lose their forests and rivers shifting their course to the sea.

With our minds trapped in modern categories, we tend to think of the region as an assembly of nation states—sharply defined and often antagonistic blocks of land labeled "China," "Japan," "North Korea," and "South Korea." For most of recorded history, though, it was a shifting ebb and flow of peoples, pulled together and spun apart by the changing shape and fortunes of its central force—Zhonghua, the "Culture that Flowers at the Center," the Chinese empire. From the viewpoint of the literati of the Chinese center, the smaller kingdoms and nonstate communities lying on the horizons of knowledge could be organized into encyclopedic lists of "barbarians." There were tribute givers, like the Koreans to the east, whose ways were well known; and beyond such tribute-giving kingdoms were a multitude of other barbarians known by rumor rather than experience: to the west, lands of white people and black immortals; to the south, people with beaks like birds; and to the east, a Land of Gentlemen whose inhabitants (according to one account) were polite and always accompanied by two tigers.[2]

When the Chinese empire weakened, the barbarians seized their chances: the Jurchens in the twelfth century, the Mongols in the thirteenth, and the Manchus in the seventeenth century all in turn swept southward to occupy the Chinese heartland. The Mongols pressed on, southeastward as well as westward, occupying Korea and sending their fleets to Japan, only to be turned back by the divine wind of a typhoon—the origin of the term kamikaze. During the late sixteenth century, the upstart Japanese warlord Hideyoshi had his designs on the weakening Chinese Ming Empire—but his forces only reached Korea before being driven back at its rugged mountain barriers by defenders who included bands of armed monks from the temples of the Diamond Mountains.[3] The Korean Peninsula was already becoming what it has always been in modern times: a small and fiercely independent world pressed in on all sides by more powerful forces.

The lives of Chinese dynasties and those of the surrounding kingdoms were deeply intertwined—their rise and fall sometimes synchronized and sometimes syncopated. Korea itself was a shifting patchwork of contending kingdoms whose bounds overflowed the limits of the divided nation we know today, just as Chinese power at times overflowed into the Korean Peninsula. The Kingdom of Goguryeo (Gaogouli in Chinese), whose origins and extent are still shrouded in mystery and controversy, ruled an area covering much of the northern half of the Korean Peninsula and extending into what is now northeastern China at the start of the Common Era. From the third century CE, three emerging kingdoms—Gaya in the far south, Baekje in the south-west, and Silla to the southeast—engaged in increasingly fierce rivalries for wealth and power. The victor was Silla, which, conquest by conquest, gradually united most of the Korean Peninsula under its rule. Dynastic change in China hastened the collapse of Silla and the rise in the tenth century of the Goryeo Kingdom—from whom the name "Korea" originates; and the collapse of the Mongol Dynasty in China in 1368 strengthened the hand of the Korean military leader who overthrew the Goryeo rulers to create his own Joseon Kingdom—a dynasty whose rule over the peninsula was to survive into the twentieth century and was in its final days when Emily Georgiana Kemp wandered through its crumbling palaces in 1910.

Across this landscape, stitching together its immense diversity of languages, habits, beliefs, and histories, wound threadlike paths of travel, trade, and pilgrimage, which, like the rivers, gradually changed their courses, or sometimes dried up altogether: the multitude of silk roads linking the old Chinese capital of Chang'an (Xian) across the deserts to Bactria (present-day Afghanistan), and southwards, to the Himalayas and India. Eastward, minor byways of the tribute routes extended into the plains of Manchuria and thence south to the mountain ridges of the Korean Peninsula and north toward the marshlands along the Amur River, with their multiplicity of small language groups.

The farming people of Northeast Asia's plains, valleys, and rice lands might live in a world tightly circumscribed by the horizons of village life (as most people in North Korea do today). But superimposed on the self-contained village world was another geography of phenomenal journeys: tribute missions, trading journeys, and, greatest of all, the journeys of Buddhist pilgrimage.

Buddhism first percolated into China in the first century CE, and it arrived already thoroughly mixed with preexisting myth, magic, and tradition. In practice, the coming of the new ideas was not a sudden event but rather a gradual osmosis from many sources—Central as well as South Asia—over the course of a century or more. As the new ideas took hold, Chinese pilgrims traveled to the west in search of enlightenment, and Indian and Central Asian monks traveled eastward with their messages of wisdom and their copies of the sacred sutras. By the fourth century CE, Buddhism had reached the northern kingdoms of Korea by various routes, from where Korean missionary monks carried it onward across the sea to Japan, and by the sixth century it was officially accepted as the religion of the Silla Kingdom.

The journeys taken by these traveling monks were breathtaking. In the eight century, the Korean monk Hyecho traveled from the Kingdom of Silla by sea to India and then on overland to Central Asia, leaving a written record that includes descriptions of Tokharistan, Bamiyan (in today's Afghanistan), the "Land of the Arabs," and parts of the Byzantine Empire.[4] Other Silla monks journeyed to India in search of the site of the Buddha's enlightenment, their wanderings commemorated in the lyrical language of religious mysticism. Of one it is written, "Like the movement of the moon, day and night he went where his travels took him. Now he crossed over boulders heaped high where the courses of the birds were as high as the clouds; now he traversed ice that extended for a thousand leagues, walking on the wind and lying down on the clouds."[5] Monks from India, Kashmir, and Sogdian in Central Asia traveled to the Chinese capital Chang'an, where they met traveling Chinese monks and pilgrims from Korea; and from these encounters, the pilgrims brought back the mystic geography of Buddhism, which they superimposed on familiar neighboring landscapes, imbuing their seas and mountains with new sacred meaning. So the strange shaped range of mountains on the east coast of Korea came to be identified as the Diamond Mountains of the Flower Adornment Sutra, where all the bodhisattvas in the universe eternally expound the dharma. As the eighth-century Chinese monk Chengguan (himself a tireless pilgrim to the sacred mountains of China) explained,

Diamond Mountain is a mountain called Jingang [in Chinese; pronounced Kumgang in Korean] located in the east of Haidong [Silla]. Although it is not wholly made of gold [jin], up, down, all around, and when you go into the mountain's precincts it is all gold in the midsts of the sands of the flowing waters. When you look at it from a distance, the whole thing is golden.[6]

What to Take on a Pilgrimage

Two days before setting off on the journey to the Diamond Mountains, I am sitting on the floor of the untidy spare bedroom of my Canberra house, staring at a long packing list and wondering what to take on this pilgrimage. Like many people in today's globalized world, I spend much of my time on the move, barely able to absorb the sights, sounds, and smells of the endless succession of global cities through which I pass. After endless packing and unpacking of suitcases, sometimes I run out of energy, and the case remains unzipped on the bedroom floor with an assortment of tissue boxes, aspirin, spare jumpers, and other travel necessities still lying in its depths, waiting for the next journey.

Whole volumes could be written about the history of suitcases and their contents. For westerners planning travel to Northeast Asia a century ago, the process of packing was clearly a very different matter from today's flinging together of a few clothes, a toothbrush and toothpaste, and the assorted remedies needed to ward off the microscopic aliens that wait to assault our bodies the moment we board an airplane.

Nineteenth-century traveler Isabella Bird, for example, set out on her journey into the Korean interior equipped with

> a saddle, a trestle bed with bedding and mosquito net, muslin curtains, a folding chair, two changes of clothing, Korean string shoes, and a "regulation" waterproof cloak. Besides this, I took curry powder, green tea and 20 lbs of flour. . . . The kitchen equipment consisted of a Japanese brazier for charcoal, a shallow Japanese pan and frying pan, and a small kettle with charcoal tongs. . . . The "table" equipment was limited: a small mug, two plates and a soup plate, all in enameled iron, and a knife, fork and spoon which folded up, a knife, fork and spoon of common make being reserved for the "kitchen."

And that was only after she had "discarded all superfluities, such as flasks, collapsing cups, hand mirrors, teapots, sandwich tins, lamps, and tinned soups, meats, bouillon, and fruits."[7]

British philosopher and pilgrim J. B. Pratt describes (for the benefit of other travelers) the experience of arriving at a temple high in the Diamond Mountains in the 1930s, accompanied by a Korean "jiggy [jige] man" (porter), whose task was to carry visitors' luggage (and sometimes the visitors themselves) up the precipitous slopes:

> Your bedding and other luggage is unpacked, the brazier is brought out, the kettle put upon it, and a monk fans the charcoal while you make the coffee and warm up the beans which good Mr. Heinz has sent you all the way from Pittsburgh, or while you open up the jam which Messrs. Cross and Blackwell serve indifferently to you in the Kongo-San and to King George in Windsor.[8]

Kemp also brought bales of bedding on her journeys, as well as suitcases and baskets, though what these contained remains a mystery.

Earlier generations of wind-walking pilgrims presumably traveled more lightly. Indeed, for Buddhist monks, all of life was (in theory at least) a journey for which they needed only the barest minimum of possessions: their clothes, a begging bowl, a water strainer (to ensure that they did not accidentally consume insects and other living creatures), and a small rug to sit on. Some sources allow a slightly more generous list of possessions for life's journey—excluding the rug, but adding a razor, thread, and needle.[9]

For a true pilgrim, what mattered was not physical but rather spiritual and mental baggage. A pilgrimage is more than mere movement through space. It is a journey that takes us out of the routine cares of everyday life, not only into an unknown place, but also into an unfamiliar realm of time.[10] Though every pilgrimage has its goal—its sacred ground, purifying river, or holy mountain—the significance of the journey lies in movement itself, as much as in arrival. Through trials and tribulations along the road, the pilgrim experiences a foretaste of the ultimate journey into that unknown from which no traveler returns. Like the bodhisattvas who abandon the vision of Nirvana and resume the trials of earthly life to rescue others, however, the pilgrim is also expected to go home. The journey returns to its starting point: but the traveler returns as a changed person, inhabiting a world whose meaning has been transformed forever.

Motives, of course, are always mixed. Perhaps even the traveling monks of the Silla Kingdom secretly shared in the feelings that propelled the early twentieth-century traveler Kemp on her extended journeys through East Asia:

"Why do you go on journeys to such impossible places?" is a question which I am continually asked. "Can it possibly be for pleasure? How can any one like," and here the eyebrows are raised and a shade of disgust, politely veiled, is visible, "to stop in awful inns and visit cities full of dirt and smells? What is your real reason for traveling in the interior of China?"

Strange as it may seem to the comfort-loving Britisher, PLEASURE is the main lure to China, and a sort of basilisk fascination which is quite irresistible.[11]

I share Kemp's sense of sheer pleasure in travel, and for me North Korea exerts a peculiar "basilisk fascination." But modern travelers too, I think, often hope to be transformed in some way through the process of travel—to step outside the mundane world of everyday life and return to that world with changed and sharpened perceptions. Reading between the lines of Kemp's travel accounts, I think she too may have found in her journeys not only pleasure and the delight of new discoveries but also the strength to move through profound personal pain to a place of survival and tranquility.

Today, a pilgrimage to North Korea requires neither begging bowl and strainer nor jam and baked beans. But one pocket of my suitcase does contain sachets of instant coffee, since the coffee supply in the Democratic People's Republic of Korea can be erratic. Euros or Chinese yuan are needed—being the most acceptable forms of foreign exchange in a society where foreigners are not allowed to use the local currency and dollars are a symbol of U.S. imperialism—as are a good supply of Imodium and plenty of presents for the guides. Cigarettes are the recommended gifts, but I cannot bear the thought of rewarding the hardworking guides with a gift of carcinogens and have instead bought a selection of scarves and wallets, which, I hope, will be an acceptable substitute.

Then there is the delicate question of cameras. While visitors are prohibited from bringing cell phones into North Korea, still and video cameras are allowed. But photography is a very sensitive issue. An unauthorized shot of a soldier, or of anything that shows the country in a bad light, might result in the deletion of photos, the confiscation of the camera, or worse. I am planning to take a small and light video camera with me but have decided to bring an old still camera as well, just in case.

Kemp was an accomplished artist, whose work had been exhibited in galleries and even at the 1893 World's Columbian Exposition in Chicago—one of the greatest world fairs of all time.[12] Wherever she went on her travels, "she had her paint-box, her water bottle (which often had to be unfrozen at high altitudes) and her paint-brush; and paint she would and make her record—even if armed men had to be called up to guard her from brigands—till she had finished her sketch."[13] Unfortunately, I have no artistic skills. But my sister Sandy, who is joining me on the journey, is a professionally trained artist, and we are curious to see how our North Korean hosts will react to her attempts to sketch the streets of Pyongyang and perhaps (if we reach them) the northern fringes of the Diamond Mountains.

The Great Siberian Railway

Emily Kemp, our long-dead guide on this journey, arrived in the northern Chinese city of Harbin in 1910 after weeks of wearying travel by train across Europe and the steppes of Siberia, just before the winter ice began to melt.

But she had already fallen in love with China seventeen years earlier, on the day in 1893 when, at the end of a long and miserable sea voyage through the tail of a typhoon, her ship "emerged from the storm and sailed into the wonderful bay of Hong Kong."[14] The love survived even the disasters of Chinese history that engulfed her family.

Kemp was in many ways representative of that tribe of British "lady travelers" whose members traversed the surface of the earth from Alaska to Tierra del Fuego in the late nineteenth and early twentieth centuries. Like her predecessor in East Asia, Constance Gordon Cumming, and her successors, Elizabeth Keith and Audrey Harris, she had private means, an enquiring mind, and an urge to escape from the mental and physical confines of British society.[15] She was born in 1860 from the heart of the industrial revolution: in her own, slightly self-mocking description, a "mid-Victorian child."[16] Her mind and soul were molded ten thousand miles from Manchuria in the cradle of free enterprise, nonconformism, and high-minded social reform: the Lancashire town of Rochdale. In the late nineteenth century, one of the largest employers in Rochdale was the woolen textiles firm of Kelsall and Kemp, and Emily Georgiana was the fifth child of the Kelsall-Kemp partnership: her mother, Emily Lydia, was the daughter of the firm's founder, Henry Kelsall; her father was Kelsall's accountant and later business associate, George Tawke Kemp.[17]

Her parents were devout Baptists and philanthropists, and their piety and tireless benevolence to "the destitute classes" left its unmistakable imprint on Kemp's life, thought, and travel writings. Two of her four sisters became missionaries, and Kemp herself studied medicine as well as art in the hope of becoming a medical missionary. She is said to have abandoned this dream because of health problems, but given her prodigious travels in inhospitable terrains, this seems an unlikely explanation.[18] Regardless of the reason, Kemp never joined the missions herself, though she often stayed with missionaries on her travels. Her profoundly Victorian religious sensibilities are the aspect of her writings, which are most difficult for a twenty-first-century reader to digest. Every now and then—when she visited the Indian city of Benares (Varanasi) or the Central Asian city of Bokhara (Bukhara), for example— Emily would encounter people whose religious fervor was just as deep as her own but expressed in utterly unfamiliar ways, and she responded with a very imperial British revulsion: "The barbarism of Bokhara is unspeakable," she declares.[19]

She was, however, also a highly educated woman, who had been brought up to speak French, German, and Italian, "but I regret to say, not Latin—it still being considered unnecessary for girls."[20] She came, indeed, from a family of remarkable women, the most remarkable of all being her mother, Emily Lydia, who, despite being profoundly deaf, managed the family firm after her husband's early death in 1877 as well as running an assortment of philanthropic ventures for the poor of Rochdale. As the younger Kemp wrote with pride, "The present Feminist movement has had its foundations well and truly laid in many parts of our country by such women as my mother."[21]

Kemp inherited her mother's determination and independence of mind. She was among the first generation of women to study at Oxford University, entering the newly established women's college Somerville Hall in 1881, only two years after its founding, before going on to study art at the Slade School in London.[22] Her circle of friends included artists and politicians as well as intellectuals, and she became a fellow of the Royal Scottish Geographical Society, as well as being awarded a medal by the French Geographical Society for her travel writing.[23] While traveling, she read voraciously—not just the works of the major European orientalists but also English translations of Chinese classics and of the writings of Japanese scholars and diplomats.

Her dismissive comments about Bukhara are an aberration from the enthusiasm and broad-mindedness that permeates much of her writing. Unlike many of her contemporaries, she even managed to look self-critically at the privileged position of Western travelers like herself. On her second visit to China in 1907, for example, she expressed amazement at the kindness and hospitality that she encountered wherever she went, particularly in the light of the rudeness that many Chinese experienced from foreign visitors. A longtime friend described her as having "a strong sense of humour and that inestimable gift, the power to enjoy, a zest for life and all the manifestations of life."[24]

Kemp's traveling companion, Mary MacDougall, on the other hand, remains an enigma. She is mentioned once in the preface to *The Face of Manchuria, Korea and Russian Turkestan*, and similarly in two other books that Kemp wrote about the journeys the women undertook in China and its borderlands. But not a word is recorded about MacDougall's life or background, and hardly anything is said about her impressions of extraordinary experiences in the remotest corners of Northeast Asia. We catch only tantalizing glimpses: at the end of the women's great trek through China in 1907–1908, for example, Kemp writes, "The journey was one long series of pleasant surprises, and my friend expressed the feelings of both of us when, on crossing the border into Burma, she exclaimed: 'if only we could turn round and go all the way back again!'"[25] This seems to confirm a passing comment by an aquaintance, who refers to MacDougall's "equable and cheery temper."[26] Kemp herself, however, does not even tell us her companion's first name, and it was only a chance discovery that enabled me to identify her name in full: Mary Meiklejohn McDougall. Beyond that, all is silence.

When Kemp set off for Manchuria and Korea, travel on the Great Siberian Railway was still a novelty, and she was eager to pass on impressions and tips to the stream of future travelers who would follow her on this route to "the New Far East." Before the Russian Revolution, three types of trains traversed the Siberian steppes—the relatively fast and comfortable International Train, which ran one service a week from St. Petersburg and one from Moscow; the slower Russian State Express, which was more crowded and made more stops along the route; and the daily Siberian Express, which seems to have belied its name, for one passenger wrote, "We never saw it moving. It was always on a siding or at a station, forever waiting for somebody or something."[27]

Kemp advises her readers to take the International Train, whose compartments offered "ample room for two suitcases and two bags of bedding," as well as "a nice dressing-room between every two coupés, where hot and cold water is laid on," though the supply was erratic, and hot water sometimes had to be bought at a cost of 2½d.[28] Lighting was also limited, meaning that most passengers went to sleep at nightfall: "Even a first-class carriage has only a single candle for illumination, and that is placed in a lantern above the door, so that it only serves to reveal the darkness."[29]

It was with understandable relief, after weeks of travel, that she awoke "to find a glorious, dazzling sun shining on the snowy plain between Manchuria [the far northern Chinese town of Manchouli] and our terminus, Kharbin [Harbin]."

Harbin Station

Just as the Silk Road created strange oases where diasporic groups of Mongols or Central Asian Muslims were stranded for centuries, so too the "Iron Silk Road" of the Trans-Siberian Railway and its various branch lines created unexpected ethnic outposts on the fringes of Northeast Asia; and the strangest, most alluring, and most vibrant of these outposts was the city of Harbin.

As Tsarist Russia pushed eastward, attempting to consolidate its power in Siberia, Russian towns complete with boulevards and cafes, bathhouses, and Orthodox churches sprouted like mushrooms from the marshlands along the Amur and Sungari rivers. When Russian surveyors and engineers arrived on the banks of the Sungari in 1898, the place that would become the city of

Harbin was just a ferry crossing with a straggle of houses on the riverbank and a single Chinese-owned distillery nearby. It was also well within the frontiers of the Chinese empire.

Russia, however, had been granted the right to build a railway, cutting across northeastern China to link the Trans-Siberian to the port city of Vladivostok, and Harbin was chosen as the construction base for the railway. Within five years of its founding, Harbin had streets of brick buildings, flour mills, saw mills, brick kilns, and a fluid and transient population of over quarter of a million. A grandiose European-style "new Harbin" was being constructed along the river, adjoining the section of town already known as "Old Harbin"; for, according to Bertram Putnam Weale, an American journalist who visited the fledgling city in 1904,

> Unfortunately for the Russians the Sungari happened to be in flood at the time of the founding of Harbin, and no less unfortunately the railway engineers did not happen to notice it. Old Harbin was therefore built with lavish expenditure, the railway was pushed forward with ferocious rapidity, and it was not until some time had passed that the railway engineers discovered that the Sungari was a good many miles away from the budding city.[30]

The story may have been embroidered in the telling, but Harbin Station, which soon became a meeting place of nations, is indeed some distance from the river.

For Western travelers of the early twentieth century, there were four main gateways to the "Far East." The ports of Yokohama, Hong Kong, and Shanghai provided entry points for those arriving by ocean liner, whether across the Pacific from San Francisco or from London through the Suez Canal and Indian Ocean; for those who came overland, the entrance to Northeast Asia was through Harbin Railway Station, with its grand central archway flanked on either side by tall, white stucco pillars.

The world that confronted travelers as they stepped from the train at Harbin was a dizzying mixture of Europe and Asia. Putnam Weale describes a station concourse crammed with Chinese migrant laborers and a multinational mass of others on the move:

> Yellow-clad lama priests rolled strings of beads in their hands and muttered, possibly prayers, but more probably curses, on the heads of the lusty Chinese railway police, who, clad in their semi-Chinese soldier attire, wielded unmercifully heavy sticks on the heads of all who did not keep moving. Buryat cavalrymen, with high Mongol cheekbones and a purely Chinese aspect, swaggered about in their Russian uniforms. Red-turbaned Sikhs from down-town stores

and godowns chanted Hindustani at one another. Russian officers of every
grade and size ran about looking for their wives and belongings, saluting and
clicking their spurs endlessly at one another.[31]

When Kemp and MacDougall arrived there, Harbin Station had also just
acquired another and more sinister claim to fame. Some four months earlier,
on October 26, 1909, an event that symbolized the unfolding tragedies of
Northeast Asian history had taken place on its northbound platform. On
that day, Itō Hirobumi, Japan's most famous modernizing statesman and the
man in charge of the rapidly expanding Japanese interests on the Korean
Peninsula, arrived in Harbin for a meeting with the Russian finance minister.
As he stepped from his railway carriage, saluted by ranks of Cossack guards,
Itō was confronted by a slightly built young man who pulled out a revolver
from inside his greatcoat and shot the Japanese politician in the heart, before
unfurling a flag and crying out, "Long live Korean independence!"

The assassination of Itō Hirobumi on Harbin Station, seen by many as
marking the birth of Korean nationalism, also embodies many of its paradoxes. The assassin, Ahn Jung-geun, had been an enthusiastic admirer of
Japan's modernization and of Itō's political vision, until Japan's determination to control and subdue Korea became unmistakable. Ahn was arrested
by the Russians, handed over to the Japanese, and executed in Port Arthur
(Lushun) on March 26, 1910, just a few days before Kemp and MacDougall
crossed the Yalu River from China into Korea. Kemp, who followed this dramatic story during her travels, reported that Ahn "faced his death sentence
with great equanimity. As he was engaged at the time in writing a poem, the
authorities postponed his execution for ten days in order that he might have
time to finish it!"[32]

Her account is only partly correct. Ahn Jung-geun's demeanor in prison
did indeed win sympathy from his Japanese guards, and he did seek a stay of
execution in order to complete his writings. But the work he was composing
in his final days was not a poem but rather an essay on a peaceable vision of
a Northeast Asia whose countries would collaborate to resist the incursions
of the West. The essay was never completed, and, a century later, the vision
remains unfulfilled.

"There is always a thrill of expectation for the genuine traveler on crossing
the frontier into an unknown country, which even the sight of the customs
house fails to dispel."[33] So writes Kemp in the opening lines of *The Face of
Manchuria, Korea and Russian Turkestan*. Today, the sight that generally confronts the traveler entering a new country is not a customs house but rather a

long queue of weary fellow passengers penned in by the metal crush barriers in the bleak passport control zone of some international airport.

It is a sunlit day in April, and I am flying over the great expanse of Manchuria from the south, surrounded by a plane full of Chinese and Korean passengers, who chuckle quietly at an episode of America's Funniest Home Videos as they tuck in to their overcooked braised chicken and peas. Below, the flat landscape slowly unfolds, patterned like textile with long stripes of varying shades of brown. Here and there are small villages built on rectangular grids. As we approach our destination, I can pick out each house with its roof of gray tile or red terracotta and its square walled backyard where a cow or a couple of pigs forage amongst mounds of straw. This is a settler's landscape, devoid of organic curves.

My friend Emma Campbell is waiting to meet me at Harbin Airport—her shoulder-length blond hair and the black-checked Palestinian scarf round her neck instantly identifiable amongst the small group that congregates in the featureless, gray arrivals hall. Originally from Britain, Emma has lived in China and Hong Kong and worked in the travel industry before embarking on research in Asian Studies, and although she only arrived a few hours earlier from South Korea, which is her current base, she whisks me and my luggage through the hall and into a bus to the city center with practiced ease. My artist sister Sandy will be arriving via Paris and Beijing in the evening. It is almost a year since I last saw her. We meet at long intervals in random locations—Vientiane, Geneva, Kathmandu. The older I grow the more I become conscious of the loneliness of the long-distance family.

On the drive into central Harbin from the airport, Emma and I speculate what Kemp and MacDougall would have made of the city today. The Harbin that they encountered as they left the station was a fragment of Europe transported into the wilds of northern Manchuria, with neo-Renaissance brick and plaster buildings, some in the process of construction, lining its broad, straight avenues. As Kemp noted disapprovingly, the town "still looks painfully new," and she could hardly wait to leave its Russian heart and embark on the sleigh ride in search of the real China. The steep embankment of the Sungari River down which she and MacDougall plunged in their sleigh—"a most perilous descent"—is now paved with stone steps. In the wide plaza overlooking the river, the young and old of Harbin are flying kites: dragons and phoenixes, Winnie-the-Pooh, and the Japanese anime character Doraemon swoop through the air and strain at their strings against a hazy sky.

Standing on those steps in the biting wind that blows off the Siberian taiga, Emma and I watch the empty pleasure boats with their dragon-head prows bobbing on the icy waters of the Sungari. Behind us stands an old man

Boats on the Sungari River (S. Morris)

with gold teeth and a sack over his back, looking every bit like one of the indigenous Siberian traders who peddled furs on this riverbank a hundred years ago. But the young couple nearby, huddled together against the cold, are dressed in fashions straight out of the Giordano and Benetton stores that now line Harbin's main streets.

A watery gold sun gleams faintly behind the translucent clouds. For some reason, blowing bubbles is a very popular pastime in Harbin, and the couple have brought with them soapy water, thin films of which they hold up to the icy wind. The bubbles form, break free, turn and shine in the light, lift, and dip in the wind, before disappearing one by one. A few last iridescent spheres float almost impossibly far out over the Sungari, and we watch them until every single one has dissolved into air.

Missing People

Although she may not have realized it, Kemp had arrived just in time to witness Russian Harbin's fleeting moment of glory. By 1910, the Russian community was already facing invisible pressures that would, in the end, banish its people, leaving only their buildings—now lovingly restored by Chinese owners—as mementos to the city's past. For, just five years before Kemp arrived in Manchuria, Japan's overwhelming victory in the Russo-Japanese War had tipped the balance of power between the two countries decisively in Japan's favor. As she traveled southward, she would witness the retreat of Russia and the gradual but inexorable northward march of the Japanese presence in China.

The wonderful brick cathedral of St. Sophia with its green onion domes is a perfect expression of Harbin's past and present. Inside, its walls are lined with photos of the city's history: the indigenous Daur and Jucher traders who once brought their goods to sell on the banks of Sungari; the Russian mansions rising from the Manchurian mud; and the ornate departments stores of Harbin's main shopping street, which in the early decades of the twentieth century bore the fittingly confusing name "Ulitsa Kitaiskaya" (Russian for "Chinese Street"). In one corner of the cathedral is a display of posters for films, plays, ballets, and operas, recalling the vibrant cultural life of 1920s Harbin.

Cathedral of St. Sophia, Harbin (S. Morris)

After the Russian Revolution of 1917, a mass of refugees, including many artists and intellectuals, fled to this city. Their presence becomes tangible in the low-ceilinged corridors of our century-old hotel—the Modern Hotel, named in tribute to that triumphant early twentieth-century modernity whose architectural pretensions Kemp so deplored. Between the marble and gilt pillars of the hotel's dimly lit interior hang mementoes of the famous who passed through its doors. The opera singer Chaliapin stayed here while giving concerts in Harbin's American Cinema. The great political activist Song Qingling (Madam Sun Yat-Sen) took a room in the hotel in the 1920s, on her way to an anti-imperialist conference in Moscow.

The photograph of the young man seated at a grand piano, however, suggests the darker side of Harbin's checkered past. Semyon Kaspe, son of the Modern Hotel's Russian-Jewish founder and owner, was (by all accounts) a pianist with a brilliant future. But in 1933, returning to perform in his home city, Kaspe was snatched from a Harbin street corner by gangsters and was later found murdered. By then Japanese forces were in control of the city and were buttressing their power by forming alliances with shadowy groups of right-wing, anti-Semitic White Russians. Whether Kaspe fell victim to that anti-Semitism or to the schemes of the Japanese military police is still debated today.

Images of Russian musicians, entrepreneurs, and gangsters decorate the aisles of the cathedral and the walls of nearby Russian cafes. Their lives haunt the city. On Sun Island, a great sandbank in the middle of the Sungari, a collection of their abandoned dachas has been assembled into a Russian village. At the ticket kiosk we pay our entrance fees and receive, in return, a plausible replica of a Russian passport. But beyond, the dachas, with their peeling paint and overgrown gardens, have a forlorn air. Amid the tall grass and straggly hollyhocks, rusting cages contain an assortment of live animals including (oddly) some thin and angry looking cats. Each cage is carefully labeled in Chinese, Russian, and English: "Russian Eagle," "Russian Rabbits," "Russian Cats," and (with a charming little English misspelling) "Naive Russian Bears."

But the people themselves are long gone. Nowadays, the cathedral is a museum, not a place of worship, and it is an entirely Chinese choir that performs a rousing medley of Russian folksongs and American country music under the impassive gaze of the golden icons. In the wide square outside, meanwhile, the city's Chinese inhabitants rollerblade, play badminton, pose for fashionable wedding photographs, and (of course) blow bubbles.

The souvenir shops selling vodka and Russian-doll images of Vladimir Putin are run by Chinese shopkeepers. My traveling companion Emma, being tall and blond, is often greeted with cries of "*zdrazdvytye*" by Chinese who mistake her for a Russian, but in fact even Russian tourists seem scarce.

To flee from the gilded stucco of the Russian town, whose European modernity they found so offensive, Kemp and MacDougall had to cross the Sungari and travel sixteen miles to Hulan, which, Kemp noted, is "quite a Chinese town." Indeed, she observed,

> As soon as spring comes there is a steady stream of workers to be seen arriving from China proper, especially from the province of Shantung, to which they return when the harvest is ended. Many come to accumulate enough money during eight or nine years to buy land and bring their families up here to live. In fact, we met some emigrants already arriving with all their scanty possessions.

For by 1910, Manchuria was the focus of one the modern world's greatest movements of people. In the seventeenth and eighteenth centuries, China's Manchu rulers had prohibited Han Chinese from migrating to the Manchu homeland, but by the end of the nineteenth century, pressures of population and fears of foreign encroachment into Manchuria had undermined these restrictions, and Chinese settlers from far and wide were pouring into the northeastern plains. The human tide was to swell even more in the coming decades. Between 1923 and 1930, it is believed that over five million Chinese people migrated to the four provinces of the Manchurian region, and by the late 1930s, this migration was running at around one million a year.[34]

Unlike glamorous, thriving Harbin, the town of Hulan today embodies the grittier working-class face of China's economic boom. Its gray concrete Mao-era apartment blocks are crumbling and streaked with grime. But the central covered market is still abuzz with the vibrant energy that Kemp found here a century ago. Old men with beards sit by the entrance selling pale blue duck eggs, roasted sunflower seeds, and ginseng. Inside the market, one stall is piled high with an array of dried fruits—dates, kiwi fruit, and kumquats— glowing like multicolored jewels. Another has its own antiquated machine for pressing sesame oil; a third, a tempting array of kimchi (Korean pickles), presided over by a Chinese stall-keeper but produced by families from the Korean villages around Hulan.

Kemp had only a limited knowledge of the Chinese language and did not speak any Korean. Perhaps for that reason, she did not notice that, among the flood of immigrants to Manchuria whom she passed on her travels, a number were not Chinese but Korean. The place where China ended and Korea began had in early times been vague and shifting, but the modern percolation of Koreans across the border into northeastern China had begun in the nineteenth century and intensified as war, political turmoil, and the growing Japanese presence destabilized rural Korean society. In 1910, there were already over two hundred thousand Koreans in Manchuria, some beginning to settle as far north as the plains around Harbin and Hulan. By the middle of the twentieth century, their number would grow to two million. Today, ethnic Koreans still constitute one of the northeast's largest minorities, their communities sometimes providing shelter for the North Koreans who cross the border to trade or seek refuge from hunger and political persecution.

The landscape between Harbin and Hulan is almost entirely flat, but, bathed in faint afternoon light, it looks strangely beautiful. The dark earth is striated by the lines of the plough. Smoke rises from the chimneys of brick cottages. Sometimes we pass a horse-drawn cart weaving in and out of the impatient motor traffic. Elsewhere, acres of old farmhouses are being flattened to make way for new suburban developments or multinational food-processing factories.

Mr. Chou, the driver of the taxi we have hired for the day, is a descendent of the inflow of Han Chinese migrants that Kemp witnessed. A member of an extended family of over fifty people who live in a dusty little village between Harbin and Hulan, Mr. Chou is a cheerful man in early middle age. His taxi contains an image of the Buddha of Mercy alongside a glass amulet, suspended from red satin thread, containing a portrait of the late Chairman Mao.

"I believe in them both," says Mr. Chou with a calm smile.

En route, we stop at the tiny one-story brick house that he shares with his wife and twenty-year-old daughter. The front room has been converted into a beauty salon where his daughter is busy perming customers' hair. There is a red star on the door, a line of miniature cannon for launching fire crackers at the entrance, and a Japanese lucky cat beckoning customers in the front window.

"A lot of people from this part of the world go to work in Japan and send money back home," says Mr. Chou. "Some day," he adds a little wistfully, "I'd like to go too . . ."

By and large, though, he seems content with his life, and expresses little envy for the burgeoning nouveau riche of China's economic miracle. When we pass a gated community of surprisingly opulent mansions next door to a wildlife park on the outer fringes of Harbin, where a few sad remnants of the once-feared Siberian tiger are displayed, Mr. Chou gives the place a disdainful glance: "I wouldn't want to live there. You wouldn't be able to sleep, you'd be so afraid of being eaten by the tigers."

Mr. Chou's view of his Korean neighbors is revealing. He talks warmly of the Hanguoren—the South Koreans who come Harbin on business or as tourists. But the Chaoxianren—descendants of prewar Korean migrants to China—are seen as a different people altogether. The popular perception amongst the majority Chinese community, he says, is that "they eat chilies and shout at you in Korean when they've had too much too drink." But Mr. Chou is a warm-hearted and open-minded man, and happily takes us down a narrow dirt lane that leads to an ethnic Korean settlement not far from his home to meet its villagers. The collection of brick and concrete cottages, clustered closely along straw-strewn alleyways, looks much like any local Chinese village but for the great brown glazed kimchi vats that stand outside some of the front doors.

When we greet a couple of passing women, they look at us warily and respond in Chinese but then burst into radiant smiles of enthusiasm when Emma and I speak a few words of Korean. "*Bangapsumnida*—welcome, welcome!" they cry. One rushes off to fetch a brochure for the Korean restaurant that her son runs in Harbin and tells us excitedly about her daughter, who works in the South Korean city of Busan. There are handshakes and hugs all round, and we take each other's photographs in varied combinations, to make sure that no one is left out.

The human rivers that Kemp witnessed are flowing though this region again. Today, as at the start of the twentieth century, Northeast Asia is being transformed by that most powerful and irresistible of forces—the migration of people.

After the relative stasis and isolation of the Mao era, the region is once more on the move, creating a great network of human connections that spans the expanse of China and crosses national boundaries. In recent years, more than one hundred million Chinese people have been migrating between countryside and city each year, and since the nation began to open up in the late 1970s, thirty-five million people have left to seek new lives abroad. Over five hundred thousand Chinese citizens now live in South Korea, though more than two-thirds of them are ethnic Koreans from northeastern China, who receive an ambivalent reception when they return to the homeland that their grandparents or great-grandparents left many decades ago. Some one hundred thousand Chinese have settled in Siberia, many moving back and forth across the border, and Chinese immigrants have recently overtaken Koreans as Japan's largest ethnic minority.

This constant multidirectional movement involves social dislocation and sometimes friction but also weaves the region together in new ways. Wherever we go we meet people with relatives in Guandong or Inner Mongolia, Osaka or Seoul.

But still no Russians.

It is not until my last day in the city that I finally encounter the Russians of Harbin. By chance, a grand reunion of Harbin Russians—the first of its kind—is taking place in the city, and suddenly the lobby of the Modern Hotel rings again with the sound of animated Russian conversation and impromptu accordion renderings of "Moscow Nights" and "Katyusha." At breakfast, an aging woman with a fox-fur stole and the poise of a ballerina sits at the table next to mine, greeting new arrivals with multilingual rapture: "Darling! It's been years! *Kak dol'go!* And this must by little Katya. *Milaya, milaya!*"

And listening to the voices, I finally understand what became of the Russians of Harbin. For the conversations in the lobby are interspersed with unmistakable accents of Texas, South Africa, and my own homeland, Australia. The man who sits opposite me in the lobby as I wait to check out comes from Brisbane—the city where his parents settled as refugees in the late 1940s, when he was seven years old. The woman who joins in our conversation has just flown in from California to rediscover the Harbin where her Russian parents lived before the war:

"My Pa once hit the jackpot in a lottery, and he and Ma spent a whole year living in a suite in this hotel," she says.

"How wonderful!" I exclaim.

"It was the worst decision of their lives," she responds darkly.

With the rise of Japanese influence in Manchuria, many Russians left Harbin and those who remained often struggled to survive. In the mid-1930s, journalist Peter Fleming encountered a Harbin whose diverse cast of characters—"the Red engineer working on the Chinese Eastern Railway; the White Russian lady in exile, grown fat on the luxuries of nostalgia, for ever fantastically scheming the downfall of the Soviets"—were firmly under Japanese direction, for "behind Harbin's hybrid façade it is to-day the Japanese, and the Japanese only, who count."[35]

Another visitor to the city in 1935 described an urban landscape where "most shops are shuttered and everything is listless."[36] Ever since the influx of refugees from the Russian Revolution, the fight to succeed in this city of light and darkness had been hard—"Harbin may have been the only city in East Asia in which Caucasian beggars outnumbered Asian beggars," writes one historian.[37] War, civil war and the Chinese revolution, accelerated the impoverishment and destruction of the community. Just a handful—mostly children of mixed marriages between Russians and Chinese or Koreans— braved the years of Mao's Great Leap Forward and the Cultural Revolution. By the 1950s, China was firmly in control of the city, and Russian Harbin had scattered to all corners of the earth—to Europe and the United States, and to Australia, New Zealand, and Israel.

But the exiles took with them fragments of this city in memories, music, and photographs. Through their family heirlooms and legends, their jokes, songs, and nostalgia, the dream city of Russian Harbin lives on in disembodied form, drifting around the world like the ethereal bubbles that float out across the Sungari River.

In Harbin Station today, the arches and turrets of the original building have been replaced by functional concrete and steel, and we queue in the crowded gray hallway to pass through the metal detectors that guard the entrance to every major railway station in China. The waiting room is a solid mass of people, all speaking Chinese, although there are doubtless ethnic Koreans, Mongolians, and others among them. A few minutes before our train is due to leave, the gates to the platform open and a human cascade spills out of the waiting room.

I keep one eye out for a plaque or monument commemorating the assassination that took place on this spot a century ago, but there is no sign that the tangled fates of Itō Hirobumi and his nemesis Ahn Jung-geun are remembered here.

The weather forecast posted in the Modern Hotel has provided an enigmatic prognosis for this day of our departure: "Today: Cloud. Tonight: Sun." Our train is ready to leave. We heave our cases on board and set off south, through Manchuria toward Changchun, Shenyang, the Yalu River, and the Diamond Mountains beyond.

Notes

1. See http://www.globalsecurity.org/military/world/dprk/dprk-dark.htm (accessed January 31, 2010).

2. Richard J. Smith, *Chinese Maps: Images of "All under Heaven"* (Oxford: Oxford University Press, 1996), 18–19.

3. Korean Buddhist Research Association, ed., *The History and Culture of Buddhism in Korea* (Seoul: Dongguk University Press, 1993), 196.

4. Hyech'o, *The Hye-Cho Diary: Memoir of the Pilgrimage to the Five Regions of India*, trans. and ed. Yang Han-Sung (Berkeley, Calif.: Asian Humanities Press, n.d.).

5. Kakhun, *Lives of Eminent Korean Monks: The Haedong Kosŭng Chŏn*, trans. Peter H. Lee (Cambridge, Mass.: Harvard University Press, 1969), 93.

6. Quoted in Richard D. McBride II, *Domesticating the Dharma: Buddhist Cults and the Hwaŏm Synthesis in Silla Korea* (Honolulu: University of Hawaii Press, 2008), 132.

7. Isabella Bird Bishop, *Korea and Her Neighbours* (New York: Fleming H. Revell Co., 1898), 67.

8. J. B. Pratt, *The Pilgrimage of Buddhism and a Buddhist Pilgrimage* (New York: Macmillan, 1928), 422.

9. John Kieschnick, *The Impact of Buddhism on Chinese Material Culture* (Princeton, N.J.: Princeton University Press, 2003), 87.

10. Chris C. Park, *Sacred Worlds: An Introduction to Geography and Religion* (London: Routledge, 1994), 260.

11. E. G. Kemp, *Chinese Mettle* (London: Hodder and Stoughton, 1921), 11.

12. Two etchings by Kemp ("Study after Vandyck" and "The Coming Storm") are listed in the catalogue of the Keppel collection of engravings, which was displayed in the Columbian Exposition's Woman's Building, to show "what has been done by women engravers during the past three centuries." See Jeanne Madeline Weimann, *The Fair Women: The Story of the Woman's Building, World's Columbian Exposition, Chicago, 1893* (Chicago: Academy Chicago, 1981), 300–304.

13. Helen Darbishire, "In Memoriam: Emily Georgiana Kemp," in *Somerville College Chapel Addresses and other Papers*, 10–13 (London: Headley Brothers, 1962), 11.

14. E. G. Kemp, *The Face of China: Travels in East, North, Central and Western China* (London: Chatto and Windus, 1909), 1.

15. On Cumming, Keith, Harris, and other women travelers in Asia, see Jane Robinson, *Wayward Women: A Guide to Women Travelers* (Oxford: Oxford University Press, 1994).

16. E. G. Kemp, *There Followed Him Women: Pages from the Life of the Women's Missionary Association of the Baptist Missionary Society, 1967 to 1927* (London: Baptist Missionary Society, n.d.), vii.

17. See E. G. Kemp, *Reminiscences of a Sister: S. Florence Edwards, of Taiyuanfu* (London: Carey Press, 1919), 9; "Driving Force Was Right from Waterloo," *Rochdale Observer*, March 20, 2006.

18. See Judy G. Batson, *Her Oxford* (Nashville: Vanderbilt University Press, 2008), 65.

19. E. G. Kemp, *The Face of Manchuria, Korea and Russian Turkestan* (New York: Duffield, 1911), 224.

20. Kemp, *Reminiscences of a Sister*, 10.

21. Kemp, *Reminiscences of a Sister*, 28.

22. Darbishire, "In Memoriam: Emily Georgiana Kemp."

23. On Kemp's study at Somerville, see Darbishire, "In Memoriam: Emily Georgiana Kemp"; Vera Brittain, *The Women at Oxford: A Fragment of History* (London: Macmillan, 1960), 83, 186–87; and Batson, *Her Oxford*, 65. (Batson's work is also the source of information on the medal from the French Geographical Society.)

24. Darbishire, "In Memoriam: Emily Georgiana Kemp," 11.

25. Kemp, *The Face of China*, viii.

26. Letter from Marcus Dods to Miss Emily G. Kemp FGRS, August 31, 1907, in Marcus Dods, *Later Letters of Marcus Dods DD* (London: Hodder and Stoughton, 1911), 270.

27. Mrs. John Clarence Lee, *Across Siberia Alone: An American Woman's Adventures* (New York: John Lane, 1914), 109.

28. Kemp, *The Face of Manchuria, Korea and Russian Turkestan*, 152.

29. Kemp, *The Face of Manchuria, Korea and Russian Turkestan*, 153–54.

30. B. L. Putnam Weale, *Manchu and Muscovite* (London: Macmillan, 1904), 137.

31. Putnam Weale, *Manchu and Muscovite*, 138.

32. Kemp, *The Face of Manchuria, Korea and Russian Turkestan*, 106.

33. Kemp, *The Face of Manchuria, Korea and Russian Turkestan*, 3.

34. Bruno Lasker, ed., *Problems of the Pacific, 1931* (Chicago: University of Chicago Press, 1932), 438; J. R. Stewart, "Chinese Migration to Manchuria Setting New Records," *Far Eastern Affairs* 9, no. 18 (August 28, 1940): 214–15.

35. Peter Fleming, *One's Company: A Journey to China* (London: Jonathan Cape, 1934), 68.

36. Audrey Harris, *Eastern Visas* (London: Collins, 1939), 24.

37. Joshua Fogel, "The Japanese and the Jews: A Comparative Analysis of Their Communities in Harbin, 1898–1930," in *New Frontiers: Imperialisms New Communities in East Asia, 1842–1953*, ed. Robert Bickers and Christian Henriot, 88–108 (Manchester, UK: Manchester University Press, 2000), 94.

CHAPTER TWO

Manchurian Ghosts
Changchun and Shenyang

Lost Countries

Like Saxony, Walachia, and the Kingdom of the Khazars, Manchuria is a lost country. A vast and vaguely bounded area once inhabited by a kaleidoscope of cultural groups—Jurchen, Khitan, Daur, Nanai, Korean, Han Chinese, and many others—Manchuria has now vanished from the map, being transformed into the much more prosaic "Northeast China." The flowing script of Manchu, the native tongue of China's last imperial dynasty, still adorns monuments all over Northeast China, but this is virtually a dead tongue, a language with only a handful of living speakers. According to Chinese censuses, more than ten million people belong to the Manchu ethnic minority, but Northeast China has a population of 107 million. Traveling through the land that Emily Kemp knew as "Manchuria," we have met Han Chinese, Mongolians, Koreans, Russians, and others, but we have yet to meet anyone who claims to be Manchurian.

Yet, the Manchurian presence lingers on in the substratum of history. Veins of Manchurian culture run through the dress, food, architecture, and ritual that we unthinkingly label "Chinese," and distant paroxysms in this "cradle of conflict" still faintly reverberate through the politics of China, Japan, and North and South Korea today.[1] Speeding south in our train from Harbin toward Shenyang, along the line once controlled by Japan's mighty South Manchurian Railway Company (SMR), we are gradually being drawn back into the lost world of Manchuria.

In the first half of the twentieth century, railways were the arteries of empire, and those who controlled them had powers of life and death over the lands through which they ran. The railways of Manchuria were particularly vital because the trains that crossed the Manchurian plains linked the great population centers of East Asia to the Trans-Siberian Railway, and so to Europe overland.

As Emily Kemp noted, in 1910 the section of railway running from Harbin to Changchun was still in Russian hands, "and one's attention is continually arrested by the large numbers of soldiers who are kept along the line to guard it."[2] Japan's victory over Russia in 1905, however, had given it control of the southern sections of the railway beyond Changchun, and since the Japanese section of track used a narrower gauge than the Russian one, Kemp and her fellow passengers had to change trains at that point. At Changchun station, imperial rivalry was made palpable. By the time Kemp and Mary MacDougall arrived, Japan's SMR had already constructed a grand new station building, fronted with neoclassical columns and towering over the more modest Russian-owned station next door. And this was just the beginning; for, as Kemp foresaw, the Japanese annexation of Korea was indeed about to open the "highroad into Manchuria."

The SMR, founded three years before Kemp's visit, was already in the process of becoming an empire in its own right. This was surely one of the most ambitious business ventures in the history of the world: a corporation with a hubris to rival that of the British and Dutch East India Companies three centuries earlier. As well as running transport, the SMR owned huge tracts of land, administered entire sections of cities, acquired factories and mines, and operated its own police force and massive intelligence-gathering network. The hotel where Kemp and McDougall spent the night as they passed through Changchun had been opened by the SMR the year before they arrived and was called the Yamato Hotel ("Yamato" being the ancient and poetic name for Japan). Kemp described it with enthusiasm as "a brand new Japanese hotel just opposite the station, which was radiantly clean and fresh, such a contrast to the Russian one at Harbin."[3]

The railway line from Changchun to Mukden (today's Shenyang) was also "kept admirably clean," but, to Kemp's disappointment, the cars were "long open corridor ones," unlike the more private compartments of European trains. On the Japanese stretch of the line, she observed, "the trains always have military officials on board, who usually go only short stages, being replaced by others whenever they get out."[4] Indeed, the SMR's proliferating network of lines provided Japan with the excuse to station growing numbers of troops throughout northeastern China and to intervene ever more deeply in the troubled political life of the region. As Gotō Shinpei, the SMR's first president, put it (in words succinctly summarized by an employee), "Japanese imperialism in its advance into Manchuria . . . chose to assume the form of a railroad company."[5]

The high-speed train that carries us toward Shenyang (which will be our base for exploring the heartlands of Manchuria) passes through a landscape that, in many places, seems little changed from the one described by Kemp: an expanse of broad horizons dotted with red brick cottages that would not have looked out of place in Kemp's native Lancashire. But signs of the Japanese empire are even more elusive than the traces of Russian Harbin—for unlike the Russian architecture of Harbin, the relics of the Japanese SMR evoke very little affection from Chinese people.

A train, as Michel Foucault once observed, is "an extraordinary bundle of relations." It takes people from one place to another; it transforms the towns and countryside through which it passes; and it also, for a few hours, creates a microcosm of society, an involuntary community of people hurtling through the ever-changing landscape beyond its windows.[6] Our carriage, like Kemp's, is a "long open corridor one," but its tight rows of airline-style seats provide only limited scope for interaction. Emma Campbell has entered into conversation with the small, soft-spoken man in the seat next to her, who is recounting his life story. Otherwise, our carriage is largely quiet apart from the occasional snores of passengers and the chime of cell phones. The military presence has disappeared from the railway, and today it is a small embodiment of the new, dynamic, commercial China that speeds southward toward Shenyang.

The man sitting next to Emma comes from a remote village in Inner Mongolia but has managed to gain a degree from a prestigious university. Now he is an engineer living in Shenyang with his wife and children, and supervising construction projects for the Chinese branch of a giant European supermarket chain.

While he tells his story, the sun sinks toward the flat horizon, turning deep red as evening falls. The smoke from the cottage chimneys settles in the still air, gradually forming a thin layer of haze over the endless ploughed fields. It is growing dark as we reach Shenyang, but we can still just make out Dickensian slums on the city outskirts. When we approach North Shenyang station, though, the city rises glittering before us, its soaring postmodern architecture bejeweled with multicolored neon lights. Shenyang, with its official population of seven million (and many more unofficial residents) is to the twenty-first century what the cities of Lancashire were to the nineteenth.

We take our suitcases down from the racks and head for the exit. The man from Inner Mongolia looks out of the window at the lights of his new hometown.

"Life in Shenyang is good," he says.

And then, a little sadly, "But whenever I have holidays I go back to Mongolia, back to my village, to see the white sand, and the green grass, and the blue sky, and to ride horses . . . "

The Manchu Tombs

The great American scholar of China's frontier regions Owen Lattimore, writing twenty years after Kemp visited this region, described Manchuria as "the storm centre of the world."[7] It was the place where three empires—Chinese, Russian, and Japanese—collided, and it was also at the heart of a rhythm of history, a tidal ebb and flow, which recurred across the centuries and millennia of the Chinese past.

As Chinese imperial dynasties weakened, they became prey to attacks from the martial, horse-riding Manchu and Mongol societies on their northeastern border. But in the end the northern invaders themselves, having burnt, destroyed, and conquered the lands to the south, were (to a greater or lesser extent) always culturally subdued by those they had militarily defeated. Each wave of outsiders in turn adopted the trappings of Chinese culture and, "gradually losing the characteristics of conquering aliens, became essentially a Chinese ruling class."[8] The pattern was repeated in the Liao Dynasty of the tenth to early twelfth centuries, the Jurchen Jin Dynasty of the twelfth to thirteenth centuries, and the mighty Yuan Dynasty of the Mongol emperors (1217–1368). The last of these great tidal movements—the rise and fall of Manchu Qing Empire—began with cataclysmic turbulence on the plains around present-day Shenyang in the early seventeenth century and ended with bizarre pathos in Changchun in 1945.

When Kemp and MacDougall arrived in Shenyang in the spring of 1910, the last representative of that dynasty still ruled all of China, and their first expedition was "naturally to the Foo Ling tombs to see where the great founder of the Manchu Dynasty lies buried." They traveled in a "weird glass chariot, quite suggestive of Cinderella's coach; it had windows the whole way round, and was lined with mouse-coloured plush, not to mention a fine mirror opposite us."[9] In the early twentieth century, such excursions were no simple matter. English-language guide books were nonexistent, and the imperial tombs and palaces were not open to the general public, so, here as elsewhere, Kemp relied on her missionary connections to arrange the visit and to obtain the special permit needed to enter the tomb precinct.

Following in her footsteps, on our first day in Shenyang we hire a less exotic form of transport—a regular Shenyang taxi—to take us first to the tombs (whose name is now normally written "Fuling") and then to the Imperial Palace in the center of Shenyang—a place that, to Kemp, had a special significance as a point where her own troubled life and the history of the Chinese empire intersected.

The Fuling Tombs of the empire builder Nurhaci and his empress Yehenala are now on the eastern fringes of Shenyang suburbia, past the massive power station, the slums of crumbling brick houses (each with a surprisingly neat stack of cardboard boxes outside the door), and the gated community of huge new architect-designed villas. In front of the main entrance to the tomb complex there is the usual clutter of ticket offices and public toilets, but inside the long Venetian red wall that runs around the complex, we are in a landscape that seems hardly to have changed since Kemp walked here a century ago, or indeed since the Qing emperors came to perform their ancestral rituals three hundred or more years ago.

The Fuling Tombs, Shenyang (S. Morris)

The day is glorious, and the sunlight illuminates the delicate veins of the trees' new leaves. There are few visitors at the tombs: just a couple of family groups strolling on the ramparts or foraging for wild herbs beneath the pine trees that line the long, sacred way, watched over by the impassive gaze of a parade of stone camels, horses, lions, and griffins. (The herbs, we are told, are particularly good for flavoring dumplings.) The main sound to be heard is birdsong. Striped squirrels and curious little marmotlike creatures dart though the shadows, and a cuckoo calls softly in the distance.

Beyond the sacred way, a steep flight of stone steps leads up to the ceremonial courtyard, which is enclosed by high gray-stone ramparts. In the gateway to the courtyard, a great granite bixi—a mythical being shaped like a turtle—holds aloft a stele inscribed in Chinese, Manchu, and Mongolian script. The bixi's nose is smooth and shiny from being rubbed for good luck by many hands. A gold sash has been laid across its neck, and a mass of small coins thrown by visitors cover its back. On rainy days, according to local legend, the spectral outline of a beautiful ghost woman appears in the stone on the reverse side of the stele, but on this clear spring morning the stone is smooth and devoid of phantoms.

We wander along the top of the ramparts, treading warily to avoid the swarms of ladybirds that have gathered to sun themselves on its warm stone. A hoopoe appears for a moment, alighting on the ornate roof of the Eastern Hall, once used to store funeral silks that were burnt as part of the Qing ancestral rites. The hoopoe's crested head, among the parade of little sculpted animals on the ridgeline, seems to reflect the gold of the glazed tiles that overhang the roof's blue ornamented eaves. At the far end of the courtyard is a further ritual hall with a curious array of stone creatures in a pit behind it, and beyond that, the walkway curves in a semicircle around the simple mound of the grave itself, which is covered in wild violets.

The man who lies beneath the violets, Nurhaci hala-i Aisin-Gioro (to give him his full Manchu name) was born in 1558 into a chiefly family belonging to a tribe of horse-riding farmers and hunters in the mountainous borderlands where China and Korea meet. His rise from this relative obscurity to become the patriarch of the Qing Dynasty was, as Kemp put it, "like a romance, and no parallel to it is to be found in the pages of history."[10]

At the start of the seventeenth century, when Nurhaci was at the height of his powers, the tides of Chinese dynastic history were turning. The once mighty Ming Dynasty was in disarray, undermined by corruption, famines, and epidemics, and further weakened by the consequences of the failed attempt by Japanese warlord Toyotomi Hideyoshi to invade Korea and China. Nurhaci, a brilliant strategic leader, began to consolidate his power over his fellow Manchus and the neighboring Mongols and, in 1616, declared himself their khan. Inspired by the Manchu tradition of hunting in groups, Nurhaci formed his followers into disciplined military bands, each possessing distinctive colored banners that (like the pennants of modern sports teams) symbolized structure and identity. At first, his rise was welcomed by China's Ming court, which rewarded him with titles and favors.

But Nurhaci had greater ambitions. By the middle of the 1620s, he had established his capital in Shenyang and was ready to launch an all-out assault on the Ming Empire—then riven by internal rebellion.

Nurhaci did not live to see the final victory: he died of wounds received in battle in 1626. It was left to his son Hung Taiji to consolidate the Manchu victories, subdue the Koreans (who loyally insisted on continuing to pay tribute to the dying Ming Dynasty), and proclaim the new dynasty of the Qing—meaning "pure." And it was only after the sudden death of Hung Taiji that Nurhaci's grandson fulfilled the imperial dream, being enthroned as emperor of China in Beijing's Forbidden City on June 6, 1644, two months after the last of the Ming emperors hanged himself.

Meanwhile, the cultural assimilation of the conquerors by the conquered was already underway. Nurhaci's palace in Shenyang, though resplendent with colored tiles and adorned with golden dragons, is octagonal—representing the original eight Manchu banners. The palace of his son Hung Taiji has

The Imperial Palace, Shenyang (S. Morris)

spaces for conducting the shamanic ceremonies of the northeastern tribes. But the tomb that Hung Taiji built for his father, like the tomb in which he himself lies buried, carefully replicates the Confucian and Daoist iconography of the Ming emperors' tombs.

Rather than becoming wholly Sinified, though, the Qing rulers and their bannermen preserved elements of Manchu tradition even as they became Confucianized and Chinese speaking: Manchu shamanism as well as Confucian ritual shaped the rites that were performed by generations of Qing rulers at the Shenyang tombs. Constant ethnic and cultural mixing revitalized the Chinese dynastic system, and under the Manchu Qing emperors of the seventeenth and eighteenth centuries, imperial China experienced its final blaze of political glory and intellectual creativity.

By the time Kemp came to Shenyang in 1910, however, Qing rule had in its turn succumbed to inertia, corruption, and foreign pressures, and was in a state of terminal decay. The walls of the tomb compound that Kemp visited on her first day in Shenyang were riddled with bullet holes left by the Russian and Japanese forces that had, just five years earlier, turned the surrounding landscape into a battlefield. The Imperial Palace of Nurhaci and Hung Taiji was filled with treasures, but its precious porcelains were "piled in endless heaps in glass cases, which probably remained unopened for decades."[11] Aisin-Gioro Pu Yi, a tenth-generation descendant of Nurhaci, and destined to be China's last emperor, occupied the Dragon Throne in Beijing, but he was a four-year-old child. Less than two years later, he would be deposed in the republican revolution.

The Last Emperor's Unfinished Palace

On the New People's Avenue in central Changchun, I almost walk straight past the dead woman without seeing her. Her presence, amongst a group of people waiting at the bus stop, is so unexpected that it would be easy not to notice her.

The sky is clear, the spring sun casts a sharp light on the pillars and turrets of the city's buildings, and the cherry trees are all in bloom. The dead woman's companions are smoking and chatting quietly, but she lies absolutely still on a low canvass trolley. From her toes to her forehead, she is covered with a flowered counterpane. Only her hair is visible, streaming like a dark frozen waterfall over the end of her stretcher. She must have died a few hours earlier, and from the sheen of that thick, black hair, I guess that she died young.

The life and death of Jilin University Number One Hospital, whose somber brick facade looms over this street corner, flow out from the building onto the pavements around. A man in striped pajamas and bedroom slippers wanders down to the bus stop for a smoke, his head thickly wrapped in crepe bandages. A group of young cadet policemen in crisp, blue uniforms approach us. Are they worried about the presence of the corpse at the bus stop? But no; such things are entirely normal. Instead, one cadet shyly produces his cell phone.

"Excuse me," he says to Emma, "Can I have my photo taken with you?"

"Me too, me too," echo his comrades.

So we take a succession of photos of Emma and the young policemen in various poses, while a few meters further down the road, a dusty private van draws up, the dead woman is gently loaded by her companions through its rear hatch, and she sets off on her last journey home.

It is not only the encounter with the dead woman that leaves me with the sense that Changchun is haunted. It is also the city itself: its immensely wide boulevards, its faintly menacing 1930s architecture (of which Jilin University Number One Hospital is a fine example), and its huge, almost empty parks, sections of which are rapidly being turned into construction sites. Over everything, it seems, stretches the shadow of this city's uneasy history.

For, between 1932 and 1945, this unremarkable Chinese provincial town was briefly "the New Capital"—Xinjing (Shinkyō in Japanese)—one of the twentieth century's most extraordinary (and short-lived) attempts to create a global and multicultural metropolis. Inspired in part by Walter Burley Griffin's design for my own hometown, Canberra, Xinjing was conceived on a far more imposing scale. This was intended to be a symbol of the world's grandest experiment in imperial social engineering, the place where the revived glories of the last Chinese empire and the new energies of an expansionist Japan would be combined.

Having lost his imperial throne at the age of six and regained it for less than two weeks at the age of eleven (when he was briefly restored in an unsuccessful coup), China's last emperor was to be installed on the throne for a third time in 1934—but this time, on the throne of a political chimera: Manchukuo, whose showplace capital was to be the planned city of Xinjing.[12] His first enthronement as Chinese emperor had been engineered by a dying dowager empress; his second, by a prominent Chinese warlord. His reincarnation as emperor of Manchukuo was orchestrated by the Japanese troops guarding the SMR. After staging a fictitious "terrorist attack" on the rail line at Shenyang in 1931, the Japanese military used this as their excuse to seize control of Manchuria, which they then proclaimed the independent state of Manchukuo.

Manchukuo was the fulfillment of that Japanese advance in Manchuria that Kemp predicted in 1910—and which she lived to observe from afar, as an old woman in the 1930s living alone in a house on the edge of London's Regent Park, her traveling days mere memories.[13] Shunned by the most of the world as a facade for Japanese expansionism, Manchukuo was the most paradoxical of short-lived modern states. Its creators included idealistic Japanese bureaucrats with grand dreams of multicultural social engineering but also power-hungry Japanese military and business leaders; Chinese still loyal to the old Qing Dynasty, as well as Manchus and Mongols with ethnonationalist ambitions. Investment by giant Japanese firms like Nissan fuelled Manchukuo's industrial development, but the new country's government bonds were (initially at least) underwritten with the help of profits from the opium trade. Chinese (who were always officially referred to as "Manchukuoans") occupied all the main political posts in the country, but real power was firmly in the hands of their deputies, who were always Japanese. Such was the realm over which Pu Yi reigned (but did not rule) from 1934 to 1945.

The planners of Manchukuo's New Capital Xinjing envisaged an imperial palace fronting onto a great avenue—the Avenue of Obedience to Heaven (now known as the New People's Avenue) lined with the state's major public buildings: an arena that could be used for events to outshine the mass political rallies of Mussolini's Rome, Hitler's Nuremberg, or Stalin's Moscow. Just as Shenyang's Imperial Palace and tombs reflect the intermingling of Manchu and Han Chinese culture, so the architecture of the Manchukuo capital reflected cultural confluences, for Manchukuo was a modernizing state, where (in theory) industry and commerce would flourish and Han Chinese, Manchu, Mongols, Koreans, and Japanese would live in utopian harmony.[14]

The space surrounding Pu Yi's never-completed palace embodies the dream, the reality, and the ironies of his insubstantial empire. On one side of the avenue stands the building that once housed Manchukuo's State Council, symbol of the nation's loudly proclaimed independence. But looking at this building, whose facade survives almost unchanged today, I realize there is something oddly familiar about it. It is bears an uncanny resemblance to the Japanese parliament building in Tokyo—no coincidence, since the construction of both buildings was overseen by the same Japanese designer.[15] And on the other side is the great, dark building once occupied by Manchukuo's Ministry of Military Affairs, from where Japan's Kwantung Army oversaw a massive and multiethnic apparatus of social control, responsible both for propagating the utopian vision of Manchukuo and for rooting out any resistance to this vision: a task they pursued with energy, discipline, and a great deal of violence. Among the enemies they unsuccessfully pursued was a communist guerilla band operating in eastern Manchuria and led by a young Korean named Kim Song-Ju, who, under his alias Kim Il-Sung, was later to become Eternal President of North Korea.

The diminutive Pu Yi, meanwhile, lacking all power to make real political decisions, engaged in interminable debates with the Japanese military and the SMR about the one thing he could determine: the design of his projected palace. He wanted a Chinese design, and he wanted it to have a garden laid out according to the principles of the traditional Chinese vision of the universe, with himself, the Son of Heaven, occupying the center of the cosmos.[16] After a lifetime of being manipulated by others, it seemed that, on this one matter, Pu Yi was about to win the battle.

But by then much larger battles were already being lost. In August 1945, with the palace still unfinished, Japan was defeated in the Asia-Pacific War, and Pu Yi's Manchukuo dissolved as suddenly as it had appeared. A few years later, China's new communist government took over the grand monuments of the Manchukuo capital and (with a conscious sense of rectifying history) turned the headquarters of the Ministry of Military Affairs into the medical center now known as Jilin University Number One Hospital.

Such is the weight of history that lay over the deathbed of the young woman whose corpse we encounter lying under her flowered bedspread at the Changchun bus stop. During the days that follow, I find myself thinking about her—wondering who she was, how she died, and what images floated through her mind as she journeyed inexorably toward darkness in a ward in the former Manchukuo Ministry of Military Affairs. Do Changchun's citizens today, as they confront the everyday struggles of life and death, sense the presence of the uneasy ghosts of history who lurk in their public spaces?

The grand villa on the city's outskirts where Pu Yi waited in vain for the completion of his palace is now a carefully reconstructed museum. Multilingual placards on the walls condemn the "traitors" who collaborated with the Manchukuo puppet state, the last emperor's state train stands stationary in the garden, and a waxwork likeness of his opium-addicted first wife lounges on her chaise longue. A boisterous group of Taiwanese tourists is going round the museum when we visit, but entry costs eighty yuan, and our taxi driver, who has lived in Changchun for twenty years, has never been inside.

"What's it like?" he asks eagerly after we come out of the museum, adding, "I'd love to see it, particularly the train. But I can't afford a ticket."

The following day, however, we meet one group of people who have come here especially in search of Manchukuo. I am in the Imperial Palace built by Pu Yi's ancestors in Shenyang, looking for the Manchu treasures—that jumbled mountain of porcelains, jades, and bronzes—which Emily Kemp glimpsed in the palace storehouse in 1910. I can find no sign of them. Perhaps these treasures are preserved in museums elsewhere. More likely, though, decades of war, civil war, revolution, and cultural revolution have simply swept them away. Instead, I find myself caught up in the fringes of a tour group from Japan, on a five-day trip to see the highlights of the old South Manchurian Railway Company.

In Shenyang today, only a few buildings from the era of Manchukuo and Japanese domination survive, but a new Japanese presence is visible everywhere. Our hotel lobby is full of businessmen in gray suits negotiating joint ventures with Chinese partners. The great industrial complex of Tiexi, on the outskirts of Shenyang, was built during the days of Pu Yi's empire to accommodate Japanese investors in Manchukuo. After the communist revolution it become known, in succession, as a showplace of socialist heavy industry and then as one of the most polluted places on earth. Now resurrected as an "Economic and Technology Development Zone," it hosts a mass of multinational corporations including Japanese giants like Sanyo, Mitsubishi, and Panasonic. Meanwhile, droves of young Japanese come to live and work in Northeast China for a few years, and tourists from Japan (some of them elderly people born in prewar Manchuria) arrive on Manchukuo nostalgia tours.

The nostalgia has rather uncomfortable overtones. This tour group, I discover, comes from Hiroshima, so its members have more reasons than most to remember the disastrous results of Japan's imperial ambitions. Their travels have taken them to see the grand prewar buildings that still line the waterfront in the port city of Dalian, and now to Shenyang to see the Imperial Palace here. But they are not going further north, to confront the bleak complex of ruined archways and factory chimneys that stands on the fringes of Harbin: the remains of an immense industrial research laboratory where the Japanese Imperial Army once manufactured chemical and biological weapons, and tested them on captive Chinese and allied prisoners of war.

The Japanese tourists are attentive and polite.

"I think some Chinese people still resent us Japanese because of, you know . . . what happened during the war," murmurs one, when I ask her about her impressions of China.

She is, unfortunately, right. The comments we have heard along the route about Japan's contemporary presence in the region have ranged from tact to ferocious nationalism: "I hate the Japanese," said one particularly forthright taxi driver, "I could kill the lot of them." (But, then again, he loathed the imperialistic British, too.) Japan's government has not made things any easier. Promoting economic engagement while avoiding the subject of the past until pushed into reluctant apologies, Japan's leaders have failed to appease the unhappy ghosts of empire, which continue to trouble relations between this region's two greatest powers.

It remains unclear whether new flows of migration and finance will make relations easier for the next generation. The Hiroshima tour group is guided by a young Chinese woman. She tells me that she has never lived in Japan. Yet, her spoken Japanese is so flawless that she can explain the symbolism of Nurhaci's gilded octagonal pavilion and describe life in the quarters of the imperial concubines with eloquent ease.

"I'm taking this lot back to Dalian tomorrow," she tells me as her Japanese charges disperse to snatch a few final photographs. "Where are you headed?"

"We want to see a bit more of the region around Shenyang first. Then we're going to Dandong and North Korea."

The guide's eyes widen with surprise and curiosity. "North Korea!" she says. "Very strange! Very dangerous!"

Notes

1. On the notion of Manchuria as "the cradle of conflict," see Owen Lattimore, *Manchuria: Cradle of Conflict* (New York: Macmillan, 1932).

2. E. G. Kemp, *The Face of Manchuria, Korea and Russian Turkestan* (New York: Duffield, 1911), 8.

3. Kemp, *Face of Manchuria, Korea and Russian Turkestan*, 8.

4. Kemp, *Face of Manchuria, Korea and Russian Turkestan*, 8–9.

5. Itō Takeo, citing the SMR's first president Gotō Shinpei, in Itō Takeo, *Life along the South Manchurian Railway: The Memoirs of Itō Takeo*, trans. Joshua Fogel (Armonk, N.Y.: M. E. Sharpe, 1988), 5.

6. Michel Foucault, "Of Other Spaces (1967): Heterotopia," trans. Jay Miskowiez, at http://foucault.info/documents/heteroTopia/foucault.heteroTopia.en.html (accessed December 22, 2009).

7. Lattimore, *Manchuria*, 4.

8. Lattimore, *Manchuria*, 38.

9. Kemp, *Face of Manchuria, Korea and Russian Turkestan*, 16–17.

10. Kemp, *Face of Manchuria, Korea and Russian Turkestan*, 11.

11. Kemp, *Face of Manchuria, Korea and Russian Turkestan*, 21.

12. See Shin'ichi Yamamuro, *Manchuria under Japanese Dominion*, trans. Ezra Fogel (Philadelphia: University of Pennsylvania Press, 2006).

13. According to information kindly provided by David Munroe of the Scottish Royal Geographical Society, Kemp's address was 26 Hartley House, Regent's Park. She was a member of the Scottish Royal Geographical Society from 1906 until her death on May 8, 1940.

14. On the design of Xinjing, see David D. Buck, "Railway City and National Capital: Two Faces of the Modern in Changchun," in *Remaking the Chinese City: Modernity and National Identity, 1900–1950*, ed. Joseph W. Esherick, 65–89 (Honolulu: University of Hawaii Press, 1999); and Qinghua Guo, "Changchun: Unfinished Capital Planning of Manzhouguo, 1932–1942," *Urban History* 31, no. 4 (2004): 100–117.

15. Guo, "Changchun," 115–16.

16. Guo, "Changchun," 108–14.

CHAPTER THREE

Of Sacred Mountains
Liaoyang and the Thousand Peaks

Light in the Mirror

The vision of sacred mountains is much older than Buddhism itself. These wild and rugged places—their summits vanishing into the clouds and their crags sculpted by wind and ice into transcendent forms—have been seen since ancient times as links between the human world and the world beyond. In the Daoist realm of the early Chinese dynasties, "mountains were revered for their own power to protect the welfare of the communities, or the state as a whole," but also as cosmic pillars: "the intermediary realms in man's communication with heaven, or with heavenly spirits."[1] Their numinous power evoked both wonder and fear, for mountains were "a zone of sacred horror."[2] By the time of the Han Dynasty, each emperor was expected to perform rituals to harness the power and avert the horror at the mountains that marked the outer limits of his empire to north, south, east, and west, and at Mount Song, which marked the center.

Unlike Buddhism, which spread throughout Northeast Asia, Daoism had only limited influence beyond the limits of the Chinese empire, but in Japan and Korea local nature worship and shamanic beliefs also imbued mountains with supernatural forces. In Korean art, the mountain spirit Sansin, "evident to human senses through vitality, power and mystery of the physical landmass as well as in dreams and visions," is depicted as a bearded man who rides upon a tiger.[3] The Korean landscape itself was said to be home to the spirits of longevity, who were lured to the peninsula by its mirror lakes and soaring mountains, and who "dwelt principally on three lofty peaks": Mount Paektu in the far north, the Diamond Mountains in the east, and Mount Halla on the southernmost island of Jeju.[4]

Buddhism infused these old beliefs with new layers of meaning. To the litany of China's holy mountains were added the Buddhist sacred peaks of Mount Wutai in the north, Mount Jiuhua in the south, Mount Putuo in the east, and Mount Omei in the west. The austere and lonely heights of the mountains became places for the practice of the ascetic rituals surrounding the Maitreya, the Buddha of the Future, whose cult flourished along the Silk Road, in early Tang Dynasty China, and in Korea's Silla Kingdom. Korean devotees of the Maitreya Cult made pilgrimages to the holy mountains of the Korean Peninsula and beyond. The monk Sunje is said to have first encountered the Maitreya Buddha in a vision on China's Mount Wutai, and he in turn trained the famous Korean Buddhist master Jinpyo who traveled the length and breadth of the peninsula teaching the rituals of the Future Buddha, eventually founding the eighth-century Paryon Monastery on the Diamond Mountains' Maitreya Peak (Mirukpong).[5]

Officials and literati followed in the footsteps of the monks. Kwon Geun (1352–1409), whose vision of sea clouds and jade lotus is quoted in the first pages of this book, was born "just a few hundred *ri* away" from the Diamond Mountains but in his early life had never seen their landscape with his own eyes. In 1396, he was sent as Korean envoy to the Chinese imperial court, and—diplomacy in fourteenth-century China being a very different matter from today's hasty meetings behind closed doors—one of his diplomatic duties was to compose poems on a series of subjects set for him by the Chinese emperor. Among the works ordered by the emperor was a poem on the Diamond Mountains. Kwon Geun was forced to admit he had not seen the mountains but thereupon resolved that on his return he would travel to their heights and so "assuage the deep desire that I have so long felt."[6]

Yi Kok, who served for years as an official of China's Mongol Yuan Dynasty and died the year before Kwon Geun was born, wrote one of the earliest of many Korean travelers' diaries of a journey to the Diamond Mountains, adorned (as all such diaries were) with poems distilling his vision of the landscape. Over 650 years ago, sitting by the shores of Samilpo ("Three Days Lake"), the circular lake that lies between the mountains and the sea, he wrote the following:

> The water brims with the light of heaven, as limpid as a mirror.
> The mountains which pierce the autumn sky are lucent as crystal.[7]

The White Pagoda, Liaoyang (S. Morris)

In modern times, a new belief system has been added to the atmosphere of awe and mystery that surrounds sacred mountains: the religion of nationalism. Mountaineers plant national flags on summits; China and Korea passionately contest their rights to the soaring peak that the Koreans call Mount Paektu (Baekdu in South Korean romanization) and Chinese call Changbaishan, straddling on their common border. Complex national symbolism is deployed by both sides in the pas de deux of political estrangement and rapprochement between North and South Korea over access to the Diamond Mountains. Heading through Northeast China on the way to those mountains, I speculate whether the long drawn-out Six Party Talks on North Korea might be more fruitful if their participants spent less time discussing politics and more time setting each other themes for poetry writing.

The Walls of Liaoyang

Here and there, the paths of tribute and diplomatic mission that led to the Chinese capital intersected with paths linking the Buddhist sacred mountains, and one such point of intersection was the city of Liaoyang, where the tribute route from Korea to the imperial heartland met the pilgrimage route to China's Thousand Peaks (Qianshan).

Emily Kemp described Liaoyang in 1910 as "the most beautiful of Manchurian cities, for within its walls are orchards of plum, cherry, apricot and pear, which look radiantly lovely against the somber background of the walls." Standing just outside those walls, she painted the massive gateway "through which the Korean envoys used to pass when bringing tribute," its great masonry archway dwarfing the diminutive figures that moved through its shadows. Although the walls were more than three hundred years old, "the bricks," she wrote, "look as new in most parts as if they had just been built."[8] The only signs of ruin were breaches made by bombardment during the Russo-Japanese War for, less than six years before Kemp's visit, Liaoyang had been the site of one of the fiercest battles of that conflict. The fighting around the city left almost ten thousand Russian and Japanese soldiers dead; how many local people were also killed is not recorded.

Strolling down toward the Liao River that wound its way around the outside of the walls, Kemp and MacDougall looked across the landscape to the hills on the horizon, which "wore the lovely golden colour of an Egyptian scene," and picked out in the distance the knoll known as "Kuropatkin's Eye" where, in 1904, the Russian forces under the command of General Alexei Nikolaievich Kuropatkin had created an encampment overlooking the plain in the months before their defeat in the Battle of Liaoyang.

After reading Kemp's elegiac account of the city, it is depressing to turn to the Internet today and find the following description: "Liaoyang is a city in China, Liaoning Province, located in the middle of the heavily polluted Liaodong Peninsula. . . . Liaoyang suffers from air pollution in its metropolitan and industrial park areas. There is very limited nightlife in karaoke bars and clubs with lavish neon lights to attract customers near the downtown area."[9]

Our expectations are therefore low as we set off from Shenyang for the hour's drive along the wide motorway to Liaoyang in search of the Korean Gate and Kuropatkin's Eye. Signs of industrial pollution certainly abound. The farm fields between Shenyang and Liaoyang are dotted with slag heaps, and run-down heavy industrial factories ring the city center. As we enter Liaoyang, we pass a mule cart laden with massive wire coils, the mules' hooves slipping on the cobbled road as the beasts of burden strain at their load.

But the deep past of this city remains embedded in its industrial grime like jewels in tarnished metal, and most beautiful of all is the thirteen-story White Pagoda. Built in the twelfth century, at the time of the Jurchen Jin Dynasty—and today no longer white but smoky gray—the pagoda still soars over Liaoyang's central park. On each of its six sides, Buddhas sit serene in their crumbling niches, looking out with unmoved gaze across the centuries. Around the base of tower the devout have placed little Buddha figurines and honey-colored ceramic pots for holding incense sticks. And, as though to ensure that no traveler neglects this sacred landmark, the city authorities have added two large plaster Bugs Bunny statues, which welcome visitors to the White Pagoda with raised thumbs and goofy grins.

Beyond the pagoda, a huge and recently reconstructed temple bears testimony to the vibrant religious life of post-Mao China. A glass booth in the middle of the forecourt sells statues, CDs, and cell phones with Buddhist ringtones. The temple is freshly painted in vivid, primary colors, and at the foot of the broad flight of steps leading up to its main hall stand two stone elephants, their heads and eyes covered with large, red handkerchiefs, as though they are bashfully veiling themselves from public gaze. The hall itself contains a vast gold-plated statue, constructed in 2002 and billed as the largest seated Buddha in the world.

At the entrance, we buy some rather overpriced pink candles in shapes of lotus flowers to place at the feet of this gleaming colossus, and as we do so, a monk appears from the shadows, his face radiant with delight at the sight of foreign visitors. He is, as he explains, a latecomer to the monastic life. He left his family and the pleasures of the material world when he was already in his fifties and is eager to share his experience of enlightenment with others:

"I was living a bad life," he explains, "and so the Buddha punished me, sending me ill-health and ill-fortune. That was when I gave up my old ways and came to the temple. Now I've purified my mind and body. I eat only vegetables, only good things."

The monk's voice is musical and flows with the rhythms of one retelling a tale told many times before. He steps softly toward the sunlit veranda surrounding the temple, where another foreign visitor has appeared: a young South Korean man sporting a motorcycle jacket and an Elvis haircut. "The Buddha," continues the monk without a pause, "is for everyone, not just for Indians and Chinese and Koreans but for westerners, too. If you eat good things and remain pure, you too can become as healthy as me. Wise teachers tell us that our energy comes from within. The Buddha mind supplies all the energy we need. If you're truly pure and truly filled with the Buddha mind, you can be nourished even if you do not eat any food at all."

The monk's enthusiasm is infectious, and his unlined face and beaming smile seem the best of advertisements for his beliefs. Only his teeth are rather bad—but perhaps that is a legacy of his old, impure life.

Outside the dark red wall that surrounds the temple compound, other belief systems are on display: a group of fortune-tellers squat in a patch of

Fortune-tellers, Liaoyang (S. Morris)

shade, waiting for custom. Emma Campbell approaches one elderly man with a tall, black hat, long beard, and deep wrinkles around his dark and gleaming eyes. He rattles his fortune sticks and offers them to Emma, and a curious crowd gathers around to watch, joke, and proffer advice. The fortune sticks promise Emma wealth, long life, and something else about a horse, which causes much merriment amongst the crowd.

Here, as at the White Pagoda, we ask for directions to the city walls but are met with puzzled frowns. Walls? Gateways? Liaoyang has no city walls.

"A construction company's building a wall on the other side of town," offers one bystander helpfully.

Fragments of memory and myth survive for centuries, embedded like lichen in the cracks of ever-changing political systems. But sometimes the most monumental of human structures disappear like dust on the wind. The massive city walls that survived the bombardments of the Battle of Liaoyang have now vanished entirely, leaving no visible trace even of their foundations, and a century of upheavals, invasions, and revolutions, it seems, has also washed away memories of the Russo-Japanese War itself. As we stand by the river, looking toward that golden range of hills on the horizon where Kuropatkin made his encampment, a couple of men in a car pull up and ask us if we are lost.

The Korean Gate, Liaoyang (E. G. Kemp)

"Are you investors?" one asks hopefully.

Alas, Emma explains, we are merely historians, looking at the place where the Russians fought a great battle a century ago.

"Russians?" says the man, his face furrowed by bewildered amusement, "No. That's impossible. We've never been at war with the Russians."

The Dragon Spring Temple

Centuries before Victorian temperance campaigner Thomas Cook started organizing his rail trips for British holidaymakers or the German family firm of Baedeker began to publish its travel guides, Buddhist pilgrimages to the sacred mountains of Northeast Asia were already assuming some of the features of modern tourism. Lord Curzon, the great British imperialist who visited the Diamond Mountains some fifteen years before Kemp, noted the ubiquitous presence of "the Korean sightseer, the local equivalent to the English Bank Holiday young man on a bicycle—a character very common among the Koreans, who cultivate a keen eye for the scenery, and who love nothing better than a kukyeng [gugyeong], or pleasure trip in the country, where they can shirk all business and dawdle along as humour seizes them."[10]

Curzon was probably unaware that sightseeing trips to Northeast Asia's holy mountains had a history much older than bicycles and bank holidays. The Chinese scholar and official Chang Tai, visiting one of the most revered of Chinese mountains in the 1620s, described the daily influx of

> several thousand visitors, who will occupy hundreds of rooms and consume hundreds of vegetarian and ordinary banquets; they are entertained by hundreds of actors, singers and musicians, and there are hundreds of attendants at their beck and call. The guides are from about a dozen families. On an average day eight thousand to nine thousand visitors come, while the number can reach twenty thousand on the first day of spring.[11]

Though the focal points of Buddhist pilgrimage in China were the four major sacred mountains, there were also many lesser mountains whose spiritual power attracted poets, artists, seekers of enlightenment, and those simply escaping the weariness of everyday life; one of the most famous of these was a strange outcrop of forest-covered crags a little beyond Liaoyang known as the Thousand Peaks.

Kemp was so charmed by Liaoyang that she made a second visit on her homeward journey after traveling to Korea, and it was during this second stay that she also made her way across the plains to the Thousand Peaks. In

1910, the South Manchurian Railway Company (SMR) was just beginning to promote tourism to the region, and soon the Thousand Peaks and the nearby hot springs of Tanggangzi would become widely publicized highlights of the tourist itinerary, attracting visitors from all parts of the Japanese empire and beyond.

One of the most interesting of these Japanese tourists was the famous poet Yosano Akiko, who, together with her husband Yosano Tekkan, made a journey through Manchuria, taking in many of the places visited by Kemp eighteen years earlier. Yosano came to Tanggangzi and the Thousand Peaks in 1928, when the Japanese empire had tightened its grip on the region. But she was, like Kemp, a well-educated woman with an independent mind and feminist inclinations, and her writings on the region make an intriguing counterpoint to Kemp's.[12] Staying in an inn in Liaoyang, which was full of Japanese soldiers, she noted, in irate tones (which Kemp would surely have appreciated), how "imperialism and the smell of liquor rippled through, and the atmosphere of this inn became thoroughly incompatible with our desire to write poems about the gentle White Pagoda and the willow catkins."[13]

On a plateau above a rust belt of steel works (once run by the SMR), the gleaming glass of "Greenland IT City"—the area's newest technology park—stretches almost to the foot of the mountains themselves. The foreign visitors who come here today are businessmen and scientists rather than pilgrims, and none of the guidebooks that I could find provided information on the route to and through the Thousand Peaks. So, for this part of our journey, we have sought out the help of a tour company guide: a round-faced, ebullient, and talkative young man who uses the English name Adam.

When Kemp came to the Thousand Peaks in the company of staff from a local Christian mission, they traveled in mule carts, which had to be bodily hauled and dragged over the final rocky, rugged ascent. Eighteen years later, Yosano Akiko and Tekkan, accompanied by two friends from the SMR, made the same journey on horseback, with Akiko traveling alongside in a palanquin, and the whole party being accompanied by two grooms, four men to carry the palanquin, and six "coolies" bearing bedding, white rice, boxed lunches, sugar, and various canned goods.[14] Today, life is less complicated. Electric golf buggies wait at the entrance of the mountain range to ferry visitors toward the major landmarks. The day we visit is a minor Buddhist holiday, and a steady flow of people of all ages moves through the temple precincts.

The sacred survives through endless metamorphosis; the spirit persists by taking on new embodiments and new meanings for successive generations.

Kemp was hazy about the history of the Thousand Peaks, merely describing the view over a secluded temple as one "to charm a Chinese artist of the old school."[15] Yosano Akiko was much more specific: like most prewar Japanese with a good education, she could read classical Chinese and tells us that the oldest Buddhist temples of the Thousand Peaks date back to the Song Dynasty (960–1279) and that the Longquan Temple, described and painted by Kemp, was built "in the fifth year of the reign of the Longqing Emperor, Muzong, of the Ming dynasty (1566) and had been repaired on several occasions during the Qing Dynasty."[16]

Kemp stayed in Longquan, which had once been the most august of the mountains' Buddhist temples, but by the time Yosano Akiko and her traveling companions arrived there in the 1920s, the temple was in decline and its monks were decadent. To find true Buddhist tranquility, they had to travel higher into the mountain peaks, to temples that retained simpler and more austere ways.

The highlight of today's pilgrimage to the Thousand Peaks, however, is a marvel that Kemp and Yosano may both have seen but that neither of them recognized or recorded, since it was officially revealed to human understanding only in the 1990s—the miraculous Natural Sitting Buddha of the Thousand Peaks, inaugurated as a sacred site in 1993.

The pathway to the Buddha begins in a large temple compound at the foot of a steep mountain. The wide central courtyard is bathed in sunlight and surrounded by stalls selling incense and copies of the sutras. A gray-robed monk sits at one stall, his left hand thumbing the beads on his Buddhist rosary while his right hand busily composes text messages on his cell phone. We strike a giant bell to seek blessings for our journey and then climb the steep and narrow path, up flights of stone steps and through tunnels of sunlight-dappled forest foliage. Here and there along the way smaller temples cling to rocky footholds on the mountain face, or giant figures of Guardian Kings loom out unexpectedly from the living rock into which they are carved. As we climb, the resonant tolling of the bell rises ever more faintly from the world below. Lilacs and jasmine overhang the path, and brilliant blue butterflies skim through the shadows.

High up on the cliff face stands a recently constructed temple. In the place where you would expect to see an altar, however, there is nothing but a great, clear glass window looking out toward a weathered pink granite mountaintop festooned with sashes of crimson cloth. For this is the mountain of the Natural Sitting Buddha.

"You see," Adam eagerly points out, "there's the Buddha's head. And the long rocks on either side—those are his ears."

As we gaze at the mountaintop, straining (without much success) to perceive the sacred shape within its giant boulders, Adam helpfully poses in the shape of the Sitting Buddha—one hand on knee, the other outstretched in a gesture of blessing—to guide our unaccustomed eyes toward the shape we are supposed to see.

There is something mesmeric about the atmosphere of these mountains. At one turning in the path, a group of musicians in dark robes materializes suddenly from behind a haze of incense smoke with a clamor of horns as though to wake the dead. And in the Longquan Temple, which lies below, in a sheltered gully surrounded by towering rocks, we find that we have suddenly stepped back a century, for the terrace of courtyards opening one into the other is exactly as Kemp painted it in 1910.

A hundred years ago, the secular dimensions of pilgrimage were already much in evidence in the Thousand Peaks. Kemp and MacDougall found their stay at another nearby temple disrupted by a swarm of a hundred students in blue uniforms from a local commercial college: the era of the school excursion had already arrived. Yosano Akiko in the 1920s was even more disconcerted to discover that the Longquan Temple's monks wanted to sell her souvenir walking sticks and to question her husband about the latest movements on the currency exchange markets.[17]

But in the twenty-first century, with most sightseers lured away to the site of the Natural Sitting Buddha, a strange tranquility seems to have returned to the Longquan Temple. Its courtyards nest one within the other like Chinese boxes. The recorded sound of repetitive chanting drifts across the compound, saffron-robed monks flit swiftly and quietly between the dark brick pavilions, and an elderly man with a sad face shuffles along the paved terrace to light his sticks of incense. In an arched grotto beneath the main building, the Dragon Spring for which the Longquan Temple is named creates its own natural music as it trickles in an endless stream from the mouth of a white marble gargoyle.

In the course of our time in the mountains, we seem somehow to have slipped through a crack in the mundane world and entered the space of the surreal. From the Thousand Peaks, our guide Adam conducts us to a giant greenhouse on the fringes of the technology park. Inside is a tropical forest that echoes with the raucous cries of peacocks. A huge, plaster Santa Claus sits in the center of the forest (serenely oblivious to the fact that this is mid-May and the temperature in the greenhouse is in the high twenties Celsius), while elegantly dressed young waiters and waitresses glide around him on rollerblades, serving dishes of traditional Manchurian cuisine to tables set amongst the orchids and lianas. We appear to be their only customers.

From there we are driven to the hot springs of Tanggangzi, and to the Dragon Palace Hotel, once operated by the SMR and frequented by the last emperor Pu Yi. The hotel is large and must once have been imposing, but today its rooms are crumbling and haunted by the cabbage smell of bad drains. Where tiles have fallen from the walls, the holes are stuffed with yellowing newspaper. Outside is a great park dotted with buildings between which uniformed nurses wheel skeletal and limbless patients who have come here to bathe in the restoring waters. A chain of ponds and lakes has been carved out of the sulfurous white earth, and half-ruined bridges lead to islands and to dilapidated stucco pagodas lit with fairy lights. Part of the park contains the remnants of a zoo, and, walking through the grounds at dusk, we are startled to be confronted by an ostrich that pops its head out through the shrubbery and glares at us with baleful, yellow eyes.

But the hot spring baths where Pu Yi's empress Wan Rong supposedly once bathed are magnificent. Moisture drips from the vaulted golden ceiling, and phoenixes rise from the ashes in ceramic frescos around the walls. Sandy and I lie back in the healing warmth of the spring water and recite the poems of our childhood under the bemused gaze of the bath attendant.

It is only later that I discover the poem that Yosano Tekkan wrote while staying at this same hotel:

Plants, trees, and soil in Tanggangzi all dimply white,
the memory is terribly sad.[18]

On Calvary's Mountain

"Divided we move," writes the sociologist Zygmunt Bauman.[19] Travelers move across landscapes, sometimes intersecting with each other and with local people. But the modern world has sliced and layered space, so that, as often as not, we pass one another by, seeing the same earth and sky and mountains, and yet remaining in utterly separate worlds.

Today's space of international travel is created by global business and by its worldwide archipelago of international hotels: places like Shenyang's Gloria Plaza, where we stay on our return from the Thousand Peaks. Outside the hotel's glass doors, the spring days are growing longer, and in the great park that surrounds the tomb of Hung Taiji, feathery, white fluff from thousands of poplar trees drifts across the sky, settling on its pathways and on the surface of its ponds like snow. But within the Gloria Plaza, with its four-star rooms and attentive staff, but for the signs in Chinese we could be anywhere in the world. In the elevator, we meet a Chinese businessman who speaks impeccable English. When we tell him we are seeing the sights of the city, he stares at us with surprise.

"Why do you come here?" he asks. "It's just an industrial city. There's nothing to see."

For Japanese travelers to prewar Manchuria like Yosano Akiko and Tek-kan, an enclosed space of movement was provided by the great empire of the SMR, which carried them from city to city in an almost entirely Japanese world. Here and there they were introduced to Chinese officials and intel-lectuals, but throughout most of their journey, they traveled on SMR trains, were guided by SMR employees, and stayed in SMR hotels.

Kemp, despite the language barrier, interacted rather more closely with local people. But she also benefited from a distinct space of travel, in her case provided by the network of Western missionaries in China and Korea. In Hu-lan, Shenyang, and Pyongyang, she stayed with missionaries, who guided her round the churches, schools, and hospitals that they were constructing, as well as taking her on outings to local landmarks such as the Thousand Peaks. Kemp, with her strong religious beliefs and close family connections to the missions, had a complex and sometimes contradictory view of the work of missionaries. The missions (she noted, after a later visit to China in the early 1920s) were, all too often, complicit in the sin of Americanization: "A large section of the missionaries so value their own culture that they believe they can do no better than try and denationalize the Chinese, or Indians, or what-ever other nations they may be working amongst, and transform them into Americans. In the case of China, this seems to me a most disastrous policy, and founded on a serious error."[20]

She was also critical of the "narrow sectarian missions which still abound,"[21] and above all of governments that used missionary activity to expand their own imperial power.

No more cynical statement could be made than that of the German Govern-ment with regard to Shantung [Shandong] about the murder of two German missionaries: "La Providence a voulu que la nécessité de venger le massacre de nos missionaires nous amenât à acquérir une place commercial de première importance." [It was the wish of Providence that the necessity of avenging the massacre of our missionaries should lead us to acquire a foremost commercial position.] The Chinese have long memories, and they will not forget such things. It is foolish to expect people to discriminate accurately between the actions of a foreign power and the missions of the same race.[22]

Yet, her personal contacts gave her an unshakable respect for the dedication of Christian missionaries, particularly for their educational and medical work, and she insisted on arguing (with considerable exaggeration) that "the reforms initiated in Chinese life are practically all due to missionary activity. The education of the poor and of women, the care of the sick, the blind, the insane, were all started by missions, and they are the main agencies in undertaking relief work in famine and plague measures, even in the present day."[23]

In the twenty-first century, the world of the SMR has vanished forever, but Christianity again flourishes in varied forms across the face of China. As Kemp foresaw, China has not forgotten the tendency of foreign governments to exploit the overseas presence of their missionaries, and missionaries are not officially allowed visas to conduct evangelism on Chinese soil, although some evidently arrive in other guises. Near Hung Taiji's tomb, for example, we encounter a group of South Korean women who tell us that they are here to spread the word of God and shake their heads disapprovingly when we say that we our on our way to North Korea.

But Christian churches continue to play a role in the Chinese medical and educational life, and, sitting in the MacDonald's outlet next to North Shenyang station, we meet someone whose work maintains the tradition that Kemp so admired but whose story and background also reflect the changes that have swept Northeast Asia since Kemp's day. His name is Ho Ban, and he is a small, round-faced, energetic Presbyterian pastor, originally from South Korea, who has built and now heads a dental technicians' college on the fringes on Shenyang.

Reverend Ban's life reflects the cross-border movements that have been such a feature of modern Korean history. His grandfather and uncle were among the prewar wave of Korean migrants to Manchuria, but his grandfather returned to Korea before the outbreak of the Pacific War, and his uncle joined the mass of returning migrants after the collapse of the Japanese empire and the liberation of Korea. In the 1980s, Reverend Ban and his parents joined a new wave of Korean emigrants heading overseas in search of a better life, this time to the United States. Life there, he says, was very hard at first. He spoke only a few words of English and found a job in a Chinese restaurant washing dishes before working his way up to become a partner in the restaurant business and saving enough money to go to theological college.

His first trip to China came in 1988, at a time when South Korea did not yet have diplomatic relations with the People's Republic of China. Yet, even though he was a stranger who (at that time) spoke no Chinese, he felt (in his own words) that God had called him to the country and was determined to return. After further theological and technical training in the United States, he came back to settle in Shenyang in the late 1990s, working as a lecturer in a local university before raising the money to establish his new college in Sujiatun, an outer suburb with a large ethnic Korean community—close to the place where his uncle had lived as a migrant before the war.

We rattle off in a van through the traffic-clogged streets of the city to see the newly completed college, which is waiting to receive its first intake of students, and Reverend Ban, with justifiable pride, guides us through its shining new classrooms, laboratories, and dormitories. We also admire his splendid collection of photographs of North Korea, for (unlike the South Korean missionaries whom we met in the park) Reverend Ban is a frequent visitor to North Korea. When he first arrived in Shenyang, North Korea was in the midst of the terrible famine that ravaged that country in the second half of the 1990s, and waves of North Koreans swept into northeastern China in search of any means of survival. Since his encounters with the face of this famine, Reverend Ban has been actively involved in food and development aid schemes to North Korea.

"My dream," he says, "is to set up college in North Korea to train dental technicians."

The political climate is not propitious, but the pastor's faith is practical and boundless—somehow, he says with a beaming smile, a way will be found to overcome all obstacles.

Kemp would have loved all this. On her visit to Shenyang in 1910, she toured and admired the local missionary hospital, which had been founded by Scotsman Dugald Christie in the 1880s and had recently been rebuilt after its destruction in 1900 during the event known in English as the Boxer Rebellion, and in Chinese as the Righteous Harmony Society Movement. Kemp gives a detailed and glowing description of the hospital and of the attached medical college that was then in the process of creation. She also has much to say about the ravages of the "Boxers" in Shenyang.

The Righteous Harmony Society Movement was one of a number of millennial nationalist uprisings that broke out in China and Korea during the chaotic decades of the late nineteenth and early twentieth centuries. Its underlying causes were social disruptions brought about by the decline of the Chinese empire and by foreign incursions and exploitation, aggravated in some regions by drought and conflicts between neighboring villages. In many Western writings of the time, the "Boxers" were depicted as irrational fanatics, driven by primitive superstition to attack the missionaries, who were presented as the bringers of civilization and enlightenment to China. (I still remember comic book images from my childhood in 1950s Britain of heroic European Christians perishing at the hands of a stereotyped Asiatic horde.) Yet, in retrospect, the mixture of faith and fear that inspired the European missionaries and their converts seems, after all, not so far removed from the beliefs and fears that fueled the Righteous Harmony Society Movement. Both sides saw life as a battle between the forces of good and evil; both believed in the reality of evil spirits and in the power of signs and miracles.

In a time of fear and uncertainty, these rival visions of Righteous Harmony took on a violent logic of their own. The chaos and suffering brought by the uprising and its aftermath were enormous, and by far the greatest number of victims were Chinese, but over 180 foreign missionaries were also killed. Kemp described how the occupying Russian forces during the Russo-Japanese War discovered documents in Shenyang's Imperial Palace demonstrating the complicity of China's dowager empress Cixi in these massacres.

The largest killing of foreign missionaries occurred not in Shenyang but in Taiyuan, Shanxi Province, where the local governor encouraged forty-four members of the local missions to surrender themselves to him, promising them protection from their attackers. Once they were in his custody, he had them beaten to death and decapitated, and hung their heads from the city walls as a warning to others.[24] Meanwhile, the foreign legations in Beijing had been besieged by the Righteous Harmony Society Movement, and the imperial powers (including Japan) responded by sending their military battalions to China and forcing the dowager empress to flee the capital. The deaths of the missionaries (like the earlier killing of German missionaries in Shandong) were used by the Western powers to advance their own commercial and political interests by extracting a punitive indemnity from China and demanding the right for foreign legations to maintain their own security forces on Chinese soil.

There is one resounding silence in Kemp's writings. She speaks of the killing of missionaries and of Chinese Christians during that year of violence and praises both local Chinese and Japanese interests for helping to rebuild the Shenyang hospital, which had been destroyed during the uprising. Nowhere in any of her travel books, however, does she mention the fact that among the missionaries murdered in Taiyuan were her own much-loved eldest sister Jessie, Jessie's husband Thomas Piggott, and their thirteen-year-old son Wellesley Piggott. In all her works, although she writes warmly of her happy memories of staying with Jessie and her family in Taiyuan during her first visit to China, and speaks obliquely of Jessie's "premonition of the coming doom" as she was "nearing her Calvary,"[25] there is just one place where she writes explicitly of their deaths.

Her most personal of memoirs contains this single sentence: "They were all put to death on July 9th, 1900."[26]

Ebenezer Henry Edwards, who was the husband of Kemp's second-oldest and favorite sister Florence, wrote an influential and passionate book soon after the Boxer uprising, in which he described the killing of the missionaries in great detail and called on the imperial powers to intervene more deeply than ever in the country that he called "the sadly misnamed 'Celestial Empire.'"[27]

But Kemp responded differently. She blamed the dowager empress and governor of Shanxi for the killings, she remained silent about the details of her sister's death, and she went on loving China. In a book published nine years after the massacre, she wrote words which have a curiously strong resonance today:

> The whole civilized world looked on with astonishment and admiration at the rapid evolution of the Japanese nation in recent times, and now the Chinese Empire has resolved to make a similar change. It has a much more difficult task to achieve, and one which, on account of the size of the Empire, is likely to have a far greater importance for the world at large. The Chinese are strongly animated by the spirit of patriotism; they have great qualities and heart and mind, and a set determination to carry through the necessary reforms. In the dark ages of the past they were pioneers of art, science and philosophy; therefore one can with hopefulness look forward to a yet nobler future.[28]

If she had been asked to explain her unfaltering love for China, I imagine that Kemp might have said something about the Christian virtue of forgiveness. But, although her religious beliefs were undeniably profound and real, they can hardly explain her attitude, for history is full of examples of devout Christians who have conducted vendettas rather than offering forgiveness or who have condemned whole races and nations for the wrongs committed by one or two individuals.

Kemp was one of those who found their personal lives unexpectedly caught up in the great events of political history and who, as a result, suffered a terrible personal tragedy. I do not know what experiences or traits of personality enabled her to find a way through the enmities of international politics to the human faces that lay beyond. But sometimes I think of her, as she traveled around China and Korea, as being like those Buddhist pilgrims who set out on astonishing journeys to the sacred mountains, climbing impassable crags and enduring seemingly unbearable physical deprivations in the hope of reaching a place above the clouds where the air is thin, the light is clear, and the mind is serene.

In the front of Kemp's first book, *The Face of China*, which was published in 1909, there is a self-portrait of the author. It shows a strong-featured, rather wrinkled face with gray-brown eyes that gaze out at the reader from behind thick spectacles. She could pass for the admired but slightly intimidating headmistress of a girls' boarding school, but for one detail. She has chosen to portray herself in the garb of a traveling Chinese scholar, in a high-collared brocade robe, fur-lined jacket, and broad-brimmed straw hat, gripping a carved wooden staff in her hand.

I look at Kemp's self-portrait—at the steady gaze of her eyes—and wonder whether the reticence and apparent calm conceals the endless reverberations of a silent scream or whether in the course of her travels she found a kind of calm and human understanding beyond unimaginable pain.

Notes

1. Kiyohiko Munakata, *Sacred Mountains in Chinese Art* (Urbana: University of Illinois Press, 1991), 12.

2. Paul Demiéville, quoted in Edwin Bernbaum, *Sacred Mountains of the World* (Berkeley: University of California Press, 1997), 26.

3. Lauren W. Deutsch, "Searching for Sanshin: An Interview with Hi-ah Park Manshin, Lover of the Mountain Gods," in *The Sacred Mountains of Asia*, special edition of *Kyoto* magazine, 1993, 79–84, 79.

4. Percival Lowell, *Chosön, Land of the Morning Calm: A Sketch of Korea* (Boston: Ticknor, 1887), 209.

5. See Richard D. McBride, *Domesticating the Dharma: Buddhist Cults and the Hwaŏm Synthesis in Silla Korea* (Honolulu: University of Hawaii Press, 2008), 49–50.

6. See Norbert Weber, *In den Diamantbergen Koreas* (Oberbayern, Germany: Missionverlag St. Ottilen, 1927), 7.

7. Yi Kok, *Dongyugi*, reproduced in *Keumgangsan Yuramgi*, ed. Kim Dong-Ju (Seoul: Dongseo Chulpan Eseupero Mungo, 1992), 65.

8. E. G. Kemp, *The Face of Manchuria, Korea and Russian Turkestan* (New York: Duffield and Co., 1911), 42–43.

9. Wikipedia entry on Liaoyang, at http://en.wikipedia.org/wiki/Liaoyang (accessed April 15, 2009).

10. George Curzon, *Problems of the Far East* (London: Longmans Green, 1894), 105.

11. Pei-Yi Wu, "An Ambivalent Pilgrim to T'ai Shan in the Seventeenth Century," in *Pilgrims and Sacred Sites in China*, ed. Susan Naquin and Chün-fang Yü, 65–88 (Berkeley: University of California Press, 1992), 74.

12. Yosano Akiko, *Travels in Manchuria and Mongolia*, trans. Joshua A. Fogel (New York: Columbia University Press, 2001).

13. Yosano, *Travels in Manchuria and Mongolia*, 43.

14. Yosano, *Travels in Manchuria and Mongolia*, 24.

15. Kemp, *Face of Manchuria, Korea and Russian Turkestan*, 53.

16. Yosano, *Travels in Manchuria and Mongolia*, 28, 37.

17. Kemp, *Face of Manchuria, Korea and Russian Turkestan*, 54–55; Yosano, *Travels in Manchuria and Mongolia*, 37.

18. Yosano, *Travels in Manchuria and Mongolia*, 23.

19. Zygmunt Bauman, *Globalization: The Human Consequences* (New York: Columbia University Press, 1998), chap. 4.

20. E. G. Kemp, *Chinese Mettle* (London: Hodder and Stoughton, 1921), 27.

21. Kemp, *Chinese Mettle*, 27.

22. Kemp, *Chinese Mettle*, 195.

23. Kemp, *Chinese Mettle*, 207.

24. Alvyn Austin, *China's Millions: The China Inland Mission and Late Qing Society, 1832–1905* (Grand Rapids, Mich.: Eerdmans, 2007), 413.

25. E. G. Kemp, *Reminiscences of a Sister: S. Florence Edwards, of Taiyuanfu* (London: Carey Press, 1919), 25.

26. Kemp, *Reminiscences of a Sister*, 60.

27. E. H. Edwards, *Fire and Sword in Shansi: The Story of the Martyrdom of Foreigners and Chinese Christians* (New York: Fleming H. Revell Co., 1903), 110; for further information on Edwards and the aftermath of the Righteous Harmony Movement, see Austin, *China's Millions*, 423–26.

28. E. G. Kemp, *The Face of China: Travels in East, North, Central and Western China* (London: Chatto and Windus, 1909), 270.

CHAPTER FOUR

Borderlands
From Shenyang to Dandong

The Crescent Moon

Spring dusk is settling over the city of Shenyang. Outside the covered market, street sellers are lighting lamps in their glass booths. We are looking for a place to eat dinner and instead find ourselves wandering into yet another dimension of the extraordinary world that is contemporary China.

The entrance to the market lies through a blue, arched gateway, decorated in white with Chinese script above and Arabic script below. Within is a row of small shops on either side of a dark concrete passageway. The shops are just closing for the night, but in some, wares are still on display: headless carcasses of lamb lie spread-eagled on stone slabs. On an upper floor of the market, the restaurants are beginning to open. At the far side, the passageway gives onto an open space where a group of men, some in Muslim caps and others in faded Mao suits, stand around a charcoal brazier of sizzling kebabs. We are hungry after a long day's exploring, and the smell of the kebabs is irresistible.

The men watch us warily—a bunch of intruding foreign women who have clearly lost their way—and then one, with a shy smile, offers us a kebab.

"Where are you from?" they ask—a simple question to which there is no honest simple answer. Where are we from? We are globalized nomads, transients who have forgotten our origins. We are from Britain and Ireland via Australia and Nepal and various parts of Europe and East Asia.

"I live in Korea," explains Emma Campbell; "she [pointing to me] is from Australia, and this is her older sister, from France."

71

The men around the brazier shake their heads in understandable bewilderment. The kebab is charred on the outside but juicy within and at this moment tastes like one of the best things I have ever eaten.

"Are you Uyghur?" we ask, betraying our profound ignorance. In the outside world, Islam in China has come to be identified with the Uyghur people of the far western Chinese borderlands and with their struggle for political and religious autonomy. The men around the brazier laugh at our obtuseness.

"No, no. Hui. We're Hui," they say. "All round here," with vague gestures at the unremarkable concrete apartment blocks behind the market, "it's all Hui people."

"Do you have a mosque?" asks Emma.

"Come, I'll show you." This from a small, elderly man in an olive green Mao suit, who waves to us to follow and promptly sets off at a brisk pace along a path between the apartment buildings. The buildings, picked out in cream and blue, are cracked and fading in places, and seem to date from the same era as our guide's suit. The paths and courtyards between the apartment blocks are dotted with small gardens and clumps of tall grasses. Children play in the warm evening air, and a few adults chat in the doorways. The ground floor of one building is a kindergarten, its windows pasted with crayon drawings. I notice that, although many men wear caps, the women do not cover their heads.

When we ask our guide about this, he shrugs his shoulders and gives a small smile, "Why should they?" he asks.

Beyond the apartments lies a mellow brick wall surmounted by gray Chinese roof-tiles and pierced by a gateway. I would have taken it for the wall of a Daoist temple, but in fact, it surrounds the compound of the mosque. Passing through the gate, we find ourselves in a place quite apart from the surrounding bustle of metropolitan Shenyang. The courtyard is tranquil and filled with lilac trees, whose pale flowers seem to glow faintly in the fading light, infusing the still air with their scent.

Beyond is an inner courtyard enclosing the mosque itself. There is no dome, and I can see no sign of a minaret, but the weathered tile roof is surmounted by the metal curve of a crescent moon. We look up at the sky, where the last faint trace of day still lingers on the horizon, and there in the blue far above hangs the real moon—a perfect mirror image of the mosque's crescent.

In a brightly lit room to the right of the mosque we are greeted by the Imam, a youngish man with a round, olive-skinned face and a warm smile.

"How long have you been at this mosque?" we ask.

"Three hundred and eighty years," comes the reply. He is, it seems, a twelfth-generation Imam, whose family memories go back to the days of Nurhaci.

Unlike the Uyghurs, who were incorporated en masse into the Chinese empire as it expanded westward, swallowing up the Muslim Khanates of Eastern Turkestan, the Hui are a quintessentially diasporic people. Their origins are varied and include merchants who traded along the Silk Road and craftspeople brought back by Mongol Yuan rulers from forays into Central Asia. Hui communities are scattered all over China, although the largest groups are to be found in the northwest.

Emily Kemp, who visited a Hui mosque "built exactly like a Buddhist or Taoist temple" in the town of Ashiho (Acheng) near Harbin, noted that "Moslems in China do not attempt to proselytize openly, and they adhere less rigidly than elsewhere to their religious observations." She suggested that this flexibility might be the result of persecution, for "in past times there have been terrible massacres of Mohammedans in China whenever they have tried to withstand Chinese customs."[1]

Today, China's Muslim minority faces new political and cultural pressures. The Imam is eager to tell us that growing numbers of young people attend his mosque: "Not just Hui people. Now Han and Manchu and other people are coming too." But asked what it is like to be Muslim in twenty-first century China, he looks pensive.

"It's fine," he says. "There are no big problems. . . . But, perhaps for some people it is a little difficult . . ."

As we leave the mosque compound, we meet two of the younger members of its congregation. Both are students, and one is from Tanzania. While our Mao-suited guide had greeted us with a warm shake of the hand, the young men, clearly more observant of ritual than the older generation, conspicuously avoid the dangers of physical contact with women. The young African man tells us that he is a medical student and is in the final stages of his degree at a Shenyang university.

"What's it like living in Shenyang?" I ask.

"It has been good to study here," is the hesitant response. "It is quite nice. But sometimes it's hard. The cold and the wind and the dust are difficult to get used to. Soon I will go home . . ."

Back at the covered market, we eat our dinner in a Hui restaurant. The meal (which is excellent) is fried lamb and vegetables, washed down with beer.

"You serve alcohol?" we say in surprise.

"Of course. Why not?" replies the waitress with a smile.

Mohammedan Mosque, Ashiho (E. G. Kemp)

The Friendship Bridge

The weather breaks as we travel from Shenyang toward the North Korean border. To the south, past the coal-mining town of Bensi with its blackened factories, rusting pipes, and crumbling chimney stacks, the landscape becomes first hilly and then mountainous. Unlike the empty expanses further north, here we see many people working in the fields, some tilling the earth with mule-drawn ploughs. An elderly man is trimming the willows in the neat allotments beside the railway line.

After Bensi, the rain begins in earnest, slashing against the train windows. Fruit trees are in flower everywhere, and the hillsides are dotted with the purple of wild azaleas. The brick cottages have cobs of corn neatly stacked beneath the eaves, their facades decorated with red and gold symbols of good fortune. I am surprised to see how many also have solar panels on their roofs. As we approach Dandong, rice paddies appear in the valleys, as well as fields planted with what seem to be grapevines.

It is the eve of the May Day holiday, and the train carriage is packed solid with people heading home for the vacation. Emma chats to the family who shares her section of seating—a middle-aged couple taking their grandson, who lives in Jilin, home with them for a month in their village near Dandong. They have been traveling since midnight, and the grandson, who is seven years old, is fidgety and a little overexcited. He shows off his picture book filled with photos of motor vehicles and recites the name of every brand of car in the book: Brilliance, Saab, Hummer, BMW, Mercedes Benz . . . "When I grow up I'm going to sell automobiles," he announces. Another man in the carriage is an ethnic Korean who lives in Heilongjian, seventeen hours away, and is on his way to stay with relatives near Dandong. He tells us that his family speaks both Korean and Chinese at home, but he is clearly more comfortable using Chinese.

When Emma mentions our impending visit to North Korea, a young man further down the carriage joins the conversation, insistently repeating a refrain we have heard before: "North Korea is very dangerous." From the Chinese viewpoint, indeed, North Korea, once viewed as a convenient buffer against a possibly hostile world, is now a source of deep concern. As regional politics have changed, China has been drawn into playing the central role in preventing North Korea's unending Cold War from spiraling out of control. But however much the Chinese government (perpetuating centuries of tradition) would like to treat North Korea as "little brother," the Democratic People's Republic of Korea (DPRK) determinedly insists on going its own erratic way. In taking a lead in efforts to resolve the North Korean crisis, China may (as a former official of its Foreign Ministry observes) find itself "riding a tiger, afraid to dismount."[2]

Our train pulls into Dandong station shortly before noon. Outside in the wide square, a bronze effigy of Mao holds up its hand in frozen greeting to the arriving passengers. Dandong has the feel of a port city: there is a distant scent of the sea in the suddenly cold air.

"Unfortunately," Kemp noted on her arrival in Dandong, "there is no bridge of any kind. The permanent line will necessitate the building of a bridge, but it is not expected to be ready within the next two years, though the Japanese are straining every nerve to complete the line." For Kemp and Mary MacDougall, the crossing of the Yalu River into Korea had to be made in a "wretchedly small and crowded tug," which looked "sadly unequal" to the task of picking a course between the menacing blocks of ice that still drifted on the river's surface when they made their journey.[3]

But Kemp had underestimated the determination of Japan's railway builders: the bridge across the Yalu was in fact opened in 1911, the year after her visit, creating the final link in a rail network running continuously from Busan on the southern tip of the Korean Peninsula to the French port of Calais. Today, that bridge is known as the Broken Bridge. It was pounded to fragments by U.S. air raids during the Korean War, and just one-half survives, running out from the Chinese side into the middle of the river, where it comes to an abrupt halt. It provides tourists to Dandong with an excellent viewing platform for looking out toward North Korea.

The hotel we have booked via the Internet turns out to stand on the bank of the river, right in front of the Broken Bridge, and overlooking the parallel Friendship Bridge, which now provides the main link between the

Bridges over the Yalu River (S. Morris)

two countries. Our room has a ringside view of the small glass booth where Chinese customs officials check arriving and departing vehicles as they cross the bridge to and from the North Korean border city of Sinuiju, clearly visible through the veils of rain on the far side of the Yalu. The border check is, to all appearances, quite cursory, and a steady flow of trucks—perhaps one every five or ten minutes—rumbles over the bridge. The more tensions between North and South Korea rise, the more this bridge becomes a lifeline for the North Korean economy.

The train journey from Shenyang to Dandong, which took us about four hours, involved two days' travel and an overnight halt in Kemp's day. Her train carriage was full of Japanese soldiers, who were served bentō: multilayered Japanese lunch-boxes filled with tiers of rice, vegetables, "rissoles, fish and other savories."[4] The Yalu near Dandong (then known as Antung) had been the site of fierce battles that helped to seal Japan's victories in both the Sino-Japanese and the Russo-Japanese wars, and the town itself was divided into Japanese and Chinese sectors, with the Japanese town "situated quite apart from the Chinese."[5]

Checking a prewar map of the city, I can see that our hotel stands squarely in the middle of what was the Japanese town, in an area once filled with Japanese-owned timber mills. The colonial Japanese presence has entirely vanished, but Dandong was then and still is a quintessential border town, full of that strange mixture of drifting and enigmatic characters who are drawn to such places. In the early twentieth century, these ranged from the emigrant Japanese geisha who entertained guests in the riverside inns, to the Swiss-Russian businessman Jules Brynner (grandfather of the Hollywood star Yul Brynner)—a Vladivostok-based entrepreneur who (in Kemp's time) visited this region to conduct shadowy and politically sensitive timber dealings along the Yalu.[6]

Today, the cast of characters who make up the population of Dandong is just as diverse and intriguing. Across the road from our hotel stands a North Korean–owned restaurant, staffed by the beautiful and specially trained waitresses who are selected by their government for these overseas assignments. Similar DPRK restaurants exist in Shenyang and even as far away as Bangkok. The young women, clad in pastel-colored *chima jeogori*—the flowing national dress of their country—are (like the Japanese geisha a century before them) chosen for their musical entertainment skills and charm, and in the North Korean case presumably also for their political reliability. They are welcoming and gentle, and their voices have the distinctive musical lilt common to North Korean women. As we eat a late lunch of grilled meat and kimchi in the largely empty restaurant, a group of sturdily built middle-aged men in blue suits emerge from a curtained-off alcove where they have been eating and drinking—clearly identifiable by their lapel badges as North Korean cadres on a shopping spree.

"Those North Korean bureaucrats come across all the time," a Dandong taxi driver later tells us disapprovingly. "They have lots of money to spend and they stay in the best hotels, but they're standoffish and unfriendly." But then again, as we are to discover, North Korean officials have their own, sometimes unflattering, views of their Chinese neighbors.

By the time we have finished lunch, the rain has lifted, though an icy wind still blows off the river. Beside its turbid waters men sit fishing or simply gazing out at the land on the other side. In some places, enterprising locals have set up stalls where Chinese women tourists can dress up in Korean *chima jeogori* and be photographed against a distant background of North Korean scenery. But today there are few takers, and the gauzy folds of multi-colored *chima jeogori* flutter in the wind like wilting flowers.

By the Friendship Bridge stands a small, old man with a weathered face, dressed in military uniform and proudly displaying his array of Korean War medals. He is begging. A grand memorial museum on the hill above the town displays the devastation wrought by U.S. bombing on North Korea and on Chinese border areas—including Dandong itself—during the Korean War. I suddenly feel more acutely conscious than ever of my Western appearance. Like the Japanese tourists whom I met in Shenyang, I have an unresolved burden of history embodied in my very being.

Strolling further along the esplanade by the river, we are greeted by a friendly couple who turn out to be South Koreans. They live in Shenyang but are engaged in trade with North Korea, which they conduct via Dandong, since they are not allowed to cross the border.

"It's so sad," comments the husband, "young people in South Korea no longer care about reunification. They've barely even heard of the Korean War. All they want are the latest consumer gadgets. I hope my trading business is going to contribute something toward reunification. After all, it's not us Koreans who decided to be divided. It's Japan and the Americans and the rest of them who forced division on us."

Tourists and Smugglers

Dandong's Friendship Bridge may be the main lifeline between an isolated North Korean state and the outside world, but as we watch the Yalu River from the vantage point of our hotel room, and travel along its banks to take our boat trip on the river, it soon becomes clear that movement on and across the river is not confined to this official gateway.

The river is full of life. Family groups, who appear to be relatives of the Chinese customs officials, take advantage of the public holiday to go for outings on border-control boats. Tiny wooden craft set out on fishing trips from the North Korean side. Skeins of geese move silently through the sky across the waters of the Yalu that divide and converge around shifting sandbanks. In the broader stretches of river, a couple of dark, rickety wooden boats lie silently at anchor, with washing hanging out to dry on their decks.

As we drive back toward Dandong from our excursion on the river, through orchards of pear trees that cover the hillsides with pale pink blossom, our taxi driver suddenly says, "Would you like to meet a real North Korean soldier?"

"Of course," we say, with a mixture of surprise, enthusiasm, and skepticism.

He pulls abruptly off the main road and onto a muddy sidetrack. There, two young men are waiting to guide us (for a fee) to a point where the dividing line between China and Korea is little more than a narrow stream. As they stride down the track between farm fields, they explain that tourists can buy food from a woman who lives in a cottage on the border.

"You take the food down to the stream and stand there," they explain, "and then the woman will come out and call '*chingu, chingu*' [friend, friend] to the North Korean border guards. They're not there all the time, but with any luck, some North Korean soldiers will appear on the opposite bank of the stream to take the food. You can ask them questions if you want."

This is starting to sound uncomfortably like feeding animals at a zoo, and I am relieved to discover when we reach the narrow border stream that, although there is a farm cottage with chickens pecking beneath the trees in its overgrown orchard, there is no sign of the woman nor of any North Korean soldiers. Indeed, the only thing to be seen is a large, empty ploughed field on the North Korean side and a flock of swans gliding serenely over a marshy pond that straddles the border. The young men, both aged twenty, explain that they regularly slip across the border unofficially to trade.

"People from the other side don't dare to cross over here," they say, "but we can do it. We only trade with soldiers. We take all sorts of food to sell them."

"Do you speak Korean?" we ask.

"Just a few words. But that's enough."

They are, they explain, saving up the profits from this foray into free enterprise to buy a motorcycle.

Looking at the brown waters that ripple between the boulders and over-hanging bushes, I think of the North Korean refugees whom I have met in South Korea and Japan, and remember their descriptions of the terrifying experience of crossing the river at night into a strange land, never knowing when a false step will plunge them into icy depths or when the searchlights and guns of the border guards will pick them out in the dark. But refugees seldom attempt crossings near Dandong. The favored spots are much further inland, where the river is narrower and the population more sparse.

Dandong is full of border crossings. Our hotel is preparing for a wedding, and in true Chinese fashion, two massive portrait photos of the happy couple are on display in the lobby for public inspection. On the morning of the wedding, the hotel staff adorns the front entrance with a red, inflated plastic arch born aloft on the backs to two inflated plastic golden elephants. A battery of canon for setting off firecrackers is set up in front of the building, their muzzles pointing alarmingly at the Yalu River, as though about to fire the first salvo in a war with North Korea. They are, however, merely waiting to shower a blizzard of golden confetti over the bridal convoy, which arrives with festoons of pink and purple balloons billowing from the roofs of its black limousines.

Although the gloriously uninhibited excess is typically Chinese, the bride, as it turns out, is Japanese. Her groom's family comes from Dandong but has been living in Japan for some fifteen years. This is in fact the second Chinese-Japanese wedding that we have come across in our travels through Manchuria, and I wonder whether it is just coincidence or whether we are witnessing a small corner of a wider trend of grassroots human alliance building.

Ever since 2002, when the North Korean government admitted to having abducted thirteen Japanese citizens during the 1970s and 1980s, the Japanese media has been filled with demonic images of the DPRK. Japan has been assiduous in imposing sanctions on North Korea for its attempts to develop nuclear weapons, and airports all around Japan display signs reminding Japanese citizens that they should "voluntarily refrain" from visiting North Korea. Against this background of fear and loathing, it is surprising and somehow rather touching to hear the cheerful clamor of Chinese and Japanese voices as the bridal party arrives at the hotel to celebrate the wedding on the Chinese-North Korean border. I silently wish the couple well and hope they may be an omen of new forms of international connection in this long-troubled region.

Border Controls

We have finally made contact with Mr. Sin from the DPRK travel bureau, who has promised to come to our hotel today to sort out our North Korean visas. During the anxious days of waiting, I have built up an image of him in my mind as a grim-faced official, complete with shiny suit and party badge, and am surprised when he turns out to be a casually dressed young man with a thatch of unruly hair and a warm smile. He speaks fluent Chinese but only a few words of English. After wishing us a pleasant stay in the DPRK, somewhat to our alarm, he departs with our passports, promising they will be returned to us tomorrow (the day of our departure for Pyongyang) by "my Chinese colleague, Mr. Chan."

Retracing the travels of Kemp, I have realized how the changing nature of the nation-state has transformed frontier controls over the past century. Here and there in her writings, Kemp mentions customs inspections, but she says nothing at all about passports or visas. In her day, indeed, a "passport" meant something very different from the vital token of national identity with which we are all familiar today.

My knowledge of Kemp's passport documents comes from a declassified file of confidential political correspondence held in the archives of the British Foreign Office. When I first discovered the existence of this file, intriguingly labeled "Chinese travel of Miss Emily G. Kemp and Mary M. MacDougall," I briefly wondered whether I had stumbled upon some unexpected secret. Was there more to this story than met the eye? Were these unassuming lady travelers really British spies, or had someone else been spying on them? The truth turned out to be much more mundane but still sheds a fascinating light on early twentieth-century travel.

In August 1912, two years after their journey through Manchuria and Korea, Kemp and MacDougall set out on another daring venture—to cross the Karakorum Mountains from India into far western China. The terrain was rugged and the area was in political turmoil. To allay the fears of their families, Kemp and MacDougall promised that, on arriving safely in the town of Kashgar on the Chinese side of the border, they would telegraph the word "good" to Emily's sister Lydia and brother George in Rochdale, to confirm that all was well.

Lydia and George Kemp waited anxiously until October, at which point they finally received a telegram from Emily in Kashgar containing five meaningless words that they were entirely unable to decipher. Seriously alarmed,

George, who had served in parliament since 1895 and was about to be elevated to the peerage, used his personal connections with foreign secretary Sir Edward Grey to make enquiries about Emily's welfare. The result was a circuitous series of telegrams from the Foreign Office to the Indian colonial government, and from India to Kashgar. Meanwhile, Foreign Office officials checked Kemp and MacDougall's travel documents, which showed that, although the two women had received a "passport" from the Chinese ambassador in London, they did not have any British travel papers.

Before the First World War, passports were not necessary for foreign travel. A passport in those days was simply a letter from a suitably exalted official that, it was hoped, would help to protect the traveler in case of problems. Kemp and MacDougall's letter came from the Chinese ambassador (who notes that "Miss Kemp is known to me personally"). Written in Chinese with an English translation, it requests "all Chinese authorities en route to allow the holders to proceed on its production without let or hindrance."[7] Where particularly difficult or dangerous travel was to be undertaken, it was common for European travelers to seek a similar letter from their own government, but (as the Foreign Office noted in disapproving tones) Kemp and MacDougall had not done so. If they had, one official pointed out, "they would have been advised not to go," since His Majesty's Foreign Office was "not at all sure that Kashgar is a suitable tourist resort for ladies."[8]

As it turned out, all was well. Kemp and MacDougall had crossed the Karakorums safely (though not without adventures), and Kemp's telegram had simply been mangled in transmission. She would, I suspect, have been both irritated and amused by all the fuss. And, if she had had a chance to read the ensuing confidential correspondence, she might well have been simultaneously amused and furious at the British bureaucratic views of women travelers that it exposed. The Foreign Office was clearly annoyed at having been asked to undertake this task for George Kemp, and they proceeded to spend almost a year pursuing him for reimbursement of the costs of the telegrams between London, New Delhi, and Kashgar, which had purportedly amounted to the exorbitant sum of eight guineas. For, as John Shuckburgh of the India Office put it, in almost audible tones of patrician distaste for such follies, "Lord Rochedale ought to pay. If he will let his feminine relations go on these journeys, he must accept the consequences."[9]

For Kemp and MacDougall, the loss of their joint passport would have been an annoying but relatively minor inconvenience. For us, it would be a disaster. Our passports are our identity, our proof of existence, our ticket to membership in the nation—and thus to all the rights and protection that the nation-state (in theory at least) provides to its citizens.

We are therefore very relieved when the precious documents, along with our train tickets to Pyongyang, are duly restored to us first thing the following morning by the ebullient, leather-jacketed Mr. Chan ("call me Jackie"). There are still no North Korean visas in the passports, but we are assured that these will be issued to us on the train. Emma is leaving us today, flying back to Seoul to continue her research on the attitudes of young South Koreans to nationalism, while Sandy and I head south to Pyongyang. We have a brief moment of fond farewells before Emma dashes off to catch her northbound train back to Shenyang, and then Jackie Chan guides Sandy and me through the exit formalities at Dandong station.

The station, which has just been remodeled, is vast and gleaming with plate glass and polished marble. It has a separate section for "international arrivals and departures," clearly anticipating the day when the 38th parallel will be opened, and the Yalu Bridge at Dandong will again become a gateway on a great Iron Silk Road stretching from the Yellow Sea to the Atlantic. Meanwhile, however, international passengers are few, and after being X-rayed for hidden weapons and thermally scanned for harmful viruses by white-coated medical staff, we relax in the soft mock leather sofas of the station's opulent and empty waiting area until it is time to board the train.

Jackie Chan tells us that he regularly takes groups of Chinese tourists across to North Korea for one-day or three-day coach tours. It is relatively cheap, and Chinese visitors who can remember the Mao era seem to gain a bittersweet pleasure from the nostalgic emotions evoked by visiting the DPRK. Indeed, while some people have warned us of the dangers of North Korea, other Chinese take a more relaxed and philosophical view of their Korean neighbor. As one Dandong taxi driver said to us, "It's a really poor country. But it'll change. You'll see. After all, we were like that just a couple of decades ago."

Our train—with its olive green and dark blue carriages, looking just like the long-distance European trains I traveled on in childhood—is already standing at the platform, but we have a long wait before we are allowed to board. Passengers are busily making last-minute calls on their cell phones, since these must be handed in at the North Korean border. We must once again surrender our passports, this time to an inspector on the train, who promises to hand them back complete with the long-awaited visas at Sinuiju, our first stop on the North Korean side of the river. Finally, we are allowed to haul our backpacks and bags on board, and find our four-berthed compartment, where two North Korean men are already stretched out fast asleep.

Then, with much creaking and shuddering, and with almost agonizing slowness, the train pulls out of the station and onto the Yalu bridge.

Notes

1. E. G. Kemp, *The Face of Manchuria, Korea and Russian Turkestan* (New York: Duffield, 1911), 146.

2. Anne Wu, "What China Whispers to North Korea," *Washington Quarterly* 28, no. 2 (2005): 35–48, 44.

3. Kemp, *The Face of Manchuria, Korea and Russian Turkestan*, 61–62.

4. Kemp, *The Face of Manchuria, Korea and Russian Turkestan*, 59.

5. Kemp, *The Face of Manchuria, Korea and Russian Turkestan*, 61.

6. On geisha in Dandong, see Hubert Jerningham, *From West to East: Notes by the Way* (New York: E. P. Dutton, 1907), 232; on Jules Brynner, see Rock Brynner, *Empire and Odyssey: The Brynners in Far East Russia and Beyond* (Hanover, N.H.: Steerforth Press, 2006).

7. "Translation of a Chinese Passport Issued in Favour of Miss Emily G. Kemp and Miss Mary M. MacDougall," February 12, 1912, in "Chinese Travel of Miss Emily G. Kemp and Miss Mary M. MacDougall," Foreign Office 371, 1912, volume 1342 (China Political), file 6962, reproduced in Paul L. Kesaris, ed., *Microfilm Edition of Confidential British Foreign Office Political Correspondence, China, Series 1, 1906–1919, Part 3: 1912–1914* (Bethesda, Md.: University Publications of America, 1997), reel 35.

8. "Chinese Passport for Miss E. G. Kemp and Miss M. M. MacDougall," memo dated February 16, 1912, in "Chinese Travel of Miss Emily G. Kemp and Miss Mary M. MacDougall."

9. Letter from J. E. Shuckburgh, India Office, September 13, 1913, in "Chinese Travel of Miss Emily G. Kemp and Miss Mary M. MacDougall."

CHAPTER FIVE

Across the Bridge
To Sinuiju and Beyond

Another World

Everything was a strange contrast from what we had left; the cold co-
louring of Manchuria was replaced by a warm red soil, through which
the first tokens of spring were beginning to appear. Instead of the blue
clothing to which we had been accustomed, every one here was clad in
white, both in town and country. Rice fields greet the eye at every turn,
for this is the main cereal grown. The only things that were the same
were the Japanese line and the Japanese official, no more conspicuous
here than in Manchuria, and apparently firmly rooted in both.[1]

Crossing into Korea from Manchuria in 1910, Emily Kemp experienced a
vivid sense of entering a new world. She had traveled through China several
times before, but this was her first sight of Korea. The visit from the start was
beset by problems: friends in China had cheerfully assured her that Chinese
was understood everywhere in Korea, so she and Mary MacDougall had hired
a Chinese guide, Mr. Chiao, to accompany them on their travels.

It was true that in the early twentieth century all Korean literati could
read Chinese characters, but the travelers quickly discovered that most of the
people they met on their journey were not literati. Spoken Korean and spoken Chinese are about as mutually comprehensible as English and Russian,
and the hapless Mr. Chiao spent much of his time hunting for local scholars
or officials with whom he could communicate through messages written on
scraps of paper or scratched into the dirt of unpaved roads. His task was not

helped by the fact that their itinerary through Korea had been planned on a German map that rendered some place names into Germanized approximations that were utterly impossible to correlate with Korean, Japanese, or Chinese equivalents.

In spite of these handicaps, with the help of missionaries, English-speaking Koreans and Japanese, sign language, and Mr. Chiao's Chinese characters, Kemp and MacDougall managed somehow to find their way through the country, record a wealth of information and impressions, and sometimes even engage in conversations with local people. The exchanges of ideas that she achieved across the language barrier left Kemp with a generally warm and positive image of Korea: "The people," she wrote, "are naturally peaceful and diligent, and under a wise rule the land ought to become an ideal one."[2]

Korea, "somewhat larger than Great Britain," had a population that in 1910 was estimated at around twelve to thirteen million, though the figures were inexact, as the first attempt at a census had been taken by Japanese officials, and (Kemp noted) many people had avoided being counted for fear that the records would be used to impose new taxes.[3] When we visit, a brand new census, whose accuracy some outsiders question, has just put the population of the Democratic People's Republic of Korea (DPRK) at twenty-four million (almost exactly half the size of the South Korean population). Like many of Kemp's observations of Korea, her comments on the first census are a reminder of how firmly the country was already under Japanese control by the first years of the twentieth century. The formal annexation of Korea in August 1910 was the culmination of a long process of colonial penetration, rather than its beginning.

Sinuiju, on the Korean bank of the Yalu River immediately opposite Dandong, was at that time a small railway and port town where Japanese companies were rapidly developing mills for lumber that was floated down the Yalu from forests further inland. The streets were being set out in a grid pattern, and the town center, inhabited mainly by Japanese officials and settlers, was labeled with the unmistakable litany of names that Japan's colonial planners scattered all over the face of East Asia as the empire expanded: Sakura Machi (Cherry Tree Town), Yamato Machi (Japan Town), and Asahi Machi (Morning Sun Town).

As our train approaches Sinuiju station, we look down from the Friendship Bridge, at the tiny figures on the shore below who are checking long fishing nets trailing far out into the murky waters of the Yalu. Our train shunts onto a new track, where it is coupled to a local express, and we have a glimpse of central Sinuiju through the trees: a large square with trim box hedges and lilac bushes in flower, where a group of women in flowing, pink *chima jeogori* are gathered in front of a vast bronze statue of the late but Eternal President Kim Il-Sung.

Having finally reached the Korean side of the Yalu, however, we now find ourselves frustratingly sitting for three hours in the train in Sinuiju station, almost within sight of our Dandong hotel, as extra carriages are coupled onto the train and a seemingly interminable customs and passport inspection takes place. The two North Korean men in our carriage wake up and offer us dried fish and peanuts from their capacious bags of food and drink. Like Kemp and MacDougall, we suffer from a language barrier—my spoken Korean is limited to basic sentences. But one of our companions, we discover, speaks a little French. He is on his way home from an assignment in the Congo, suffering from some stomach ailment that he has picked up in the tropics, and spends most of the journey fast asleep on his bunk. What he was doing in the Congo remains a mystery.

The prolonged wait gives us ample time to read and commit to memory two large, red signs on the station, one reading "Long Live General Kim Jong-Il, the Sun of the Twenty-First Century" and the other exhorting citizens to devote themselves wholeheartedly to the 150-Day Campaign. This, it turns out, is a production drive that started on April 20 and involves the mass recruitment of people from all over the country to work on farms or in other forms of manual labor. The official aim is to "bring about a revolutionary upsurge on all economic fronts" and so "fling open the gate to a great, powerful and prosperous nation in 2012, the year marking the centennial birth anniversary of President Kim Il-Sung."[4]

A very young and rather worried-looking soldier stands to attention on the platform outside the door of our carriage, observing the comings and goings on the station. At one point, a shiny, new Toyota Crown drives onto the platform, and its driver proceeds to shift mountains of boxes—several of them filled with pineapples—from the truck and onto the train. There is much saluting from the little soldier as the owner of the pineapples boards our carriage.

I am reminded of a story I heard from a man who visited North Korea to provide aid during the terrible famine that gripped the country in the mid-1990s—an event officially known in the DPRK as "the Arduous March." Waiting at Sinuiju station, he entered into conversation with a young soldier on the platform.

"Why did you join the army?" he asked the soldier.

"Because it is the only way to get enough food to live," was the reply.

"I've come here to help provide food aid," explained the man.

The soldier looked at him sadly and asked, "Why have you come too late?"

Sinuiju railway station (S. Morris)

Once the local train is coupled to ours, North Korean passengers begin to arrive in large numbers, pouring down the staircase at the far end of the station. Many—particularly women—carry huge, blue or olive green bundles on their backs, a sight that is repeated at every station along the way. Some have great sacks that I guess contain fertilizer. Others have boxes large enough to hold television sets. Others again carry neatly folded bundles of cardboard boxes, having presumably unloaded their contents somewhere en route.

Finally the customs and immigration officials appear at our compartment door.

"Cell phone? Cell phone?" they demand.

We assure them that we have no cell phones, and they proceed to rummage in a fairly haphazard fashion through our luggage. Satisfied that we are carrying no dangerous contraband, an official appears and hands us back our passports with blue slips of paper inserted between the pages.

Our North Korean visas have arrived at last.

Red Soil, Green Rice

We have indeed entered another world, though one that, at first sight, seems far removed from the Korea depicted by Emily Kemp. She visited Korea seven years before the Russian revolution that created the first attempt at a socialist utopia. Sandy and I are witnessing the last, eccentric survival of that vast and fractured revolutionary social experiment that created such ferment in the history of the twentieth century. But as our train finally creaks out of the station through the bleak industrial wastelands of Sinuiju and rumbles south toward Pyongyang, we see the fields of red earth that Kemp described unfold on either side of the track, the ox-drawn ploughs working their way along the furrows, and farmers planting out tender, green rice seedlings from the seedbeds where they have been sheltered from the cold.

Perhaps not so much has changed after all.

People herd small flocks of ducks and geese alongside the line, unblock irrigation channels to flood the fields, or sprinkle fertilizer across the earth with a sweep of the arm that recalls the famous Millet painting of the sower. Tractors are a relatively rare sight here. Almost everywhere the hills are bare and rocky, or covered with a thin scrub of small trees, some of them in blossom. This is a landscape denuded by years of desperate energy shortage. Just here and there vivid green patches of pine trees mark recent efforts at reforestation. White egrets perch in the paddies, and at one point, to our great surprise, a large antlered deer bounds across a ploughed field.

The famine of the 1990s is past, and the last year's harvest was reportedly good, but the people in the fields have dark, stoic faces. Most are small and slightly built, the stature of young adults visibly stunted by the years of hunger. Children work alongside the adults, helping with the planting. I spot one small boy with a gaunt face eagerly devouring a bun on the embankment. A little further down the track a woman in a bright yellow cardigan waves gaily at the train, while nearby a man is painstakingly reassembling a dismembered bicycle, whose wheels and handlebars lie scattered across a dirt track by the railway.

The sun is shining, and women are out washing clothes in the streams that sparkle between the rice fields. In colonial days, the washing of clothes was a subject that attracted much attention from foreign visitors to Korea, including Kemp, who was eager to refute the negative images of Korea propagated by earlier European travelers like Lord Curzon:

> I am greatly astonished (she wrote) at the charge of dirtiness so frequently brought against the Koreans, for on the whole they would bear comparison with almost any European nation. They lavish endless time and energy on getting their clothes white and well laundered, for which they possess the most primitive implements imaginable. The garment is folded quite wet, placed on a board, and beaten rapidly with two flat sticks for any length of time. The

sound greets one's ears all day and every day in the streets, and resembles that of a stick being drawn across palings.[5]

The practice of pummeling clothes with sticks seems virtually to have disappeared, but in rural North Korea, where running water in houses is rarity, women still scrub their washing on riverside stones with great vigor, as they did in South Korea not so long ago. When I first visited the South in the early 1970s, I stayed on a small island near Incheon (the site of to-day's Seoul International Airport) where the only electricity was supplied to a few buildings for a couple of hours by a clattering diesel generator and where clothes were still washed in the stream. I vividly remember the look of incredulity with which the village women observed my pathetic attempts at clothes washing, before finally feeling impelled to intervene and show me how to do it properly. In today's high-tech South Korea, such scenes seem unimaginable, but thirty-five years ago South and North were almost equally poor countries. It was only in the last quarter of the twentieth century that the political divide was reinforced by an ever-widening economic gulf.

Clothing in general—and hats in particular—was a subject of fascination to early Western visitors to Korea. Of all the countries in the world, Korea was perhaps the one where Confucian notions of social hierarchy had the greatest influence, and the social order was tangibly expressed in costume. The basic pattern was the same for most social groups: *chima jeogori* (long skirt and short top) for women and *baji jeogori* (loose trousers and short top) for men; but colors, designs, and fabrics proliferated into a wondrous diver-

View from the train to Pyongyang (S. Morris)

sity determined by class, guild, and marital status. Commoners wore white; today's multicolored nylon *chima jeogori* is a reinvented tradition. Hats, too, defined the wearer's place in an intricate social order. "I understand a book has been written on the subject," remarks Kemp, "so numerous are the varieties in Korea." The ones that fascinated her most were a woman's mourning hat, "looking like an inverted flower, and accompanied by a long coat of stiff undressed cotton to match," and an even larger hat worn by women particularly in the Pyongyang area, which extended "over the head in front and to the knees behind."[6]

Colonialism, modernization, war, and social transformation have swept away the old etiquette of dress (even if they have not swept away social divisions). In North Korea today, the dominant color is the ubiquitous dark olive-brown of soldiers' uniforms, since most men spend seven or eight years performing military service, and the same color is repeated in the work clothes worn by farmers in the fields. But the somber monotone is relieved by the bright splashes of pink, red, and blue tracksuits, imported in bulk from China and popular particularly with children.

Fellow Travelers

As our train heads across the northwestern plains of Korea, we discover that the compartment next to ours is occupied by a charming South Asian woman who works for an international agency in Pyongyang, and together with her we make our way down the corridors of the lurching and swaying train in search of lunch. The buffet car is crowded with people chatting, drinking, and playing cards. In one corner, a middle-aged couple and their teenage daughter sit quietly, toying with their food. The daughter is ashen faced and looks as though she is seriously ill. Every now and again, the buffet and its diners are plunged into total darkness as the unlit train enters an equally unlit tunnel.

We share the train's ample set lunch, consisting of stewed beef, egg, fish in batter, kimchi, and rice. Coffee is also served, but it is cold and comes in cans. When we ask the waitress if we can have hot coffee there is much consultation, and then the cans are taken away only to be returned, about a quarter of an hour later, now faintly lukewarm.

Our South Asian companion loves life in Pyongyang. Like most employees of the UN and other international agencies, she lives in a compound for foreigners but is largely free to walk around the city center. One of her favorite places, she says, is the Sunday Tongil market, where you can buy all kinds of vegetables. After encountering initial reserve, she has become good friends with her North Korean colleagues and even invites them to meals. This is quite an achievement. Some staff of international agencies reportedly call their North Korean drivers by numbers instead of names because they find Korean names too difficult to remember.

This enthusiasm for life in Pyongyang is not shared by all foreign residents. There is also the Chinese man whom we meet in a train compartment—a large, broad-shouldered businessman with a round, shining face who looks for all the world as though he had stepped out of a historical drama set in the palaces of the Manchu Qing Dynasty. He has been based in North Korea for four years and, when the North Korean comrades are not looking, gives us a wink and a grimace. "Pyongyang! Four years!" he groans. He doesn't like Korean food and makes his own Chinese meals at home.

The North Korean man in the same compartment apparently misses this disparaging aside but, while the Chinese businessman is absent in the buffet, proves equally forthright about his experiences of life in China. Casually dressed in slacks and a stylish designer polo shirt, with a small party badge discreetly pinned below its collar, he comes from a family of diplomats, has spent much of his life abroad, and speaks excellent English. He has been on a posting in Beijing but has left his teenage son with an aunt in Pyongyang to attend school. When I ask how his son is doing, he rolls his eyes despairingly, "Kids!" he says, "You know what it's like. He spends his whole time playing computer games! I don't know what to do about it. I don't want him to go to school in China though. Those Chinese kids have no manners. It's the way they're brought up, because of China's one-child policy. Chinese parents spoil their children rotten."

He finds Chinese gender relations difficult to adjust to, too. "Chinese women can be very bossy," he says. "They even get the men to do the cooking."

The man in polo shirt has traveled through much of Europe as well as to several Asian countries, conducting economic negotiations. It's a hard task. Economic sanctions and general mistrust of North Korea in the outside world mean that few countries will accept the letters of credit that are essential to international trade and financial transactions. He enjoys the chance to see foreign countries, though.

"I loved Malaysia," he says, "but I didn't like Singapore—too many regulations: no smoking; don't do this; don't do that." (I mentally save up this social critique to share with my Singaporean friends who will, I think, savor the irony.) "I've never been to Japan, though," he adds. "There are too many problems with history. Relations with that country are just too bad."

Outside, clouds are starting to gather in the spring sky. Red flags flutter outside a village where the 150-Day Campaign is in full swing. From the train we have a chance to look more closely at villages like the ones we glimpsed during our boat trip on the Yalu River. There is something about North Korean villages that touches deep echoes in the mind. You can see in them the ruins of a utopian egalitarian dream. The white cottages with their gray-tiled roofs are all alike, huddled communally within the white village wall. The only structures that stand out are the village hall and the tall, white plaster obelisks topped by a replica red eternal flame. These are the Towers of Eternity, which began to be constructed on the third anniversary of the death of Kim Il-Sung to reassure the people of North Korea that the spirit of the Great Leader was still with them. The third anniversary of Kim Il-Sung's death occurred in 1997, worst year of the famine. In 1997, the North Korean people needed a very large amount of reassurance indeed.

Men and women trudge through a ploughed field, planting vegetables in long lines, rows of cabbages alternating with rows of spring onions. We sit in silence for a while, watching the scenery passing outside the window.

"Actually," the man in the polo shirt says suddenly, in rather subdued tones, "farming in this country's very hard. They don't have machines, you see, so it's very difficult to live in the villages."

I try, and fail, to think of an appropriate answer to his comment.

On Touring Dictatorships

Kemp, before setting off for Manchuria and Korea, was warned that "great dangers" would lie in her path. There were dark references to such perils as "tigers, brigands, Hun Hutzes [*honghuzi*, armed robbers who haunted the borderlands between Russia and China], and the lowest class of Japanese ruffian."[7] The country districts of Korea in particular were said to be "quite unsafe on account of Japanese vagrants," but, Kemp adds, "we saw nothing of them, and as far as we could judge there is excellent order everywhere."[8]

Before I left Australia, when I mentioned to friends there and in Japan that I was planning to visit North Korea, the reactions ranged from envy ("I've always wanted to go there"), through incomprehension ("North Korea? What for?"), to frank disapproval ("It'll just be a propaganda tour. You're helping to prop up the regime. They'll give you a completely false picture of what life's like there"). This last comment, which I have heard many times, has left me reflecting on the morality of travel. Does travel for pleasure or pilgrimage in search of enlightenment have ethical boundaries? Travelers, of course, carry their own ethics with them like the clothes and the bags on their backs. There are certainly things that should not be done, but are there also places that should not be visited and people who should not be spoken to?

Kemp and MacDougall's travels were hampered by language barriers, inadequate transport, and bewildering maps. They were, however, relatively free to go where they liked. Later in the colonial period, when the machinery of imperial police control was more firmly established, and suspicions of westerners were increasing, their movements would have been more restricted.[9] They would, however, certainly not have been as restricted as the movements of most foreign visitors to North Korea today. The DPRK is a country that exerts extraordinary control and surveillance over travel both within and across its borders. On the train from Dandong to Pyongyang we are not accompanied by guides, but our contact with locals is limited by the fact that we are sealed in a train that is used only by foreigners and members of the North Korean elite. As soon as we arrive in Pyongyang, we will be met by guides who will be with us for almost all of our waking hours during our stay in the country. The aim is, of course, to prevent foreigners from seeing undesirable sights and to persuade them of the virtues of the North Korean system, while earning much-needed foreign currency along the way.

But in a country like North Korea, there are some things that no amount of careful guiding can conceal—chance encounters, scenes glimpsed from train and car windows or down narrow back streets: a woman in trim skirt and blouse riding a bicycle along a bumpy rural road with a large sheet of plate glass delicately balanced behind her (glass windows are a valuable luxury here); a driver muttering dark imprecations at a tiny, runny-nosed soldier who has stopped him on the highway and demanded to see his papers; a woman soldier by a roadside peering intently into a large sack of corn that is being held open by two other middle-aged women. Is the soldier checking suspect baggage, or are the three of them engaged in a little unofficial commerce?

Sometimes, information learnt outside the country, when put together with the scenes before our eyes, can help to fill missing parts of the picture. In the 1960s, tens of thousands of Koreans living in Japan, almost all of them originally from the southern part of Korea, were resettled in North Korea under an agreement between the Japanese side (which wanted to reduce the size of an "undesirable" ethnic minority) and the DPRK side (which hoped for a strategically beneficial propaganda coup).[10] These migrants and their families in Japan, as well as refugees, Chinese travelers to North Korea, and others, are channels through which knowledge of North Korea reaches the outside world, and vice versa.

Conversation with friends who have relatives in North Korea has given me fragments of information that help my imagination to work on the landscape that rolls past outside the train window. The 150-Day Campaign is just part of an effort by the state to reimpose socialist discipline in a country where by sheer force of necessity chaotic unlicensed market activity, again and again, breaks through the crust of command economy, as blades of grass push through street paving.

Safely out of sight of visitors like ourselves, little huddles of market stalls appear in back streets and are closed down by the authorities, only to reappear in new forms. Unable to display their wares in public, women sit by the streets with pieces of paper advertising the goods they have for sale—pairs of shoes, soft drinks, electrical goods from China—pieces of paper that can quickly be concealed from the prying eyes of an approaching policeman. I have even heard from refugees and others of contraband cars pulled across the ice of frozen rivers from China by North Korea's unofficial private entrepreneurs. Ironically, as the world's most state-controlled economy struggles to survive, hard currency becomes the key to anything and everything, easing the way (according to the accounts of refugees) even to medical care and all-important party membership.

The simmering contradictions of North Korea's economy are inescapable. The government longs to proclaim its country's modernity but struggles to repress the consumerism that modernity brings with it. While state subsidies and the withered remnants of a public distribution system keep the cost of a few basic items very low, the prices of other consumer goods are soaring, making life a struggle for ordinary people with little cash income. Meanwhile, the government tries to keep the lid on the black market with a string of prohibitions: price controls on items sold in the legal farmers' markets; a prohibition on trading by women aged under forty, later extended to cover all women aged under fifty.

As our train draws into the station of a rural town, we pass blocks of apartments, five or six stories high. Most are painted pink or faded peppermint green. The apartments have balconies, some of which are sheltered from the cold with sheets of polythene. All around the blocks, the ground is carefully cultivated and planted with vegetables. Outside one building, a pile of straw is being unloaded onto the earth from an oxcart. Sandy and I will never see the inside of these buildings, but I have heard stories of the daily life within and project these remembered stories onto the buildings as we pass them. There will be no functioning elevators inside, so it is much better to live near the bottom than near the top, particularly if (as is often the case) the taps do not work and water has to be carried up the stairs in buckets or hoisted up through a window by rope. Cooking is probably done on a wood or coal briquette stove that fills the apartment with fumes.

We will not see the northeastern part of the country, which is both the poorest and the most tightly restricted area. It is also home to the most notorious of North Korea's numerous labor camps—Yodok. Officially known as Control Area (Kwalliso) 15, Yodok, like other places of punishment for political dissidents, is not so much a "detention camp" in the normal understanding of the word as a whole area of countryside, including villages, farms, and mines, enclosed behind heavily guarded electric fencing.[11] In these Control Areas, detainees are exposed to all the extremes of violence that occur when people who fear for their own lives are given absolute powers of life and death over others: torture, public execution, and sexual and psychological abuse. Needless to say, we will not be allowed anywhere near a Control Area.

We know that such places exist; how much our guides know is another matter. The testimony of camp survivors shows that many middle-ranking members of the North Korean elite are unaware of the existence of the camps unless they or their immediate family have the misfortune to be sent to one.[12] We will carry this knowledge around in our heads as we view the sights that the guides present to us, but it will not be spoken about.

Knowing these things, should we be in the country at all?

All modern nations use tourism to present a smiling face to the world. When Kemp visited Korea, the Japanese government was soon to embark on a careful and effective campaign, conducted via pamphlets, advertisements, photographs, and film, to encourage foreign visitors to tour the empire, witnessing the "remarkable cultural progress of the peninsula" achieved by the "civilizing work" of Japanese colonization.[13] The counterparts to this were the tours of Japan organized for carefully selected groups of Koreans, to persuade them of benefits of rule by their more powerful neighbor. Former U.S. president Theodore Roosevelt—a great admirer of Japanese colonialism (as well as an advocate of U.S. imperial expansion)—enthusiastically described how

> tourist parties of Koreans are formed to visit Japan and study its advanced systems of agriculture, industry and education. The visits are generally timed so as to see a national or some local exhibition. . . . The Japanese are endeavouring to introduce their language, culture and industry into the country, and are taking very practical steps to introduce the Koreans to the high modern civilization of the new rulers of the land.[14]

Roosevelt's comments were based, not on personal observation, but rather on his reading of an essay by Terauchi Masatake, Japan's first colonial governor-general of Korea, but some westerners who saw Korea for themselves also came away convinced of the virtues of Japanese colonial rule. One was Herbert Austin, a British army officer who visited Korea two years before Kemp and was guided around Pyongyang and Seoul by senior Japanese officials. Rather surprisingly, Austin was given a tour of Pyongyang's two prisons, one for Japanese prisoners, which he described as "clean, well-ventilated and airy," and a separate establishment for Korean prisoners, where "criminals were herded together, from lack of accommodation, to the number of from twenty-five to thirty in a cell perhaps 12 to 14 feet square."[15] He found the second prison troubling but still returned from his travels with a cautiously optimistic view of Japan's rapidly expanding power in Korea. Although he wrote that "there was little room for doubt that the whole nation [of Korea] has been most hardly and unjustly dealt with by Japan," he concluded that "Korea is incapable of managing her affairs" and that Japan was rapidly learning the skills of successful colonization. Once these skills had been more finely honed, Austin predicted, "Korea should be destined to form a bright jewel in the crown of the Rising Sun."[16]

A few foreign visitors, though, perceived a far darker side to the colonial order. Journalist Frederick A. McKenzie was, by 1908, already expressing anxieties about the growing power of the military in Japan, prophetically warning that this might lead to "harsher rule in Korea, steadily increasing aggression in Manchuria, growing interference with China, and, in the end, a Titanic conflict, the end of which none of us can see."[17] His criticism was to grow more strident after the annexation of Korea in 1910, and particularly following the mass Korean protest against colonial rule in 1919, to which the authorities responded with the imprisonment without trial and torture of large numbers of political prisoners.[18] Kemp was less vociferous in her condemnation but developed a complex and critical view of Korea's colonial rulers as she traveled through the country. No one, however, seems to have suggested that these foreigners should not have visited Korea because the country had been colonized without its inhabitants' consent or because the colonial authorities tortured prisoners.

When I first visited South Korea in the 1970s, that country was under the authoritarian rule of Park Chung-hee, many of whose political opponents languished in grim prisons.[19] The South's political prisons in the 1970s were not as extensive as the North's today. (They had been larger in the 1950s, in the days of South Korea's first president, Yi Seungman [known in the English-speaking world as Syngman Rhee].) In some ways, however, my feelings toward North Korea echo today the emotions I felt on first visiting the South Korea of Park Chung-hee: a sense of despair at the nature of the political regime and a deep respect for the ordinary people who manage somehow to live within the narrow spaces left to them, and to live without losing their humanity.

There can be no absolute answer to the question of whether one should or should not walk on the soil of nations where people are tortured and killed for their political beliefs. But I believe that traveling with open eyes and an open mind may help to open fissures in the walls that surround dictatorships and disrupt the cycles of mutual dehumanization that block international communications and hamper political change. If we close the shutters, if we treat some countries as pariahs beyond the reach of all communication, and if we fail even to attempt to peer through the cracks, we will also fail to see the complexities and paradoxes that beset even the most repressive societies. And then it becomes too easy to build an imagined "rogue state" in our minds and to devise comfortingly simple—and almost certainly miscon-ceived—solutions to its profoundly complicated problems.

Dusk is falling as we enter the suburbs of Pyongyang. A little boy, super-vised by an older sister, is shakily learning to ride a bicycle on a strip of dirt beside the track. A guard comes down the train corridor and abruptly closes the curtains on the window of our compartment. This, of course, only whets our curiosity as to what is outside, and we try discreetly to peep round the sides of the curtain but see nothing more remarkable than forests of tall, graying apartment blocks and the outline of the unfinished pyramid hotel—Pyongyang's most striking and symbolic landmark.

Two guides—Ms. Ri and Mr. Ryu—are waiting to meet us on the platform of Pyongyang station. Ms. Ri is bright and crisp in a neatly tailored pink suit and high-heeled shoes. Mr. Ryu is older and seems a little quieter, and has a long, gentle, slightly sad face and a streak of gray in his hair. The station is vast, dimly lit, and echoing, like a giant barn, utterly devoid of seats, wait-ing rooms, kiosks, or shops but crammed with a mass of people, most in dark clothes and weighed down by bundles.

As we head toward the exit, Ms. Ri asks us for our train tickets.

Train tickets? We realize with a sudden sinking feeling that we gave them to the guard on the train but have no memory of getting them back again. Focused on anxieties about passports and visas, we had forgotten all about tickets. While Sandy and the guides run back to the carriage to look for the tickets, I wait near the exit, watching the darkness deepen and the station gradually empty of people. At last they return with no tickets, but the young woman at the barrier seems unconcerned. She asks us where we come from and waves us through the station gate with a smile. Ms. Ri, enormously amused, tells us that we are the first foreign tourists who have ever managed to lose our train tickets, and for the rest of the week the missing tickets become a topic of ongoing jokes with the guides and our driver, Mr. Kim.

Our hotel is a short drive from the station. Its large lobby is dominated by a picture of Kim Il-Sung and Kim Jong-Il against a red rising-sun background. To the left is the reception desk and, beyond, a restaurant and a surprisingly large gift shop, selling groceries as well as the usual assortment of *chima jeogori*, artworks, and purses decorated with Mickey Mouse. (Mickey Mouse is very big in North Korea.) Up the broad stairs is a bookshop. Our room overlooks a square and, on the far side, the headquarters of a newspaper company—a building painted the color of pistachio ice-cream. The building is surmounted with a large, red sign.

My Korean has improved a little since this morning: I can read the sign instantly and without effort. It says, "Long Live General Kim Jong-Il, the Sun of the Twenty-First Century."

Notes

1. E. G. Kemp, *The Face of Manchuria, Korea and Russian Turkestan* (New York: Duffield, 1911), 62.

2. Kemp, *Face of Manchuria, Korea and Russian Turkestan*, 63.

3. Kemp, *Face of Manchuria, Korea and Russian Turkestan*, 63.

4. "Agitation for Victorious 150-Day Campaign," *Korea Central News Agency*, May 15, 2009 (Juche 98), at http://www.kcna.co.jp/item/2009/200905/news15/20090515-12ee.html (accessed May 14, 2010).

5. Kemp, *Face of Manchuria, Korea and Russian Turkestan*, 71.

6. Kemp, *Face of Manchuria, Korea and Russian Turkestan*, 69, 76; see also Homer Hulbert, "Question and Answer," *Korea Review* 2 (1902): 22.

7. Kemp, *Face of Manchuria, Korea and Russian Turkestan*, x.

8. Kemp, *Face of Manchuria, Korea and Russian Turkestan*, 133.

9. It is interesting to compare Kemp's account of her travels through Korea with that of British traveler Audrey Harris, who made a similar journey in 1936. By the 1930s, transport and communications were much better, but Harris had far more encounters with Japanese officials who repeatedly questioned her about her background and her travel plans. See Audrey Harris, *Eastern Visas* (London: Collins, 1939).

10. See Tessa Morris-Suzuki, *Exodus to North Korea: Shadows from Japan's Cold War* (Lanham, Md.: Rowman & Littlefield, 2007).

11. On North Korean *kwalliso*, see, for example, National Human Rights Commission of the Republic of Korea, ed., *North Korean Human Rights: Trends and Issues* (Seoul: Author, 2005).

12. See, for example, Kang Chol-Hwan and Pierre Rigoulot, *Aquariums of Pyong-yang: Ten Years in the North Korean Gulag*, trans. Yair Reiner (New York: Basic Books, 2001).

13. Government General of Chosen, *The New Administration of Chosen* (Seoul: Author, 1921), 3.

14. Theodore Roosevelt, *Fear God and Take Your Own Part* (New York: George H. Doran, 1916), 295.

15. Herbert H. Austin, "A Scamper through Korea," in *Korea: Its History, Its People and Its Commerce*, by Angus Hamilton, Herbert H. Austin, and Masatake Terauchi (Boston: J. B. Millet, 1910), 185.

16. Austin, "A Scamper through Korea," 206.

17. F. A. McKenzie, *The Tragedy of Korea* (New York: E. P. Dutton, 1908), 261.

18. F. A. McKenzie, *Korea's Fight for Freedom* (New York: Fleming H. Revell, 1920).

19. On the South Korean political prisons of the Park era, see Suh Sung, *Unbroken Spirits: Nineteen Years in South Korea's Gulag* (Lanham, Md.: Rowman & Littlefield, 2001).

CHAPTER SIX

Diversion
On Time

Timetables

Emily Kemp, in her travel writings, allowed space to triumph over time. Chronology was reorganized to fit geography. Her first book, *The Face of China*, wove together two separate journeys: one made in 1893–1894 when Kemp stayed with her missionary sister Jessie in Taiyuan; the other, in 1907–1908, several years after the murder of Jessie and her family.

The two journeys, however, were melded by Kemp's writing so that the reader can seldom tell whether the scenes being described were seen in early 1890s or more than a decade later. In recounting her journey through Manchuria and Korea, Kemp also shifts events such as her visit to the Thousand Peaks, rethreading them like beads on a string according to the logic of place rather than the actual sequence in which they occurred.

A true child of the industrial revolution, she was an enthusiastic reader of timetables and planner of schedules, molding and disciplining time to the needs of her travel itinerary, and she observed with surprise the lives of those who moved to other rhythms. In Manchuria, she wrote, "the people have the vaguest conception of time and are accustomed to wait hours at the station," and even Japanese bank clerks in Seoul pursued their transactions at a pace that she found exasperatingly slow: "Time seemed to be of no importance."[1] Her desire to keep things moving at her own brisk tempo was almost to lead to disaster in the Diamond Mountains. For, as one friend observed, Kemp had "an indomitable will: what she intended to do she did in spite of warning, in spite of opposition."[2]

The attempt to re-create Kemp's journey requires a similar subduing and reordering of time. The places she visited still exist, but in some cases the connections between them have been totally severed. The road from Wonsan to the Diamond Mountains, which Kemp and Mary MacDougall reached by boat from Busan, for example, can now only be approached from the northern side, and we embarked on it via a detour from Pyongyang in the company of Ms. Ri, Mr. Ryu, and the driver Mr. Kim. I shall describe it, however, after following Kemp's path through Pyongyang, Seoul, and Busan—using words and imagination to weave together the sundered connections into something resembling the landscape that existed a century ago.

Calendars

On this pilgrimage in search of the end of the Cold War, I am conscious of moving through many overlapping layers of time. The pulse of Kemp's world was that of high modernity: progress was forever sweeping away the old and opening up the new. However much she mourned the relentless march of modernity across the landscape, Kemp could never quite repress a thoroughly modern sense of time as an enemy to be subdued. Wherever she went, she described the monuments of the past as "dimmed," "injured," or "ravaged" by the hand of time.

In today's North Korea, the modern belief in the power of progress and the urge to control time finds its most extreme and ironical expression. Juche Thought, the idiosyncratic departure from Marxism-Leninism that was created by Kim Il-Sung as North Korea's official ideology, teaches that "man is the master of everything and decides everything." This means that the forces of material progress move eternally forward but also that a small and poor country like North Korea, by sheer human determination and willpower, should be able to leapfrog over the preordained stages of history and become the vanguard of the world. Like many revolutionary regimes, North Korea has its own calendar: the Juche Calendar, in which Year 1 is 1912, the year of Kim Il-Sung's birth. This calendar, however, was not introduced at the moment of revolution but retrospectively in 1997, when North Korea was in the midst of one of the worst famines of the late twentieth century. And in the end, the attempt to leapfrog history has left the country trapped in a strange time warp from which there is no obvious or easy exit.

Around the rock of Juche time flow the currents of Northeast Asian history—the slow shift from a Chinese-centered to a Japanese-centered world, and now the shift of the center back toward China again. Viewing the past century from the perspective of the present, the temporal perspectives sometimes seem surprising. Japan's colonization of Korea, which casts such a long historical shadow over the region, officially lasted only thirty-five years—a mere half-lifetime—though de facto Japanese dominance over the region lasted almost twice as long. The division of the Korean Peninsula has continued for sixty years—almost a whole lifetime—and though the imminent demise of North Korea has been repeatedly predicted for the past two decades, the system stubbornly clings to life. Even now, its end is impossible to predict, though the signs indeed point to impending change.

Meanwhile, I travel through a region gripped by a day-to-day sense of crisis. One moment, the North Korean government is rattling sabers and threatening war; the next, it is offering olive branches. One week North and South are deep in negotiations about reopening their closed border crossings; the next, the talks have been broken off amid acrimony and mutual recriminations.

And far beneath all these surface currents moves the slow, almost imperceptible rhythm of a much older sense of time: the vision of the Buddhist pilgrims in which individual human lives were imperceptible flecks in the innumerable and vastly long *maha-kalpa*—the cycles of creation, stability, decline, and extinction, each said by some to last 320 million years. In this vision—at least in one version popular in China, Korea, and Japan—the goal of pilgrimage is the point where each world with its "encircling ring of diamond mountains" is flooded by the light of Amitayus, the Buddha of Infinite Life, "as it will be at the kalpa's end when a great flood will submerge the myriad things and there will be nothing visible as far as the eye can see except a vast expanse of water."[3]

Notes

1. E. G. Kemp, *Face of Manchuria, Korea and Russian Turkestan* (New York: Duffield, 1911), 56, 105.

2. Helen Darbishire, "In Memoriam: Emily Georgiana Kemp," in *Somerville College Chapel Addresses and Other Papers*, 10–13 (London: Headley Brothers, 1962), 11.

3. "The Larger Pureland Sutra: Sukhavativyuha Manifesting the Land of Bliss," at http://www.amidatrust.com/amidashu/lpls.html (accessed May 14, 2010).

CHAPTER SEVEN

The New Jerusalem
Pyongyang

The Water Carriers of Pyongyang

Korea is a peninsula divided, not just by barbed wire, mines, and all the monstrous machinery of modern warfare, but also by words. The old differences in regional dialect between North and South have been sharpened by ideology; foreign words imported since division in 1945—"helicopter," "cable car," and so on—have been translated differently on either side of the 38th parallel. Our driver Mr. Kim gives a broad smile, revealing the gleaming gold fillings in his teeth, when I use the phrase *ireopseumnida*, which in North Korea is polite and means "it's not a problem" but in South Korea means "mind your own business." The rival governments on either side of the divide have developed different systems for converting Korean characters into the Roman alphabet, causing endless problems for people (myself included) who write books in English containing place names in both North and South.

Most troublesome of all is the divide in the name given to the country itself.

When Cold War Germany was divided in two, both halves at least still called themselves Deutschland. But in Korea, the regimes on either side of the Cold War dividing line chose to inherit different versions of the historical name for Korea. The North became the Democratic People's Republic of Choson (Joseon in South Korean romanization), using the name by which Korea had been known for most of its history since the fourteenth century. (Choson is often translated into English as "Land of Morning Calm," though Emily Kemp, more correctly, translates it "Land of Morning Freshness.") The

South became Daehanminguk ("Great Nation of the Han People"), "Han" being another archaic term for Korea, briefly revived by the modernizing Korean empire between 1897 and 1910. The search for a shared name is just one of the multitude of roadblocks that litter the path toward reunification.

The problem of names also has other, more subtle effects. Not only Koreans themselves but also their neighbors, the Japanese and Chinese, have come since 1945 to use their own versions of the two different names for the two halves of the peninsula and its people. The people of the North are known in Japanese as Chōsenjin and in Chinese as Chaoxianren; the people of the South are Kankokujin in Japanese and Hanguoren in Chinese. When Japanese people remember their country's annexation of Korea, they use the term Kankoku Heigō, which roughly (and ambiguously) means "unification with" or "absorption of" Korea—but the term for "Korea" in this phrase is the word that today means "South Korea."

The approaching centenary of Kankoku Heigō prompts much debate in the Japanese media about appropriate ways for Japan and its neighbor Kankoku—South Korea—to collaborate in commemorating this event. But the debate also serves to deepen a strange shadow in Japanese memory—a shadow that obscures recollections of colonial expansion in the northern half of the Korean Peninsula. Few if any Japanese people, as they watch the military parades in Kim Il-Sung Square that regularly accompany news items on the North Korean "rogue state," think of Kim Il-Sung Square as the place that once housed the offices of the Japanese-run telephone exchange and Chōsen Bank in the city of Heijō (the Japanese colonial-era name for Pyongyang). Few of the Japanese media consider how Japan and its other neighbor, North Korea, might come together to commemorate the memory of the annexation. As time goes on, Japan's colonial rule in Korea is increasingly remembered as a colonization of South Korea, while the colonial history of the North is consigned to uneasy oblivion.

As Emily Kemp and Mary MacDougall arrived in Pyongyang in the early afternoon, and climbed into the sedan chairs prepared by a Korean Christian missionary who was waiting to meet them, they saw the "handsome large new red brick barracks" and the "Japanese suburb" that were rapidly growing up around Pyongyang station. With interpreter Mr. Chiao and the Korean missionary walking behind while conducting a silent conversation in written Chinese characters, the two women were carried in their chairs through streets lined with stalls selling a multitudinous array of unfamiliar foods: "dried cuttle fish hang up in rows, and are a tasty dish in the eyes of the natives, and all kinds of other fish are dried and hung up in strings to form artistic designs for the adornment of the shops, as well as for the benefit of the purchasers."[1] Kemp was delighted by the exotic clutter of these alleyways, but (as she had in Harbin) lamented the steady spread of architectural modernity across the face of the city: "It is sad," she wrote of Pyongyang, "to see every place being disfigured by European-looking erections of the ugliest and most aggressive type."[2]

Kemp's ambivalence toward the Western presence in Northeast Asia is mirrored in her ambivalence toward the Japanese presence on the Asian continent. As the child of a socially conscious industrial revolution pioneer, she wholeheartedly welcomed the modern medicine, hygiene, and education that foreign intruders brought to Manchuria and Korea. But, as a traveler who delighted in the exotic landscapes, sounds, and physical sensations of Asia, she lamented the vanishing traditions displaced by modernity.

A sight that instantly attracted her attention in the streets of Pyongyang was the presence of water carriers, since all the city's water was still drawn from the river. Unlike other parts of Korea, where the heavy work of water carrying was often done by women, the water carriers of Pyongyang were mostly men, who bore their precious burden in pails on their backs. By 1910, however, the Japanese authorities, already in de facto control of the city, had just completed new waterworks on the banks of the broad Taedong River that flows through the center of Pyongyang and on Rungna Islet in the middle of the river itself. The waterworks were a highlight of the Pyongyang tourist itinerary, and as she visited them, Kemp observed wistfully that "soon that picturesque being—the water carrier—will be nothing more than a memory; but undoubtedly the advantages of a good water supply will reconcile the inhabitants to the change."[3]

The waterworks were just part of a profound colonial reshaping of the city, whose influence can still be seen throughout the center of Pyongyang today. Visiting Pyongyang almost two decades before Kemp, the missionary James Gale had found an ancient city still enclosed in high walls. In the remote beginnings of recorded history, the area around Pyongyang was a place of intense interaction between Korean and Chinese kingdoms, and high on Moranbong, the forested hill overlooking the Taedong River, stood a weathered monument that for almost a millennium was revered as the tomb of the semimythical Chinese figure Kija. Known as Jizu in Chinese, Kija was said to have fled from Shang China to Korea more than a thousand years before the start of the Common Era and to have ruled the northern part of the country from Pyongyang.[4] When Gale passed through the city in the early 1890s, aristocrats who claimed descent from Kija still lived in the hills to the south, while in the hills to the north was a "citadel" of Buddhist temples, whose "beauty and strength of situation gives one an idea of the power Buddha once possessed" in Korea.[5]

But, in 1894, disaster struck Pyongyang. The city had the misfortune to lie in the path of Japanese troops as they marched northward toward the Yalu River, and of the Chinese army as it sought to confront them, and so became the site of one of the fiercest conflicts of the Sino-Japanese War of 1894–1895. After the battle, the city of Pyongyang, wrote Gale,

> was strewn with corpses, and the once busy streets were silent, for the inhabitants had scattered, no one knew whither. A Korean with his wife and three children, escaped through the thick of the fight, and by climbing the wall reached safety. He had been a man of some means, but of course had lost everything. He said he was thankful he had his three children spared to him. The little black-eyed girl had heard and seen that night what she would never forget—the rattle of Murata rifles and the other hideous accompaniments of war.[6]

Japan's growing domination over Korea following its victory in the war provided an opportunity to impose a new geometry of modernity on the shattered city. The "Japanese suburb" that Kemp saw springing up around the station was part of an urban design that prefigured the grand Japanese experiment of Manchukuo's "New Capital." A broad, straight avenue—Teishaba Dōri (Japanese for "Station Avenue")—was laid out from the railway station to the Taedong River, where a new town of shops, offices, and warehouses, planned on a grid pattern like that of American cities, accommodated around six thousand Japanese settlers, alongside the old city's Korean population of some thirty-six thousand.[7]

In this new Pyongyang, however, parts of the old were carefully preserved. From the colonizer's perspective, Kija's role in Korean history was evidence of the country's historical subordination to China and, therefore, of its lack of cultural creativity. Kija's tomb became a key exhibit in a new Japanese colonial version of history that challenged Korea's claims to independence and was a landmark visited by most foreign travelers to Pyongyang in the first half of the twentieth century. Kemp climbed the forested slope of Moranbong and found the tomb surrounded by a dense grove of pine trees. It was "tightly shut and barred," but she and MacDougall were able to catch glimpses of the grave mound with its surrounding retinue of stone animal and human guardians. Like most visitors, they were captivated by the breathtaking view from Moranbong over the sparkling river and the fields and hills beyond. But, as Kemp noted sadly, the walls of Pyongyang, dating according to legend from the days of Kija himself, were "now in the course of demolition." This, she added wryly, "synchronises with the coming of the first party of [Thomas] Cook's personally conducted tours!"[8]

Three years later, Korea's new colonial rulers would begin the construction of a grand wooden hall with steeply sloped thatched roof on the hill near Kija's tomb. This was to be Pyongyang's Shinto shrine, where not only the city's growing Japanese population but more particularly the indigenous Korean inhabitants would be required to pay homage to the descendant of Japan's primordial Sun Goddess, Amaterasu Ōmikami: the Japanese Emperor in distant Tokyo. Needless to say, no trace of the Shinto shrine remains in today's Pyongyang.

The further she traveled in Korea, the more Kemp became aware of a dark side to colonial modernity—a cultural violence that went beyond the irresistible retreat of the past in the face of encroaching modernity. Even in these final months before the formal annexation of Korea, the Japanese government continued to disavow any plans for full-scale colonization, insisting that their presence was merely a protectorate exercised with the consent of the Korean king. But, Kemp observed,

> instead of trying to make their protectorate as conciliatory as possible, they too often do the reverse. . . . In many ways they are doing a great deal which should benefit the country, but in such a manner as to make it thoroughly obnoxious. It is little use to repudiate the idea of annexation, when they trample on the dearest wishes of the Korean, and treat him as a vanquished foe.[9]

The Sound of Silence

The Pyongyang landscape that entranced Kemp when she visited Moranbong can be seen in even greater splendor from the landmark to which every foreign visitor is taken today: the Tower of the Juche Idea. Kija, with his foreign and colonial associations, has fallen out of fashion and his tomb has been destroyed, for Juche Thought is above all else profoundly nationalistic. From the summit of the soaring, white tower, surmounted by its stained-glass flame, you can look out to every side across the city and over the glittering, midnight green waters of the Taedong River flowing serenely through its heart.

The broad avenues and squares of the city are kept immaculately clean by legions of tracksuited residents, performing their required civic duties with trowels, dustpans, and brooms. The occasional truck or bus clatters past, but most of the traffic is pedestrian. The people of Pyongyang—men in black suits or army uniforms, women in demure skirts and blouses, and children in school uniforms or sports gear—move with the distinctive gait of those used to walking long distances: unhurried, heads held high, and arms swinging rhythmically by their sides. In the parks along the banks of the Taedong, with their neatly trimmed grass and disciplined topiary, the citizens fish, smoke, or squat in the shade of trees, reading books. The azaleas are in flower, and willow branches, delicate with the green of spring, touch the water's surface.

There is a strange resonance to the open spaces of Pyongyang, a deep silence lying beneath the blasts of martial music and mournful electronic midday and midnight chimes that issue from above the rooftops. Before a truck or bus appears, you can hear its approaching sound from far away, and the deepening grind of its engine continues to reverberate long after it has disappeared from view: for Pyongyang, with its population of over three million, lacks the sound that permeates every other city today—the ceaseless background hum of vehicles.

When, in my early teens, I first lived in a big city, I would wake at night and listen in terror to that sound—the deep inhuman endless roar of the metropolis. Now the sound of the city has become so familiar that (like most people) I no longer hear it, but in Pyongyang, I hear its resounding absence.

At breakfast in the huge dining room of our hotel, with its white linen tablecloths and crystal chandeliers, there is no menu but only a rather shy waitress who seems very eager to please. After some consultation and a long wait, she produces large quantities of bread and fried eggs and quite drinkable

Pedestrians, Pyongyang (S. Morris)

hot coffee. At the table next to ours an extended family, ranging from frail grandmother to small children, is conducting a conversation in a mixture of Korean and Japanese. Our guides tell us that this hotel is often used by Korean families from Japan and even the United States who have come to North Korea to meet long-lost relatives. Later, we see the same family on the steps of the hotel. The grandmother stands shakily, bent double over a walking stick. There are tears pouring down her face.

Mr. Ryu is up early, revising his text for the day as he waits to meet us in the lobby. Although he is older than his female colleague, he is (we discover) a newcomer to this job, having completed his military service and also worked as a researcher for some years before becoming a guide. His English is less polished than Ms. Ri's, but his determination makes up for his lack of experience. Every spare moment is spent memorizing information and revising texts, so that, even though he sometimes stumbles over other words, English phrases like "under the wise leadership of the Great Leader Kim Il-Sung" flow smoothly and fluently from his tongue.

"I liked the army," he says. "It was really hard work, but it was enjoyable, too. You feel as though you're an important person when you're in the army."

He does not really seem the military type, though. He looks more like a schoolteacher, which he was briefly before becoming a soldier. His black suit hangs loosely from his tall and gangly form, and the real loves of his life, I suspect, are his wife and the baby daughter whose photo he carries around with him in his wallet. In the car, as we drive beside the Taedong River, he rather bashfully shows us the little image of a tiny, round face surmounted by tufty hair, and for a moment his eyes loose their sadness and are illuminated with a smile of pure fatherly joy.

Today's Pyongyang is the product of a second wave of destruction and reconstruction, even greater than the first. Just as most Japanese people have forgotten the devastation of Pyongyang during the Sino-Japanese War, so most Americans, British, Australians, and others have forgotten the obliteration of Pyongyang during the Korean War.

The North Korean government does little to remind them. The memory of war is tangible everywhere in the city, but the stories that are commemorated are those of heroic resistance and brilliant victory. In the Victorious Fatherland Liberation War Museum in central Pyongyang, a cheerful young woman soldier proudly displays the massive dioramas depicting the great battle of Daejeon (in South Korea) where "our forces *totally* destroyed one big American military division at that time" and the titanic struggle at the Chol Pass where "the fighting spirit of the drivers of the People's Army, under the guidance of our Great Leader, *utterly* frustrated the enemy's plot to crush the Korean people." With that passion for statistical trivia displayed by guides all over Korea, she also breathlessly informs us that the depiction of Daejeon, which covers the entire wall of a circular hall with a rotating platform in the center, is "fifteen meters high and one hundred and thirty-two meters around and forty-two meters in diameter and from this place to the painting is thirteen and a half meters and on this one picture our artists have painted more than one million people." She pauses for breath before confessing, "But for me, I have continuously counted, but I cannot yet completely count them all." The Victorious Fatherland Liberation War, she explains to us, began on June 25, 1950, when

> the American aggressors attacked our country from the south, over the 38th Parallel, and our Great Leader ordered our soldiers to frustrate the enemy's challenge by going over to the counteroffensive. And on the occasion of this war our Great Leader ordered that in one month we must liberate the whole South Korea. But our soldiers had not many weapons and the American aggressors brought massive reinforcements from their own country and from the Mediterranean fleet and from the Pacific fleet, and with these reinforcements they temporarily occupied some areas of the North, including Pyongyang, so our Great Leader Kim Il-Sung ordered our soldiers to temporarily retreat to the north. But then American imperialists bombed some places in China over the Yalu River, so the Chinese sent us volunteers, and together with our People's Army, they began a new offensive and we drove the Americans south of the 38th Parallel.

The Chol Pass diorama, brought to life with the aid of melodramatic sound and light depicting enemy planes swooping low over the pass and the crackle of antiaircraft fire, is (she says) very popular with children.

But everyday stories of human suffering fit uneasily with this strident official narrative—in which North Korea the victim is instantly transformed into North Korea the victor. I look in vain for a commemoration of two days in the life of Pyongyang that I read about shortly before leaving Australia, days whose statistics seem more significant than the dimensions of the Daejeon panorama: July 11, 1952, the day when U.S., British, Australian, and South Korean planes flew 1,254 bombing sorties and dropped twenty-three thousand gallons of napalm on Pyongyang and its inhabitants; and August 29, 1952, the day when the number of sorties reached 1,403, and around six thousand citizens of the capital were killed.[10] The bombardment of Pyongyang ended a few days later, when the United States command decided there was too little left in the city to justify the effort of attack.[11] By then, 80 percent of the city's buildings were in ruins.

As we leave the museum, our Mr. Ryu remarks in passing, and without any noticeable sign of bitterness, that both his grandfathers and one of his grandmothers were killed in the Korean War. Such stories are commonplace here.

The new city that rose from the chemical-saturated rubble was revolutionary defiance expressed in concrete, stone, and marble. Pyongyang was to be the living embodiment of Juche Thought. Its buildings would be grander, its entertainments more lavish, and its culture more elevated than anything other capitals could offer. The Tower of the Juche Idea, at 170 meters, is seventy centimeters taller than the Washington Monument, which it closely resembles. The Arch of Triumph, built to commemorate Korea's heroic resistance to Japanese colonialism, is the biggest triumphal arch in the world. As Mr. Ryu explains (displaying the fruits of his careful homework), it is sixty meters high and fifty meters wide, while the French version stands at less than fifty meters in height and is a paltry forty-five meters in width.

But although North Korea's leaders proclaimed their determination to erase all traces of the colonial city, the street grid that Japanese modernizers laid out in the early twentieth century in fact provided a good foundation for the Juche capital, and its outlines can still be seen beneath the widened avenues and socialist neoclassicism of today's city. Station Avenue, successively renamed "People's Army Street," then "Willow Street," and now known as "Glory Street,"[12] still runs as straight as an arrow from the station toward the city center. The main road that once bisected the Japanese business district of Yamato Machi (Japan Town) was straightened and broadened in the 1950s and given a new name: Stalin Street. Today, it is Victory Street—like the Arch of Triumph, a commemoration of the defeat of colonialism.

The island in the Taedong River that housed the Japanese-built waterworks is home to the May Day Stadium, where North Korea's breathtaking Arirang mass games are staged. But Moranbong remains, as it was when Kemp visited, a popular picnic spot, while the museum built to commemorate the founding of North Korea's ruling Workers' Party occupies a colonial period edifice that looks suspiciously like the Diet Building in Tokyo and its alter ego, the State Council building in Manchukuo's lost capital of Xinjing. And at least until recently, North Korea's monument to the fallen soldiers of the People's Army stood on the very spot where the Japanese colonial authorities had commemorated their soldiers killed in the 1894 Battle of Pyongyang. The nationality and politics of "our glorious dead" change, but the rituals of remembrance remain much the same.

The Grand People's Study House

Pyongyang is a reward for virtue. To live in the capital is the ultimate mark of success, for (more than almost any other capital city) Pyongyang is reserved for the social and political elite. Guard posts on the roads into the city carefully protect it from any influx of undesirable rural poor. The apartment blocks that face onto the wide main streets present a bland superficial face of modernity. Kemp would be horrified. Yet, looking down from the summit of the Tower of the Juche Idea, you can see how each of the older apartment complexes forms a square surrounding and containing lines of rickety gray-roofed one-story cottages: hidden villages stowed away in the heart of the metropolis.

No building more powerfully proclaims the utopian vision of Pyongyang than the Grand People's Study House. In the early twentieth century, the gentle hill in the city center where the Study House now stands was occupied by Pyongyang's Catholic church and Methodist Episcopalian mission, the latter described by Kemp as a compound of buildings in "American style," including a fine, large church with a belfry "which can be seen as well as heard from afar."[13] Both churches were flattened during the Korean War,[14] and their space is now occupied by a palatial neotraditional structure of white marble columns and tier upon tier of jade green-tiled roofs. The Grand People's Study House, completed in 1982, is not only North Korea's national library but also a research center, adult education college, and general disseminator of enlightenment.

To one side, in a paved expanse worthy of the Palace of Versailles, torrents of surprisingly clear water flow though a series of fountains, waterfalls, and ponds, between the crags of miniature mountains, around gnarled pine trees, and over rocky causeways. A group of boys in pioneer uniforms—red scarves round their necks and the cuffs of their white shirts and blue trousers rolled up—balance perilously, with shrieks of delighted fear, on the boulders in the middle of the torrent. Mothers have brought their toddlers for a picnic in the square, and one wipes her little daughter's sticky fingers with a flannel dipped in the waters of the fountain.

Nearby, a newlywed couple—the bridegroom in a gray suit and the bride in a high-waisted, wide-skirted, pink *chima jeogori* adorned with golden flowers—laughingly play the scissors, stone, and paper game as their wedding photographer darts around them selecting the best angle for his shots. There seem to be few guests in attendance, but several passersby stop to offer smiles and waves of blessing at the couple.

North Korean marriages are still often arranged in traditional fashion by a go-between, who helps to check the political and social pedigree of the part-ners. Our guide Mr. Ryu's wedding, he tells us, was arranged by his superior in the army. But here as elsewhere in Asia, arranged marriages do not preclude love, and Mr. Ryu promises us that, when his fellow guide and driver are not around to hear, he will tell us the story of how he fell in love with his wife.

"*Chima jeogori* are so beautiful," remarks Sandy to Ms. Ri as we watch the bride pose in front of the fountains.

"Yes," replies the guide, adding, with a surprising and conspiratorial smile, "also, very useful if you happen to have any little accidents between your engagement and your wedding."

Inside the echoing gray and pink marble entrance hall of the Grand Peo-ple's Study House, a huge, white statue of the late Kim Il-Sung sits in front of a frieze of Mount Paektu, staring out into the distance, as monumental and impassive as the great golden Buddha of Liaoyang. We are shown around the building by a librarian from the international exchange section, who reels off the inescapable litany of numbers: "The stone used to build this hall comes from all the nine provinces of our country. The Grand People's Study House consists of ten buildings and one hundred rooms and contains over thirty million books . . ."

The ideals seem admirable. The library employs its own staff of eminent academics, who conduct research and are on hand to answer visitors' ques-tions on recondite subjects. In a large room filled with rows of computers, the people whom the library serves are busy conducting their own research using North Korea's homegrown Kwangmyong Intranet.

"The network's limited to our country at the moment, but soon we will connect to the Internet," the guide assures us.

Meanwhile, however, North Korea remains the country most hermeti-cally sealed off from the impact of the Internet revolution, while the South is the most digitally connected place on earth. And in practice, it seems, the majority of the foreign books in the Grand People's Study House, except for technical texts, are off limits to ordinary users, as is most of its extensive collection of foreign records, CDs, and films. Yet, the doors are not entirely closed. Ms. Ri, who proves to be an excellent karaoke singer, has a repertoire that extends beyond standard North Korean favorites such as "Nostalgia" (a song said to be composed by Kim Il-Sung) to include "Climb Every Moun-tain," "Edelweiss," and "My Heart Will Go On"; *The Sound of Music* and *Titanic* were required viewing during her English-language training.

She is, as she also tells us, busy saving up for a cell phone, since these are now available in North Korea and are evidently a status symbol, even though they connect only to a very limited domestic network.

Sunday in Pyongyang

The imposing Methodist Episcopalian church, which Kemp visited and whose bells rang out over central Pyongyang, was at that time just part of a rapidly growing network of Christian churches throughout the city. In 1910, Pyongyang's population of forty thousand was said to include about eight thousand Christians, and Kemp and MacDougall were able to spend the Sunday of their stay in the city happily touring one church after another (though in the case of the Methodist church, they slipped out quietly as the sermon began).[15]

The first Western missionaries to arrive in Pyongyang had not received a warm welcome. A Scottish pastor, Robert Thomas, armed with a trunk full of Bibles, attempted to enter the city in 1866 aboard the General Sherman, an American vessel chartered by a British trading company as part of an audacious attempt to persuade the "hermit kingdom" to open its doors to trade. The voyage was a disaster that ended when the ship ran aground, the panicked crew fired cannons into a Korean crowd that had gathered nearby, and the incensed crowd set fire to the vessel, killing all on board. Korean defiance against "aggression by the American imperialist invasion ship General Sherman" still looms very large in North Korean historical imagination and is commemorated by a large stone monument on the banks of the Taedong River, symbolically placed next to the USS *Pueblo*, the American spy ship captured by North Korea in 1968.

But after initial hostility, in the first decade of the twentieth century the churches in the northern cities of Wonsan and Pyongyang experienced a sudden conversion boom—perhaps a response to the turmoil of war and encroaching colonialism. The Presbyterian Central Church, a lovely simple building in traditional Korean style, was large enough to contain a thousand worshippers, but when Kemp and MacDougall worshipped there, it was often full to overflowing, and thirty-nine new churches had been set up in surrounding areas to accommodate the growing number of converts. By 1910, Pyongyang was already gaining its reputation in missionary circles as "the Jerusalem of the East."

At the Central Church, Kemp and MacDougall met its Korean pastor, the fiery Reverend Kil, a convert to Christianity whose enthusiasm and energy seems oddly to resonate with today's 150-Day Campaign: "When his people seemed to be growing careless, he started a daily prayer meeting at 4 o'clock in the morning, and this was soon attended by six or seven hundred people, with the result that a great revival took place, and his people promised to spend over 3000 days in trying to win others to a knowledge of Christ."[16]

Kemp and MacDougall arrived at the Central Church just as a women's Bible class was starting, and Kemp was enthralled by the sight of the congregation—some wearing the giant hats with which Pyongyang women shielded themselves from male gaze—and by the children, who looked to her like "a gay group of butterflies": "Nowhere (observed Kemp) could there be found a more attractive sight than the hundreds of white clad women, carrying their books wrapped in cloth tied round their waists in front, or their children tied on behind, the little ones dressed in every colour of the rainbow."[17]

These images invite speculation. Was a devout young Korean Christian woman named Kang Pan-Sok, daughter of Presbyterian church elder Kang Tong-Uk, amongst the white-clad women who attended this gathering of

Coy Korean maiden (E. G. Kemp)

women at Pyongyang's Central Church?[18] In 1910, Kang Pan-Sok would have been eighteen years old. Two years later, she would give birth to her first son, Kim Song-Ju, who (after changing his name to Kim Il-Sung in adulthood) would then go on to become the Eternal President of the Democratic People's Republic of Korea.

After being taken on the obligatory pilgrimage to Kim's giant gleaming statue near the site of the vanished Methodist and Catholic churches, it is tempting to superimpose on that image of the gargantuan bronze figure the alternative image of a white-clad young women in her early twenties, with a butterfly-like infant strapped to her back as she said her prayers.

Chilgol, the village on the outskirts of Pyongyang where Kim Il-Sung's mother grew up, was later transformed by her son (by then North Korea's Great Leader) into "Chilgol Revolutionary Site," an open-air museum dedicated to her memory. But, rather unusually for a revolutionary site in a nation dedicated to the Juche Idea, Chilgol contains a church, built in 1992 and said to be a replica of the church attended by Kang Pan-Sok.[19] Presumably, the original must have been one of the dozens of little Presbyterian churches built by the faithful from Pyongyang's Central Church to accommodate their overflowing flock.

The Chilgol church is just one of two Protestant churches in Pyongyang. The Pongsu Church, a little nearer to the city center, is built in a similar unpretentious style and is attached to a noodle factory, where flour sent by Christian aid groups overseas is turned into meals for primary school children and the elderly. Its services are, on special occasions at least, accompanied by hymns sung by a choir of students from Kim Il-Sung University. Pyongyang also boasts Catholic and Russian Orthodox churches, and a mosque in the grounds of the Iranian embassy.

This strange presence of religious structures at the heart of an avowedly atheist country evokes all kinds of questions to which I expect no answers. Clearly, ordinary North Koreans are not free to choose their own religion. Unauthorized possession of a Bible, indeed, is likely to bring down the most terrible punishments on the head of the offender. Who, then, are the Koreans who attend the Chilgol, Pongsu, and Catholic churches? Why was Kim Il-Sung willing and even eager to reconstruct his mother's church in the heart of the Revolutionary Village? What do the students of Kim Il-Sung University think about as they sing their Christian hymns?

The further I travel through North Korea, the more I am intrigued and perplexed by that strange and elusive phenomenon that we call "belief."

The Cranes of Immortality

Beautiful scenery. Hwang Sok-Min stands lost in deep thought, gazing on the beautiful scenery. . . . The inner stage is lit up, and fairies come down on it from the rainbow-spanned sky. The poor little Sun I appears and calls "Pa-Pa!"
[Chorus]
Tell O Kumgang-san, Kumgang-san mountains
How many legends are there woven around you!
Here's a girl crying for her father.
O Kumgang-san, is her story also a legend?

Legends flourish in the Democratic People's Republic of Korea. In the revolutionary opera *The Song of Kumgang-san Mountains*, which premiered in 1973, choruses of fairies provide a backdrop to the story of a family torn apart by the cruelties of Japanese imperialism. The father, Hwang Sok-Min, who loves to play songs to his family on a bamboo flute, leaves his wife and baby daughter in the Diamond Mountains to join Marshall Kim Il-Sung's heroic partisans fighting colonialism in Manchuria and becomes a successful composer of revolutionary songs. After liberation, the mountains—long denuded by the depredations of wicked Japanese landlords—are transformed into a socialist paradise bedecked with flowers. (Japan's reinvention of the Diamond Mountains as "the future vacation land of the Far East" sits uneasily with North Korean visions of the rapacious imperialists and is absent from this story.)

The opera concludes with a moment to delight the hearts of all lovers of melodrama, when the poor little Sun I, now grown to beautiful maidenhood, is chosen to travel to the capital and sing in an opera set in her home village but performed on the stage of Pyongyang's Moranbong Theatre (which stands on the site of the long-vanished Japanese Shinto shrine). As the star-struck and nervous Sun I rehearses under the direction of the opera's famous composer, the young singer clutches an old bamboo flute that the composer suddenly recognizes. This is the very flute that the composer himself played long ago as a young man before being parted from his beloved family, and yes, Sun I is indeed his long-lost daughter.

The play-within-a-play concludes with the assembled cast heralding the glories of Kim Il-Sung, our Sun.

Kumusan Memorial Palace lies to the north of Pyongyang's city center, surrounded by a moat where swans glide through the reflections of the willow trees. Kemp, on her travels, often encountered pheasants in the forested mountains of Korea, and at Kumusan for the first time we catch a glimpse of a brightly plumed cock pheasant strutting across the manicured lawns.

The opportunity to visit this place is a rather unexpected honor. Until recently, the palace was off limits to all foreigners except official guests of the state. Its waiting room, with brown marble walls, looks like the lobby of an office suite, which perhaps it once was, for this was the heart of North Korea's political world: both Kim Il-Sung's home and the office complex from which he and the senior party leadership managed the affairs of the nation. Today, this is the mausoleum where the Eternal President lies in state.

A group of women in headscarves, who prove to be from the Iranian embassy, are waiting with us for our turn to enter the inner sanctum. It is quite a long wait, and to pass the time I read a copy of the official English-language magazine *Korea Today*, which lies on a coffee table in a corner of the lobby. The magazine contains a rather useful outline of the essentials of Songun (Army First), a policy introduced by Kim Jong-Il as a supplement to the official Juche ideology. The core "Army First" principles, we are told, are that "the army means the military, the State and the people" and that "the entire country has been entirely turned into a fortress." Turning the page, I am about to embark on an article entitled "Towards Increased Hairpin Production" when our moment to enter the mausoleum arrives.

Before proceeding further, we must hand in all our belongings except for purses. Cameras and cigarettes are particularly sternly forbidden, and a body search is carried out to make sure that none are secreted on our persons. A green plastic shoe cleaner removes the detritus of the outer world from our feet, and we step onto a conveyor belt that glides silently along immensely long corridors, over the moat and into the realm beyond. I am reminded of the beautiful Bulgugsa Temple in South Korea's Gyeongju, where a great moat once separated the transient world outside from the sacred space within.

Here in Pyongyang, the walls between which we move are lined with marble friezes of cranes—the symbol of eternal life. In North Korea, there is a legend that, on July 8, 1994, the day when the Great Leader Kim Il-Sung died, a throng of cranes descended from the sky and gathered on the roofs and walls of his palace.

Our guide Ms. Ri was just a small child on that dark day but still remembers it vividly. "I had just eaten lunch when my mother turned on the news and heard what had happened. I was too young to really understand it. I remember joining the crowds in the street. There were so many people, and for a while I lost sight of my Mum and Dad and became frightened. For about three years, no one smiled or laughed for days around the time of the anniversary. Children who laughed at that time were scolded by their parents."

For almost forty years since the liberation, North Koreans had known no other leader. Kim Il-Sung was the revolutionary hero, the focus of the state ideology, the central subject of art and literature, and the father of the nation—endlessly depicted dispensing loving smiles on crowds of children. His sudden death from a heart attack occurred at a time when the world of socialist states had crumbled and North Korea was facing the greatest economic crisis in its history. His disappearance left a dizzying and terrifying void at the heart of the nation's life. The grief was genuine and profound; its source was complex.

Beyond the corridors lies a hall watched over by female attendants clad in black velvet *chima jeogori* embroidered with golden suns. A vast statue of the lost leader is set at one end of the hall, against a background of the rising sun.

As we enter the next chamber, a black-clad attendant hands us each an audio set with an English-language explanation of the world beyond. As well as the Iranians, there are several other foreigners in the room, moving quietly through the hall amongst the large and orderly groups of North Korean visitors.

The taped narration is intoned in deep and dramatic cadences by a male voice with an unmistakable north-country English accent:

This is the very place where the Great Leader lay in state. He was the son of mankind. He labored ceaselessly and gave His very life for the people. . . .

The Great Leader is our sun, who was sent from heaven to bring happiness and light to the world. . . .

See the friezes on the wall of this room. Look how the people are weeping—old men, women, children, all weeping. Their hearts are breaking because He is gone. . . .

But this place was built by His son, our Dear Leader General Kim Jong-Il, to show us that indeed the Great Leader President Kim Il-Sung is with us for eternity.

The foreigners move through the room with downcast countenances and audio sets pressed tightly to their ears, assiduously avoiding one another's eyes.

Now we have reached the heart of mausoleum, but before we enter it, there is a further stage of cleansing. We pass through a gateway where blasts of air sweep away impurities from our clothes and bodies. In the middle of the sanctum beyond stands a glass case, with a long line of people waiting nearby. We join the line and then go forward in groups of three to bow our heads before the glass case. I look at the faces of the others in the room. A few of the Korean women wipe away a tear, but the expressions on most faces are difficult to read.

The figure in the glass case wears a suit, and his head rests on a traditional Korean pillow. No longer monumental or giant sized, with faint marks of age on his face, he looks as though he is sleeping.

In the halls beyond are the Eternal President's train carriage and Mercedes Benz, as well as glass cases filled with brass and gold: tokens of recognition from a litany of long-departed friends—Albania, Romania, Yugoslavia, Bulgaria, and the Soviet Union. Other awards presented to the deceased leader are more surprising. There are medallions from the World Intellectual Property Organization and the International Committee of the Red Cross, arrayed alongside the scroll proclaiming Kim Il-Sung's honorary citizenship of the town of Magenta in Italy, and his commemorative medal of the founding of the San Marino Socialist Party.

Later, when we eat dinner with a group of guides from another tour party, Sandy (who is better than me at asking forthright questions) says to one of them, "In your country, what do you think happens to people when they die?"

"It depends," says the North Korean pensively. "Some people like to be cremated. Some people like to be buried. Some want to come back in another life." He gives a little laugh and then says, "No, only joking. . . . But who knows. Sometimes when one person dies, another one like them is born." But all that, he insists, is quite different from the eternity of Kim Il-Sung: "He is with us forever."

Remembering the figure lying in endless state through days and long, dark nights in the glass case at the heart of the Kumusan Palace, I suddenly feel filled with sadness for all the butterfly children whom Kemp glimpsed, flying through fleeting shafts of sunshine into the winter gales ahead.

Notes

1. E. G. Kemp, *The Face of Manchuria, Korea and Russian Turkestan* (New York: Duffield, 1911), 68–69.

2. Kemp, *Face of Manchuria, Korea and Russian Turkestan*, 68.

3. Kemp, *Face of Manchuria, Korea and Russian Turkestan*, 71.

4. On the Kija myth, see Hyung il Pai, *Constructing "Korean" Origins: A Critical Review of Archaeology* (Cambridge, Mass.: Harvard University Asia Center, 2000).

5. James S. Gale, *Korean Sketches* (Chicago: Fleming H. Revell, 1898), 82.

6. Gale, *Korean Sketches*, 84.

7. See Heijō Jitsugyō Shinpōsha, ed., *Heijō Yōran* (Heijō [Pyongyang], North Korea: Heijō Jitsugyō Shinpōsha, 1909), 17; Kosaku Hirooka, *The Latest Guidebook for Travellers in Japan including Formosa, Chosen (Korea) and Manchuria* (Tokyo: Seikyo Sha, 1914), 219.

8 Kemp, *Face of Manchuria, Korea and Russian Turkestan*, 71–72.

9. Kemp, *Face of Manchuria, Korea and Russian Turkestan*, 95.

10. See Steven Hugh Lee, *The Korean War* (Harlow, UK: Pearson Education, 2001), 88; Chris Springer, *Pyongyang: The Hidden History of the North Korean Capital* (Budapest: Entente, 2003), 20.

11. Lee, *The Korean War*, 88.

12. On street names, see Springer, *Pyongyang*, 61–62.

13. Kemp, *Face of Manchuria, Korea and Russian Turkestan*, 80.

14. Springer, *Pyongyang*, 39.

15. George T. B. Davis, *Korea for Christ* (New York: Fleming H. Revell Co., 1910), 20.

16. Kemp, *Face of Manchuria, Korea and Russian Turkestan*, 78.

17. Kemp, *Face of Manchuria, Korea and Russian Turkestan*, 75.

18. On Kang Pan-Sok, see Yeong-Ho Choe, "Christian Background in the Early Life of Kim Il-Song," *Asian Survey* 26, no. 10 (October 1986): 1082–91.

19. Springer, *Pyongyang*, 105.

CHAPTER EIGHT

Both Sides Now
Kaesong, Dorasan,
and the Line in Between

The Reunification Monument

For Emily Kemp, the train journey from Pyongyang to Seoul was a nonevent. She was starting to suffer from a cold that she had picked up on her travels. Perhaps she was also busy writing the journal of her stay in Pyongyang as their train ran southward through Sariwon and Kaesong to Seoul. A couple of years earlier, when she was on a journey to China, her friend and mentor the Scottish theologian Marcus Dods (to whom she dedicated her first book) exhorted, "Be sure you write up your diary day by day, and don't disappoint the publisher and your public who wait to get some experience of unknown China at second hand."[1] Kemp returned home to England from her travels in Manchuria, Korea, and Russian Turkestan around the beginning of June 1910 and had completed the manuscript of her travel book by the end of August, which suggests she must have been following Dods's instructions.

At that time, the 312-mile (502-kilometer) journey from Sinuiju on the Chinese border to Seoul took around ten to twelve hours and cost 15.60 yen first class or 10.92 yen second class.[2] Pyongyang was almost exactly halfway between Sinuiju and Seoul, and Kemp and Mary MacDougall boarded their train at Pyongyang station in the afternoon, arriving in Seoul in darkness. Her travel account says nothing at all about the journey.

But for anyone trying to retrace her steps, this is the point at which the route is blocked by the insurmountable barrier of the Demilitarized Zone (DMZ). Under the "Sunshine Policy" promoted by the late South Korean president Kim Dae-jung, a series of breaches were made in that barrier. In

1998, South Korea's Hyundai Corporation was given permission to start tours from the South to the Diamond Mountains, initially on cruise ships, but from 2003 onward also overland by bus. By that time, North and South Korea were deep in negotiations about the building of a large joint industrial site on the fringes of Kaesong, which lies just on the northern side of the dividing line, an hour's drive from the suburbs the South Korean capital. The road link between Seoul and Kaesong was reconnected, allowing South Korean managers and technicians to travel to the complex, which by 2009 was employing over forty thousand North Korean workers.

And in 2007, to much public rejoicing, a train finally crossed the DMZ for the first time since the Korean War, opening up visions of a re-creation of the Iron Silk Road running all the way from the southern end of the Korean Peninsula to the western shores of Europe.

But these narrow apertures in the closely guarded frontier allowed only very limited movement. South Korean visitors to the Diamond Mountains were kept firmly within the high, green plastic fences that surrounded the four-star hotels and the Familymart convenience stores of the Hyundai Asan Mount Kumgang tourism resort; South Koreans working in the Kaesong industrial site were similarly enclosed in their own ghetto. As relations between North and South soured from 2007 on, the breaches in the palisade, rather than widening, were plugged by new obstacles. The shooting of Park Wang-ja led to the suspension of South Korean tours to the Diamond Mountains, and North Korea placed increasingly tight controls on movements to and from the Kaesong industrial zone.

As we set off southward from Pyongyang on a bright May morning, we know there is no possible means to cross the Cold War's last dividing line.

We travel south by car, in the gleaming black Toyota four-wheel drive provided by the state tourism authority. Toyota four-wheel drives are much favored by the North Korean elite, and I wonder whether Kemp and Mac-Dougall on their arrival in Pyongyang, born aloft in their sedan chairs, felt the same uncomfortable sense of excess privilege that Sandy and I feel in the Toyota.

On one side of the road, we catch a fleeting glimpse of the golden crosses surmounting the shining domes of the Russian Orthodox church. Beyond, we can see, rising in the distance, as we drive down the broad Reunification Avenue, a massive monument that spans the southern entrance to the city. Built of white stone and towering thirty meters high, it depicts two women dressed in *chima jeogori* who lean dramatically toward one another from either side of the roadway, their hands coming together to hold aloft a plaque adorned with a map of the Korean Peninsula: a single peninsula, unmarked by dividing line.

As we approach the monument, Ms. Ri launches into a little prepared speech on its significance. The two women, she explains, represent North and South Korea joining hands, and the map and inscription on the monument commemorate the three-point vision for reunification enunciated by President Kim Il-Sung.

"In 1971," recites Ms. Ri, "our president first announced the three basic principles of reunification: autonomy, peaceful reunification, and grand national unity. These principles were later comprehensively systematized into a concrete program for achieving the peaceful unity of the entire country."

The plan, she tells us, was for a gradual coming together, initially allowing the two sides to maintain their separate capitalist and socialist ways within a grand federation, which would ultimately lead to a complete merger of the two Koreas. The underlying philosophies may have been radically different, but the details do not sound very far removed from the late South Korean president Kim Dae-jung's Sunshine Policy, which also emphasized a gradual coming together rather than dramatic reunification. From the North Korean point of view, however, it is particularly important to demonstrate that every improvement in the relationship between the two Koreas has been the result of Northern initiative.

> "Our Great Leader president Kim Il-Sung had already taken the historic decision to visit Seoul in 1994," says Ms. Ri. "He had just signed the decree confirming his decision, but then so tragically on the very next day he suddenly passed away. After that, the South Korean leader Kim Dae-jung came to visit our country in 2000 and met our Dear Leader Kim Jong-Il. The next South Korean president Roh Moo-hyun also visited our country in 2006. But since the election of the new South Korean president Lee Myung-bak, relations have become very bad. People in the South long for reunification with their brothers and sisters in the North. But President Lee Myung-bak listens only to the Americans."

"Other countries like Germany have managed to reunify," remarks Sandy.

"Germany is completely different," snaps Ms. Ri. The example of West Germany's de facto takeover of the collapsing East is one that the North Korean elite would prefer not to contemplate.

Our guides are, however, immensely interested to know our views of the world, and particularly of U.S. president Barack Obama.

"He is very popular, isn't he, particularly in Europe," says Ms. Ri.

When we confess to sharing an enthusiasm for Obama, she remarks, "In the last U.S. election the two candidates were very different. The other candidate, Mr. McCain, was experienced, but Mr. Obama is very inexperienced. Mr. Obama is good at making speeches, but no good at achieving things."

The Road South

South of Pyongyang the land is relatively flat, and there are broad orchards of apple and pear trees, their blossom now past its best. We watch a column of people marching out from a village into a field adorned with red flags, to play their part in the 150-Day Campaign.

"Will you take part in the campaign?" we ask our guides.

"Of course," replies Ryu. "Last year too I went to work in the countryside."

"What's it like, working on a farm?"

"I enjoy it," he says. "Usually, when we go out into the countryside for work we travel by car all the time. But when we go on campaigns, we stay with farm families, and everyone works together."

The road from Pyongyang to Kaesong, North Korea's only good highway, is broad, smooth, and eerily empty. Other roads are full of people: walking, riding bicycles, pushing handcarts, carrying great burdens on their backs or heads, or sitting by the roadside resting from their work. But this is a highway for strategic objectives, not for motorists. There is virtually no traffic except the very occasional car, as dark and sleek as our own, and a few military trucks. At one point, we see two soldiers strolling down one side of the road, one with his arm slung around the other's neck in an attitude of comfortable companionship.

We pass the town of Sariwon, an old city that, unlike Pyongyang, is still a sea of one-story, gray-roofed houses, interspersed just here and there with blocks of apartments. Beyond is a roadside rest house with stalls selling dried fish and pears to the few passersby. We stop for a cup of coffee and encounter a lone Japanese tourist, looking slightly overwhelmed by his retinue of two guides and driver. He is a man in his late thirties who, it turns out, has left a career with a company to return to university.

"What brings you to North Korea?" I ask.

"I just want to see what it is really like," he replies.

I admire his quiet curiosity and determination.

The road south is not only the best and emptiest road in North Korea but also one of the most heavily guarded and surely the most meticulously cleaned. There are military checkpoints fifty, thirty, and fifteen kilometers from Kaesong, and the road cleaners are out in force on patches of embankment, removing every speck of rubbish and every protruding branch or offensive weed. Some are adults, wearing standard-issue orange, sleeveless jackets, but many are children in their brightly colored tracksuits, presumably conscripted from neighboring schools.

In some respects, it seems, schoolchildren in North Korea are not so different from their counterparts elsewhere. The girls wield their trowels and brooms with disciplined determination, while many of the boys have slipped away from the monitoring gaze of the adults and are sitting on the top of the embankment, waving madly at every passing car.

As we approach the border city, mountains appear again on the horizon. These, too, are bare, rocky, deforested mountains, with occasional dark pine trees protruding above patches of thin scrub. Kaesong is off limits to ordinary North Koreans. You need special permission to come here.

"Can people from Kaesong go to Pyongyang?" I ask Mr. Ryu.

"Yes, if they have citizen's cards and get a travel permit they can go," he replies.

Citizen's cards, as Mr. Ryu has already explained to us, are issued to North Koreans when they reach the age of seventeen, as part of a ritual of coming of age. But travel permits are another matter—according to accounts I have heard outside North Korea, a matter that often needs lubrication with cash payments.

We cross a bridge over a wide, shallow river and enter a main street, with rather grimy pink apartment blocks on either side, which cuts straight through Kaesong toward a giant statue of President Kim Il-Sung standing on a hillside at the far side of the town. Many of the side streets are lined with little old houses of dark red-brown brick and gray tiles. Streams of tea-colored water run beside the road, and women squat by the shallows, washing clothes. Bicycles and oxcarts move through the crowded alleyways. We pass an old woman bent double under a load of firewood and a mother riding a bicycle with her baby balanced precariously in the front basket. As we turn a sharp corner, a schoolboy comes skipping down the road past our car, temporarily transformed into a comically grinning ogre by a handmade paper mask.

The King and the Geomancer

Kaesong is one of Korea's oldest cities and, from the tenth to the fourteenth centuries, was the capital from which the Goryeo kings ruled the country. The hills surrounding the city are dotted with the hummocks of mysterious

tumuli—the graves of Goryeo kings and noblemen. And the most imposing
of all is the tomb of King Gongmin.

The hillslope where the tomb lies is patterned with the green of forests
that has disappeared from most of the surrounding mountains. A long series
of flights of stone steps leads upward, past a wooden cottage and between
lilac and lavender bushes to a grassy plateau, beyond which the wind blows
through the branches of tall oak and beech trees. On the plateau stand two
tumuli, surrounded and linked by granite facings engraved with scenes from
the Buddhist sutras. These are the tombs of King Gongmin and his much-
loved wife Queen Noguk, lying side by side and (it is said) linked for eternity
by an internal passageway between their grave mounds.

Around the graves are statues of sheep and tigers, and lines of stone guardian attendants. Sandy sits with her sketchbook on a block of sun-warmed
granite, looking toward a tall, conical hill on the other side of the valley,
while Mr. Ryu recounts for us the famous legend of King Gongmin and the
geomancer:

> In the period of feudal society, when a man died, a geomancer—do you know
> geomancer?—would choose the site of the grave. When his wife died, King
> Gongmin called famous geomancers and made them choose a grave site.

The tomb of King Gongmin (S. Morris)

But if King Gongmin didn't like the site they had chosen, he would kill the geomancer. Yes, kill him on the spot! One day, King Gongmin heard that a perfect site for the grave had been found, and he climbed up to see the place for himself. At that time, King Gongmin promised the subjects who came with him that, if he did not like this site of the grave, he, King Gongmin, would take out his handkerchief and wave it, and then the subjects must kill the geomancer. The handkerchief will be the signal to kill him.

Then, King Gongmin climbed up to the grave site and looked across at the sharp mountain opposite. He was so delighted to find that it was the most perfect place for the grave that in his excitement he forgot his promise and took out his handkerchief and wiped out the sweat from his forehead. The subjects thought that the king was waving his handkerchief, like this. And can you guess what happened next?

We can indeed. The geomancer was put to death on the spot. When King Gongmin descended from the grave site and realized his mistake, he reportedly exclaimed "acha!" This is said to be the origin of the name given to the conical mountain opposite the tomb—Mount Acha. Mr. Ryu translates "acha!" into English for us as "Oh, my!"—which, in the circumstances, seems oddly inadequate.

As with all Korean history—and with much history everywhere—there are multiple versions of King Gongmin's life and death. Interestingly, Mr. Ryu's account does not mention the fact that the king's beloved wife was Mongolian, nor that the king himself was also murdered, though not (it seems) in revenge for the death of the hapless geomancer. According to one version, his mistake was to alienate powerful nobles by promoting an obscure Buddhist monk to the position of his senior advisor. The romantic story of the king's love for Queen Noguk is also complicated by recent research depicting the king as "well known both as a scholar-painter-calligrapher and for pederasty with royal catamites."[3] But this is not a possible subject for discussion in North Korea, which in some respects seems trapped in an eternal 1950s. In the Democratic People's Republic, homosexuality is officially nonexistent.

The Tallest Flagpole in the World

As we drive between the rice fields from Kaesong to the small village of Panmunjom, we pass a family moving house. Their vehicle is a tractor, which pulls a large cart laden with their worldly belongings: cupboards, tables, and a couple of windows complete with glass and frames. Other farmers walk beside the unpaved roads carrying burdens on "*jige*," the Korean wooden carrying frames that were much in evidence in Kemp's day.

Approaching the DMZ, we come to a car park in front of two low, concrete buildings in vaguely art deco style. One is a souvenir shop selling postcards, guidebooks, and an assortment of brightly colored purses and fans. On the wall hangs a picture that I cannot resist buying. Carefully embroidered on canvass in vivid green and blue satin threads, it depicts the point where the Diamond Mountains meet the sea.

The other building contains a giant relief map of the DMZ, showing the high, electrified fence running along the near side of this four-kilometer-wide strip of land, the cluster of buildings in which armistice talks were held, the giant flagpole—the tallest in the world—that stands on the southernmost limit of North Korean territory, and the blue hills of the inaccessible South unfolding in distant ranges to a cloudy horizon. From here on, we and our guides will be accompanied by a military convoy.

A squirrel darts down a sidewall of the building, and as we walk through a gateway in the electrified fence, Sandy spots a pair of owls in the branches of a tree. For most of its length, the strip of land across the center of the Korean Peninsula has been uninhabited by humans for more than half a century. Ironically, this place—this sealed zone where all the sedimented dross of the Cold War has come to be concentrated—is also one of the most pristine temperate environments on earth and is believed to be home to endangered species including red-crowned cranes, black bears, and possibly even the last surviving Korean tiger.

Panmunjom is the one place within the DMZ where some semblance of ordinary human activity continues. As we drive in military convoy toward the demarcation line between the two Koreas, we pass fields where farmers work with a surreal air of normality. I watch a woman in Wellington boots, with her hair tied in a white bandana, planting rice in a flooded paddy, and wonder who she is and how it feels to live your life in this place where history has conquered geography.

The armistice between North and South Korea was signed here on July 27, 1953, by U.S. general William K. Harrison, representing the U.S.-led United Nations Command in Korea, and General Nam Il, representing the Democratic People's Republic of Korea. The South Korean government of the day opposed the armistice and refused to sign the document, and no peace treaty between the various warring parties has ever been signed. It is estimated that more than fifty thousand members of the United Nations Command, about half a million Chinese, and three million or more Koreans

were killed during the war, which ended in a stalemate with the border between the two countries almost exactly where it had been when hostilities
broke out three years earlier.

Not even the great battles of the First World War could rival this scale of
internecine futility.

When we step out of the car in front of the building where the armistice
was signed, my first thought is how peaceful this place seems. Here, as elsewhere along our route, the lilac trees are in flower. The afternoon is calm and
sunlit; and the air, clear and quiet. The armistice hall is a simple white building, looking much like a scout hall, and has a cut-out wooden dove above
the door. Our North Korean guides tell us with much pride that the defeated
Americans wanted to sign the armistice in a tent or on a ship at sea but that
the gloriously victorious North Koreans insisted on a signing ceremony conducted with proper dignity and built the hall for this purpose in just four days.

"When the American soldiers saw it," we are told, "they couldn't believe
their eyes, and they kept prodding the walls to see if it was real."

Outside is a large, roughly cut block of granite, inscribed with a replica of
Kim Il-Sung's final signature, dated July 7, 1994, and said to be copied from
the document on which he announced his plan to visit South Korea for reunification talks. As Ms. Ri once again tells us the story of this initiative, and
how it was cut short by the Great Leader's tragic sudden death the following
day, a large black and white butterfly flutters over her head, before disappearing in the direction of the demarcation line. I am curious that, at this
moment of chill in relations between the two Koreas, our guides are so eager
to emphasize the story of Kim Il-Sung's unfulfilled dream of traveling South.

At the line where the two Koreas meet, we stand on a flight of steps looking out at the row of little blue huts that marks the frontier and, beyond, at
a great, shiny modern glass and marble building, just a hundred meters away
but utterly unreachable, on the South Korean side of the line.

Soldiers with faces as rigid as the marble itself stand beside the buildings or march like clockwork between their appointed posts. The northern
soldiers wear olive green uniforms and flat caps; those on the southern side
have black metal helmets and dark glasses. There are spacious balconies for
viewing the demarcation line from the building on the opposite side, but
they seem devoid of people.

"Why are there no tourists on the southern side?" I ask.

"They used to come here," says Ms. Ri, "but now they mostly go to another viewing place, over there, beyond the flag."

She waves vaguely toward a spot to the right and ahead of us where, in the hazy distance, we can see a giant North Korean flag hanging in the sultry spring air on top of the world's tallest flagpole. A curious kink in the serpentine dividing line makes the flag appear as though it is on the southern side.

"Where?" I ask, straining my eyes.

"Behind that flag—up in the forest. They have a viewing spot where they can look down on us without being seen."

I try to follow the direction of her pointing finger but can make out only the faint outline of a wooded hill. So I mark the North Korean flag as my beacon for navigating the journey to come. I will use this landmark to connect North and South, as I pick up Kemp's route on the southern side of the border.

Then we walk down to one of the blue huts that straddle the precise dividing line between North and South Korea. We sit on brown plastic chairs at the undistinguished wooden refectory table that marks the very line itself, looking at a mirror glass window, from which we are presumably being observed by unseen eyes.

Above the window is a framed display of the flags of all the forces that fought on the southern side in the Korean War—a role call from around the world: at the top, the United States, the United Nations, and South Korea, and below them (in alphabetical order) Australia, Belgium, Canada, Colombia, Ethiopia, France, Greece, the Netherlands, New Zealand, the Philippines, South Africa, Thailand, Turkey, and the United Kingdom.

We peruse them in silence. It seems strange that the rest of the world, which intervened so massively in this unfinished war, now seems so uninterested in its ending. Sometime soon, for sure, this last Cold War barrier will give way: the forces building up on either side are just too great. The difference in pressure between the booming consumer capitalism of the rest of Northeast Asia and the small, North Korean air bubble of state-run poverty is too extreme to survive. The frictions and tensions within the North Korean system become more evident with every passing month.

How the barrier will come down is still impossible to predict but will be of momentous importance for the rest of the world. An endgame played out through military violence would be a disaster with global implications. A wholesale South Korean takeover of the North would create enormous consternation in China and might generate major conflict between the two Northeast Asian neighbors, and between China and the United States. Conversely, a regime change in North Korea backed by a newly assertive China would increase the anxiety with which China is viewed by the rest of the world. As it was when Kemp passed smoothly over this line of latitude in

1910, Northeast Asia is at the point where its future may tip in either direction: toward conflict or harmony; toward domination by a single power or cooperation between many. Which way it tips will be decided on this line.

Outside the hut, boots scrunch the dusty ground as the soldiers change guard. And then from somewhere in the distance comes a soft rumble like thunder—the sound of artillery practice, so far away it is impossible to tell which direction it comes from, or who is doing the firing.

The Empty Station

Exactly a week later, I am standing on the southern side of the dividing line, on the wooded hill that Ms. Ri pointed to, looking down at the tallest flagpole in the world, on which the flag hangs as still as ever. In the meanwhile, the weather has broken, and rain pours down relentlessly, making the flagpole barely visible through veils of water. Mist swirls over the Imjin River, which flows through the DMZ and over the main road running from the South toward the Kaesong Industrial Zone.

If I had gone by car in a straight line, the journey from the blue hut to the spot where am I now standing would have taken about ten minutes. But in fact, I have in the meanwhile traveled more than eight hundred kilometers by car and train back to Harbin and then flown a similar distance from Harbin to Seoul before boarding the tour coach that this morning has brought me and my fellow passengers to this South Korean DMZ viewing spot.

Most of the other members of the tour group are students from a multinational management training course that involves three semesters of study, one conducted in Shanghai, one in Seoul, and one in Singapore. They are a lively and enthusiastic bunch, and the bus resounds with the cheerful globalized cadences of Indian and Singapore English interspersed with Korean and Chinese. Our guide, Ms. Yoon, is almost exactly the same age as her North Korean counterpart Ms. Ri but much more casually dressed in black slacks and an orange sweater, and unlike Ms. Ri, whose English is impeccably British, Ms. Yoon's accent is unmistakably American.

"Do you know when the Korean War was?" Ms. Yoon asks us. Her audience remains silent. All have heard of the Korean War, but most are hazy about dates and details.

"After the end of the Second World War," she explains, "Korea was divided. Germany was divided in two, too, but there is a big difference between Germany and Korea. Do you know what that is?"

There is a collective shaking of heads.

"Germany caused the war and was defeated, so that was why it was divided. But Korea never caused a war, and Korea was not defeated. Korea was just the colony of Japan. Why was Korea divided and not Japan?" The question seems to be rhetorical. "The Soviets," continues Ms. Yoon,

stationed their troops in the North and the United States stationed their troops in the South to sweep away the remains of the Japanese government. It took us three years to make a government. But there were two sorts of people in Korea—the left-wing people and the right-wing people, and they couldn't agree how to make a government. South Korea had its election first, and then North Korea. In the South, Mr. Yi Seungman who was educated in the States was elected, and in the North the Soviets picked Kim Il-Sung as their puppet. At first he was really puppet, but soon he became so powerful and began to make his own decisions, and he decided to attack the South. South Korea was very weak then. In the colonial times, Japanese developed military factories in the North, but the South was kept as a farming place, so the South couldn't defend itself, and in just three days the North had occupied all of Korea except for Busan. So the United Nations came to help South Korea, but then the Chinese joined in to support the North. By 1953, both sides were exhausted, so they decided to have a rest. That is when they signed the armistice. It is not a peace treaty. Technically, we are still at war. We have been at war for sixty years.

The highlight of a visit to the DMZ from the southern side is a tour of a North Korean incursion tunnel. In the bus on our way to the tunnel entrance, Ms. Yoon remarks that she was born more than thirty years after the start of the Sixty Years' War, and "in my life I have never actually felt any danger. At times the North has launched attacks—sent spies or tried to assassinate our leaders—but I've never really felt danger. Sometimes the North sends leaflets—thousands and thousands of leaflets saying—'Come the North! Life is so wonderful!' When I was at school we used to be asked to collect them so that they could be destroyed. If we collected enough leaflets we were given something like a notebook or a pencil case as reward."

The tunnel that we visit is one of four that the North Koreans apparently dug in emulation of the underground network created by Vietnamese communist forces during the Vietnam War. When the South discovered it, says Ms. Yoon, the North pretended that it was an abandoned coalmine. The South Korean soldier who guards the entrance looks almost as young and nervous as his North Korean equivalents, although his face is rounder and softer and he wears glasses. It occurs to me that in the course of our travels in North Korea I never saw a soldier wearing glasses.

Near the tunnel's mouth is a South Korean reunification monument: this one on a more modest scale than the vast edifice on the southern fringes of Pyongyang. It features a silvery metal archway under which four human figures—two men and two women—struggle to reunite a sundered globe, in whose center lies a map of the divided Korea.

All around is dense forest full of flowering jasmine and wisteria. Rain drips from the dark pine needles and bright green oak leaves. As I stand looking out toward Panmunjom, a white egret lifts itself lazily from the dense forest on the southern side of the Imjin and flies slowly northward over the divide.

The last stop on our itinerary is Dorasan station, which stands on the line that once connected Seoul to Sinuiju via Pyongyang: the line along which Kemp traveled on her way southward through Korea. Today, the voices of a throng of Korean and foreign visitors echo through the vaults of the station's shining new glass and steel entrance hall, competing with the insistent drumming of the rain on its metal roof. There is a ticket office and a fine multicolored map high on the wall, depicting the thin, red line of the railway snaking up through the Korean Peninsula, over the border into China, on into Siberia, across the Urals into western Russia, and then branching out beyond, to St. Petersburg in the north, Lisbon in the south, and London at the center.

Only one thing is lacking: a train.

After the opening of the line across the border in 2007, freight trains were supposed to run along this line regularly taking goods to and from the Kaesong Industrial Zone, and there were high hopes that the line all the way to Pyongyang and beyond would gradually be reconnected. But today those hopes are at a standstill. Dorasan is once again the end of the line.

A group of South Korean peace activists have set up a stall in the station and urge visitors to make stenciled textile messages of hope to add to their expanding display. But when I ask Ms. Yoon about her thoughts on reunification, the answer is cautious:

"I do hope for it, but I don't think it will come soon. Really, I'm waiting for Kim Jong-Il to die," she laughs.

"When he dies," she adds, "I think things will change. But maybe there will be a lot of chaos. That is worrying, if there is chaos when he dies." She pauses, "and you know, a lot of young people here, they just think of North Korea as a burden. They don't care. They just don't want to have to pay taxes to give aid to North Korea, so they aren't really interested in reunification."

As we head south from the border toward Seoul, I am astonished at the greenness of the landscape. The hills that, just a few miles away, are almost bare of trees are here covered in lush forest. Huge electricity pylons march

Korean graves (E. G. Kemp)

across the landscape, and a steady stream of cars flows along the tangle of highways leading toward the capital. After the North, though, the fields themselves seem strangely empty of people. A tractor tills a flooded rice paddy, and here and there are acres of black plastic, covering fields of vegetables or ginseng. Unlike the North Korean hamlets with their uniform white and gray cottages, southern villages are an exuberant mixture of everything from traditional Korean to pseudo prairie homestead, often with the red brick spire of a church protruding above the roofs.

Our road crosses the still and muddy expanse of the Imjin River and then runs along its southern bank, separated from it by a high barbed-wire fence. There are guard posts at regular intervals, some manned by real soldiers and some by cardboard cutouts, which seem a curious line of defense against possible invasion from the North.

Kemp remarks that, "unlike Venice, Seoul should not be approached after dark." It should certainly not be approached on a gloomy spring day with rain pounding against the bus windows. The skyscrapers on the far side of the Han River appear and then disappear again into the murk as we enter the spaghetti junctions of the city and are instantly caught in traffic gridlock.

Eventually, the bus drops us off in the center of the downtown district of Itaewon, in a street lined by rows of brightly colored shops and stalls selling cheap clothes, shoes, and souvenirs. I have missed my lunch and am feeling cold and longing for a bowl of *bibimbap*, the wonderful mixture of vegetables, meat, rice, sesame oil, and chili paste that is a staple of Korean cuisine. But in this street, the only food on offer seems to be burgers, California pizzas, and Subway rolls, for Itaewon adjoins the U.S. military base of Yongsan, which occupies over six hundred acres of central Seoul. Over the barbed-wire-topped walls running round the base, you can just make out the dark rooftops of large brick buildings that once housed the Japanese army during the years of colonial occupation and now house the headquarters of U.S. Forces Korea.

When Kemp came here a century ago, Yongsan (Ryŭzan in Japanese) was a brand new suburb outside the walls of Seoul, its rectangular grid of streets (in stark contrast to the winding maze of the Korean town) built to accommodate the Japanese military and the colonial railway officials who already controlled the Korean rail system, for here as in Manchuria, the army and the railway company arrived hand in hand.

U.S. troops, entering Seoul in 1945, slid smoothly into the space left by the departing colonizers and have remained there ever since.

Arriving fresh from Pyongyang, it feels for a moment as though all the darkest fears of North Korean propaganda are confirmed. I can almost hear our uniformed guide from the Victorious Fatherland Liberation War Museum saying, in her sweetly reasonable voice, "You see. I told you so. The oppressed people of the South have been *totally* subordinated by their puppet rulers to the imperialist aggression of the American invaders."

Adjacent to the American military base stands South Korea's National War Memorial: a museum as vast as its North Korean equivalent but telling a story whose details have all been reversed, as though we had just passed through Alice's Looking Glass. In the museum forecourt, there is a marble monument inscribed in Korean and English with the words "Freedom is not Free" (an epigram that works much better in English than in Korean) and, nearby, a giant U.S. B-52 bomber, evidently one of the most popular exhibits.

Inside the memorial crowds of children are making the most of a rainy Saturday afternoon—but not (as I first assumed) by reliving harrowing memories of the Korean War. It turns out that almost all have instead gravitated to a special Thomas the Tank Engine event in the war memorial's basement, where, with clamors of delight, they are happily absorbed in crawling around on the floor, pushing Sir Handel and Salty the Dockside Diesel over the winding wooden rail lines of Sodor Island.

What, I wonder, would our guide from the Victorious Fatherland Liberation War Museum make of that?

Notes

1. Letter from Marcus Dods to Miss Emily G. Kemp FGRS, August 31, 1907, in *Later Letters of Marcus Dods DD*, by Marcus Dods (London: Hodder and Stoughton, 1911), 270.

2. Kosaku Hirooka, *The Latest Guidebook for Travellers in Japan including Formosa, Chosen (Korea) and Manchuria* (Tokyo: Seikyo Sha, 1914), 219.

3. Young-Gwan Kim and Sook-Ja Hahn, "Homosexuality in Ancient and Modern Korea," *Culture, Health and Sexuality* 8, no. 1 (January/February 2006): 59–65, 62.

CHAPTER NINE

In the Palace of the Murdered Queen
Seoul

The Hand of Time

In Seoul, Emily Kemp and Mary MacDougall stayed in "Miss Pinder's Rest House for Missionaries"—the very name is redolent with the smell of waxed floor boards and toasted tea cakes. After arriving in darkness and bumping over ill-lit cobbled streets to the rest house, they were delighted to wake to fresh spring light and see the city encircled in its "lofty hills of granite that change in colour at different times of day from gold to steel to deep blue."[1]

First thing in the morning, they set off for the city center, making their way down the central avenue that led to the Gyeongbok Palace—the Palace of the Prospect of Blessings. The Seoul through which they walked was a maze of narrow winding alleyways—the whole city just three kilometers wide from east to west and two and a half from north to south, surrounded by a high stone wall pierced by massive gateways. But already, Kemp noted, the walls were "rapidly disappearing to form material for building Japanese houses of truly Philistine ugliness." Stone creatures on pedestals lined the central avenue, but the old Korean official buildings on either side were also vanishing to make way for neoclassical colonial structures.

At the far end of the avenue stood the entrance to the palace, the Gwanghwa Gate—the Gate of the Dawning of Light, through which the king's virtuous radiance shone upon his realm. Beyond it, Kemp and MacDougall found themselves suddenly in an enchanted but vanishing world. The subtle greens and blues of the fading paintwork on the palace buildings contrasted with the darker green of pine trees and with the ink-wash outlines of the hills

behind. An arched stone bridge led them across a moat, "over which grotesque creatures lean towards the water as if about to plunge into it," toward
the royal audience chamber with its vaulted and ornately painted ceiling. In
the paved space before the chamber, Kemp noted the row upon row of stone
markers "like milestones" that defined the precise spot where each rank of
courtier should stand during audiences with the ruler.[2]

The travelers wandered unimpeded through a series of courtyards unfolding one into the other toward the private apartments of the king, until they
came upon a "place of delight"—a walled garden containing a broad and
tranquil lotus pond in the center of which stood an open summer house. A
flight of steps led from the summer house to the waters edge, and goldfish
glided through the depths beneath the shadows of the lotus leaves. But everywhere, wrote Kemp, "the hand of time is heavy, walls are falling down, steps
dropping asunder, and the brickwork beginning to crumble."

For this was the pleasure garden of Queen Min, and beyond lay the place
where the queen was murdered.

The reign of last royal inhabitant of the palace, King Gojong—elevated to
the status of emperor in 1897—was as troubled as it was long. When he as-
cended the throne in 1864, at the age of eleven, the intrusions of the outside
world were becoming impossible to ignore. Korea was caught in a dangerous
double bind. Because of its tributary relationship to the Chinese empire, the
Korean monarchy was expected to consult China before entering into any
relations with the outside world. But China itself was struggling ineffectually
to respond to the challenges posed by the imperial powers—learning only
slowly and by trial and error how to adjust to a world of which it was no
longer the center, a world where diplomacy was an international game of
Western chess played out with strange implements like international treaties
and extraterritorial rights.

Japan and Russia competed to lure Korea out of China's orbit, while
within the palace, efforts at reform were undermined by *yangban* (aristo-
crat) conservatives, who feared the impact of change on their own jeal-
ously guarded status. This explosive mixture of external and internal forces
ensured that the last decades of the Korean kingdom were riven by coups,
countercoups, plots, assassinations, and invasions.

The king was mild mannered and humane but also vulnerable to manipu-
lation.[3] Gojong, who came from an obscure branch of the royal family, had
been chosen to fill the empty throne when the previous incumbent died
without heir, and for the first ten years of his reign he moved in the shadow
of his domineering father, the Grand Prince (Daewongun). During these

years both father and son tried to shore up the imperiled power of the Korean kingdom through reforms based on Confucian morality, but by the 1870s, a new force was also shaping Korean palace politics—King Gojong's beautiful, strong-willed, and politically astute wife, Queen Min.

Queen Min is the stuff of which legends are made. (She was in fact to become the heroine of South Korea's very first homemade Broadway-style musical: *The Last Empress*.) Louise Jordan Miln, a British traveler with theatrical connections who visited Seoul in the 1890s, left a particularly evocative description of this unusual woman:

> The Queen is pale and delicate looking. She has a remarkable forehead, low but strong, and a mouth charming in its colouring, in its outlines, in its femininity, in the pearls it discloses, and sweet with the music that slips through it when she speaks. She dresses plainly as a rule, and in dark but rich materials. In this she resembles the high born matrons of Japan. And in cut her garments are more Japanese than those of other Korean women: she wears her hair parted in the middle, and drawn softly into a simple knot or coil of braid. She wears diamonds most often; not many, but of much price.[4]

She was also, Miln noted, the "most powerful Korean in Korea": "Her spies have been everywhere, seen everything, reported everything."[5]

Queen Min was largely self-educated and a voracious reader of politics, history, and science. She came from a leading *yangban* family, and her relatives hoped to wield power through her, but in the end it was the queen herself who learnt to maneuver her way through the factional intrigues of the court and the squalls of international politics that swirled around nineteenth-century Korea. When her father-in-law the Grand Prince attempted a political comeback in the 1880s, the queen and her supporters called in Chinese troops who unceremoniously arrested the elder statesman and carried him off to temporary imprisonment in China. Yet, the queen also supported the education of women and encouraged the sending of Korean scholar-officials to Japan and the United States to learn about the ways of the world, while trying to steer a careful and delicate course between the old hegemonic China and the new forces, Russia and Japan.

Kemp visited King Gojong and Queen Min's abandoned palace fifteen years after the queen's violent death, when its gates had been opened to visitors on condition that they paid a small fee, were respectably dressed, and did not catch birds or fish in the palace grounds. But Kemp was able to leave an unusually vivid impression of the life of the palace women in Queen

Min's day, thanks to information she received from an unnamed friend with close royal connections. The hundreds of female attendants who lived in the palace were (Kemp reported) traditionally selected for training at the age of nine or ten. They were dressed in silk jackets and "long mazarine blue skirts," and their hair, which in childhood had been worn in pigtails, was tied into knots that rested on their necks.

The palace day started late. At noon, a thundering of drums announced the royal levee, and the courtyards became thronged with people "like a busy hive of bees." The palace guards in their myrtle green tunics and breastplates prepared for official audiences, and the royal women with their retinues of female attendants, went to pay their respects to the king. At sunset, the palace gates were barred and no one was allowed to leave or enter. But within the walls, lanterns flickered as the business of the state went on, for it was at night that the king consulted with his advisors, while the queen, in her quarters beyond the lotus pond pavilion, consulted with hers.

By 1910, however, all this had vanished: not an echo of the swarming activity remained in the empty courtyards of the palace. A "Korean gentleman" whom she does not name gave Kemp a chance to draw one of the few remaining royal guards in uniform. Her image of this lone figure is embossed on the myrtle green cover of the book she published in August 1910, the month when the last Korean king lost his throne.

The Palace of the Prospect of Blessings

We are staying in an international hotel at one end of the avenue down which Kemp and MacDougall walked on their first day in Seoul and, waking to a rain-washed sky, see how the light still turns Seoul's granite hills to gold. The rocky crags rise unchanged behind the gleaming glass and steel rectangles of office and apartment blocks, but—flooding across its long-vanished walls—the city has sprawled into a megalopolis that now covers over six hundred square kilometers and contains more than ten million people.

Stone creatures still line the avenue that leads to the Gyeongbok Palace, but the Japanese offices that Kemp saw rising along this street have in their turn been swept away by history, to be replaced by the headquarters of Korean newspaper companies; by hotels and cafes and cultural centers; and by the mud-brown rectangular block of the U.S. embassy, which lies directly across the road from the palace, is fortified by concrete walls and razor wire, and instantly evokes Kemp's epithet—it is indeed of truly Philistine ugliness.

The center of Seoul itself, however, is surely one of the world's most beautiful city centers: the frenetic beat of the metropolis is counterpointed by the calm of the miniature mountains that rise above its rooflines. The contrast with Pyongyang is overwhelming—silence is here replaced by a wall-to-wall tapestry of sounds: the roar of traffic, the seductive notes of advertising jingles, the endless fragments of music (one moment Vivaldi, the next BoA and Lady Gaga) that escape from boutiques and coffee shops and department stores as you pass. As though compensating for its shadow sister in the North, Seoul blazes with lights—neon, diode, and multicolored—which flash, flow, and cascade across walls and liquid crystal screens.

I find myself walking down the road toward the Gyeongbok Palace behind a couple of young men in sneakers, jeans, and hooded sweatshirts, backpacks slung over their shoulders, who stroll along the pavement together but each engaged in separate cell phone conversations. In Pyongyang streets, people do not stroll. Parks are for strolling. But in Seoul the passerby is tempted into endless pauses and deviations, lured aside by elaborate shop window arrays of cream cakes, displays of traditional Korean paper crafts, or advertisements for super cheap cut-price flights to Shanghai and Los Angeles.

On this spring morning, the road to the palace is an obstacle course. Jackhammers are digging up sections of the paving; pedestrians weave their way past roped-off holes in the street, and the area immediately leading up to the palace is clad in cardboard hoardings proclaiming the transformation of this precinct into "Seoul's dream." South Korea's current president, Lee Myung-bak, is a former mayor of Seoul known for his enthusiastic support of grandiose urban redevelopment projects. The Gate of the Dawning of Light also has an oddly surreal quality: it is concealed behind hoardings decorated with a colorful painting of a traditional Korean gateway done in a vaguely cubist style reminiscent of the art of Paul Klee. Entry to the palace involves a long detour up a side street.

But within the walls, something extraordinary is happening: for the hand of time has been reversed.

When Kemp and McDougall wandered through these courtyards, the collapsing Korean palace buildings were rapidly being replaced by the monuments of Japanese colonialism. To the right of the entrance gateway, the Japanese authorities were erecting a boys' schools. "This," wrote Kemp, "is a hard blow to Korean pride."[6] A much harder blow was about to come.

Until 1910, the center of Japanese influence in Korea was the new suburb of Yongsan, but after the annexation, a massive new Government General Building was designed for the very heart of the old city of Seoul. Laid out in neoclassical style by German architect George de Lanade, this edifice was to be built in the shape of the character which means "sun"—the first character in the name of the new ruling power—Nippon.[7] And its site was to be the main forecourt of the Gyeongbok Palace. Completed at enormous expense in 1926, the five-story Government General Building not only dwarfed the remaining ruins of the Korean royal palace but also lay like a stone barrier across the veins of energy that, in geomantic tradition, were believed to flow from the mountains behind the palace to the city center. The beautiful Gate of the Dawning of Light was dismantled and removed to an inconspicuous spot to one side of the new symbol of power.

This act of architectural triumphalism evoked dismay even from some in Japan itself. The famous Japanese philosopher and founder of Japan's folk art movement, Yanagi Sōetsu, wrote a moving lament for the dismembered gateway:

> Oh Gwanghwa Gate, Oh Gwanghwa Gate! Your life is about to be finished. Your existence in the world is about to disappear into oblivion. What can I do? I know not what to do. The day is near when the cruel chisels and emotionless hammers will destroy your body little by little. Thinking about such an event is heartache for many, but nobody can save you. Unfortunately, the people who could save you are not the people who are sadly lamenting you.[8]

Both Yanagi and Kemp would surely be astonished to see the Gyeongbok Palace today for, in an architectural statement as bold and as political as the erection of the Government General Building itself, the South Korean government has embarked on a project to sweep away all the physical vestiges of colonialism and restore the palace to its Korean royal glory. Despite much controversy, the decision was taken to obliterate the Government General Building, which had been used as Korea's National Museum, and on the fiftieth anniversary of liberation from Japanese rule, the building was wiped off the face of the earth.

Today, not a trace of the colonial intruder remains. Instead, grotesque stone creatures again peer into the depth of the moat in front of the king's audience hall (even though the moat itself is empty of water). And all around, as though the film of history were being run backward at high speed, the buildings that Kemp saw decaying and collapsing are rising again in splendor from the ground, their faded colors brightening into fresh and brilliant hues.

Crossing the bridge over the moat I come to a great gateway that leads into the courtyard in front of the king's audience chamber. In the wide, stone-paved courtyard, the "milestones" that Kemp saw have sprung up again. A flight of steps leads up to the audience chamber itself, whose ornate eves glow once more with greens and blues against the background of the darker pine forests on the hills beyond. Peering through the doorway, I can marvel, as Kemp did, at the soaring ceiling that rises to a central design of golden dragons and see the screen behind the royal throne, decorated with the symbolic forces of nature whose power was embodied in the person of the king: the sun, the moon, and the five sacred mountains from which two waterfalls plunge in a never-ending stream.[9]

And here come the courtiers themselves in their myrtle green satin robes and breastplates, looking as though they had just stepped off the cover of Kemp's book. They stride in procession across the paved space, followed by others in long-sleeved robes of crimson and black, their tall hats and their decorated belts marking their varied ranks. It is true that some have walkie-talkies strapped to their waists and that (since it is a windy day) one has his tear-filled eyes half closed as he struggles with grit in his contact lenses. But they bear themselves throughout this resurrection of Korea's royal past with commendably aristocratic dignity, keeping their faces imperturbably straight despite the horde of giggling schoolchildren who thrust cell phones at them to capture close-up pictures. Behind the men walk the women in their turquoise and mazarine blue skirts, hands folded and heads demurely bowed beneath the ornate intertwined braids of hair. And under a great red silk umbrella walks the queen herself, with her hair tied at the back of her neck and her skirt more ornately decorated than those of her attendants.

Following their procession from one courtyard to the next, I come upon Queen Min's lotus pond, with its lovingly restored summerhouse on the island in its center. The summerhouse is built in the shape of a small, two-story pagoda, with a stone bridge linking it to the outside world. The wind furls the edges of the lotus leaves and ruffles the feathers of a white heron perched on the steps below the summerhouse.

Behind the lotus pond, near the back of the palace compound, stands a newly reconstructed building in traditional Korean style. Unlike the grand audience hall, this is made of simple unpainted wood, stone, and white plaster. Latticed doorways lead into a wide enclosed courtyard. The crowds that throng the front of the palace compound have disappeared, and here I sit alone in the sunshine, watching the wind blow through the flowering cosmos that has been planted along the wall, while above, a hawk floats silently on waves of air.

The building is new, but the reconstruction is perfect and the place unchanged—this is the spot where Queen Min met her fate.

The events that led up to her murder can be traced back to 1894, when a part-religious, part-political uprising of disaffected commoners (not unlike the Chinese "Boxers" six years later) swept across Korea. China sent troops into Korea to help suppress the rising, and Japan, fearing that China was trying to reimpose control over the peninsula, responded by sending its own army, who marched north from Seoul to capture Pyongyang and then pushed on to the Yalu River and beyond, inflicting a devastating defeat on China.

By the middle of 1895, Japan's military and political influence over Korea was enormously increased, and the chief Japanese advisor in Korea turned his attention to the task of undermining the power of the independent-minded queen. He quickly found an ally in the Grand Prince, who sought revenge for his humiliation at the hands of the queen and her clan. On October 8, 1895, Japanese legation guards, police, and civilians from Yongsan, together with Japanese-trained Korean guards, accompanied the Grand Prince to the palace to stage a coup on his behalf. An advance party scaled the walls and opened the gates from within, and the rest rushed into the palace and chased Queen Min through its courtyards toward her chambers, where, as Kemp writes, the queen and several of her attendants were "put to the sword." Queen Min's body was then dragged to a nearby knoll, doused in kerosene, and burnt.

The extreme violence of this act created international shockwaves. The Japanese government may have feared Queen Min, but even they had not expected her to be removed in such a ruthless fashion. The chief conspirators in her killing were put on trial but were found not guilty because of insufficient evidence. The immediate effects of the killing were a disaster for Japanese interests. King Gojong, who seems to have felt a genuine affection for his wife, instantly turned against Japan and sought protection from Russia, and it was only after its victory over the Russians in 1905 that Japan was once again able to assert its control over Korea, forcing the helpless king to abdicate in favor of his pro-Japanese son, Sunjong.

But Sunjong was not even to be allowed the symbolic gratifications granted to the last Chinese emperor Pu Yi in his incarnation as ruler of Manchukuo. Four months after Kemp's visit to Korea, its last monarch was removed from the throne and, although he continued to be referred to by the title "king," was in practice confined in the East Palace, not far from Gyeongbok, where he died sixteen years later. His palace was then in its turn opened to the public and transformed into a zoo.

Kemp made a drawing of Queen Min's tomb, which stood in a tranquil spot on a hillside beyond the city gates, looking out across a wooded valley toward mountains beyond (a spot from which it has since been displaced by urban development). She writes with sorrow of the queen's cruel death

The tomb of Queen Min (E. G. Kemp)

and observes, even before the formal declaration of August 1910, "It seems absurd to hear the Japanese pretending that they have not annexed Korea, for they have, practically speaking, taken control of everything in the most high-handed manner. . . . The bitterness of the bondage is aggravated by the fact that so few of the Japanese trouble to learn the language, so that misunderstandings constantly arise."[10]

And yet here, as in Pyongyang, her feelings on colonialism and modernization were ambivalent. She could not ignore the benefits of the foreign presence and wrote of a recent cholera outbreak in Seoul that had been quickly brought under control by the "splendid exertions of the Japanese."[11] And everywhere, if a little wistfully, she sought signs of hope: "It is to be remembered that this is a transitional period, and it is ardently to be desired that the Japanese Government will continue their good attempts to withdraw those who have been creating disturbances and to place a better class of officials in power."

Korea, Kemp reiterates, "is truly a land flowing with milk and honey, has a beautiful climate, and if well governed ought to be most happy and prosperous."[12]

Rebuilding the Temple

Leaving the main street, we head through a narrow cobbled alleyway, hemmed in on either side by mellow brick walls and low tiled roofs. For a moment, it feels as though I have stepped out of today's Seoul, whose consumer economy bubbles on unchecked despite recession and widening wealth gaps; for a moment, I could be back in the walled city of 1910.

My companion, a young and energetic Korean man who works for a peace group, leads me confidently through the maze of laneways and down a narrow flight of steps into a basement office. The sign on the door says, "Jogye Order of Korean Buddhism's Headquarters for the Advancement of the National Community" (Daehan Bulgyo Jogyejong Minjok Kongdongche Chujin Bonbu).

I am expecting to be greeted by solemn gray-robed monks but instead find myself shaking hands with two friendly men in their late thirties, one dressed in a tracksuit and the other wearing a stylish ski jacket: Mr. Park and Mr. Han. A humidifier steams away quietly in the middle of their small office, where a heavily pregnant woman is sorting documents in the filing cabinets. We sit at a low table sipping cups of ginseng tea. The only sign of Buddhism that I can see is the rosary of wooden beads that Mr. Han winds around his hands as he talks.

But in this basement office a remarkable plan is unfolding, a plan for an act of historical reconstruction even bolder than the rebuilding of the Gyeongbok Palace.

When Kemp visited Korea, there were more than thirty monasteries and nunneries in the Diamond Mountains, the oldest dating back to the sixth century CE. Some were little more than tiny wooden hermitages hidden away in high mountain gorges, but others—particularly the four major temples of Yuchom-Sa, Pyohun-Sa, Singye-Sa, and (greatest of all) Changan-Sa—were glorious pieces of Buddhist architecture filled with treasures from all parts of Korea and China and even from India, Tokharistan, and beyond.[13]

In a bookshop across the road from the Gyeongbok Palace, I have just bought a video containing silent film footage taken in the 1920s by the German Benedictine monk Norbert Weber. The film traces his journey to the Diamond Mountains and on to the temple of Sokwang-Sa near the city of Wonsan, whose abbots exerted far-reaching control over the monasteries of the region. The camera picks out the guardian gods who stood watch over the entrance to the temples, the richly carved doors and painted eaves adorned with symbolic figures from the sutras, and the drums and great cast-iron bell on which the monks marked the hours for prayer.

Deep in the Diamond Mountains, Weber and his party came upon a nunnery, where a tiny toothless nun in her gray hempen robes tottered forward to greet them, while young shaven-headed novices shyly appeared carrying dishes of water. Nearby, huge seated Buddha figures were carved into the living rock, dwarfing the shapes of the passing travelers. The trunks of sacred trees were half buried by cairns of stones placed there by pilgrims, and at one spot Weber's camera caught two devout visitors balanced precariously on makeshift wooden ladders as they chiseled their names into the rock-face. Although the mountains attracted seekers of enlightenment, they were also a refuge for orphans, children abandoned by their parents, or others seeking refuge from the outside world: the British philosopher J. B. Pratt found a nunnery with ten old ladies, "wrinkled as walnuts though giggly as schoolgirls," who told him they had become nuns because they were widows and had no one to support them.[14]

Pratt and Weber are among many foreign visitors who became lyrical in their search for words to describe the beauties of the temples of the Diamond Mountains. The American journalist and supporter of the Chinese revolution Helen Foster Snow described the region as "one of the most beautiful mountain places in East Asia, sacred to Buddhism since about AD 513."[15] The artist Bertha Lum recorded how, after a walk through the mountains, she crossed a stream and came to "a temple enclosure so extraordinary that I had no desire to go further but wanted to remain there for the rest of this life." This was Changan-Sa—the Temple of Eternal Peace. "The main temple," she wrote, "is the most extraordinary I have seen in any part of the Orient. Inside, as you raise your eyes, it is impossible to conceive that any mind could design the amount of carving and colour and, even after having designed it, could ever have put it in place."[16] Even the condescending Lord Curzon was moved to remark that for "lovers of the picturesque nothing more enchanting than these monastic retreats can anywhere be found."[17]

North Korean maps of the Diamond Mountains today mark "the site of Changan-Sa." For all that remains of its glory are a few foundation stones. During the Korean War, while battles raged across the mountains, the Temple of Eternal Peace was turned by North Korea into a prisoner of war camp, which at one point reportedly held some seven to eight hundred South Korean and seventy to eighty American prisoners in harrowing conditions. (According to one eyewitness account, a number of the prisoners from Changan-Sa collapsed and died from malnutrition as they were being marched from there to another nearby camp.)[18] By the end of the war, only one of the mountains' four great temples, together with a few other landmarks like the extraordinary Podok Hermitage, balanced on a cliff edge, were still standing.

According to North Korean accounts, the temples were destroyed by U.S. bombing. I have found nothing to confirm or disprove this statement. It seems curious, though, that while the destruction of Italy's Monte Casino, Germany's Dresden, and England's Coventry Cathedral still evoke intense debates about war and culture, there has been no debate at all about responsibility for the destruction of these temples, some of Asia's greatest Buddhist works of art.

Mr. Park and Mr. Han, though, are more interested in the future than the past, for their dream is to rebuild the temples of the Diamond Mountains. The Headquarters for the Advancement of the National Community is (despite its rather bland and opaque name) a body specifically dedicated to promoting Buddhist cooperation between South and North Korea. The Jogye Order is one of South Korea's largest and most powerful Buddhist denominations and is known for its active and complex involvement in the political life of the nation.

The Jogye Order's collaborative activities started in the 1990s, and the Headquarters for the Advancement of the National Community was created around the time of President Kim Dae-jung's visit to Pyongyang in 2000. Their counterpart in the North is a body known as the Central Committee of the Buddhist Federation of the Democratic People's Republic of Korea, an arm of the North Korean government that, as Mr. Park explains, "supervises Buddhist temples in the North and has an education section that provides training for Buddhist priests and monks."

Intrigued, I ask, "So, just how many Buddhist priests are there in North Korea?"

"We really don't know," replies Mr. Park. "There are about seventy temples controlled by the federation, and perhaps a few others as well. Maybe around one hundred temples altogether. There could be about three hundred Buddhist priests, but that's really just a guess. Even our North Korean counterparts can't give us a firm number when we ask them."

The Jogye group also provides food and medical aid, but their greatest efforts have gone into restoring and repairing North Korea's temples.

"In 2003," says Mr. Park proudly, "we supplied enough colored paint to repaint the eaves of every temple in North Korea. It's special paint, you know. The colors have to be just right, and the paint has to be strong enough to survive those cold, cold winters in the North." He reaches up, pulls out a book from on top of the filing cabinet, and opens the pages to show us the glorious colors of the temples restored with their paint—all those colors that

Kemp with her artist's eye so carefully named—mazarine blue, myrtle green, and Venetian red.

Their most ambitious project began in the year 2545 of the Buddhist calendar (2001 of the Common Era), when they and their northern counterpart announced a plan to reconstruct the Diamond Mountain temple of Singye-Sa. One of the region's most ancient temples, Singye-Sa was almost entirely destroyed during the Korean War, but the stone stupas and monuments that surrounded the temple were still standing.

Singye-Sa interests me particularly because it was probably the temple where Kemp intended to stay on her walk through the mountains in 1910 (although things did not turn out quite as planned).

The first task of reconstruction was to find old photographs and drawings that enabled them to create a detailed architectural plan for the temple.

"South Koreans did all the technical work—the designing and surveying and so on—and the North Korean side provided the labor to build the temple," says Mr. Park. "The North Koreans have the technical know-how to build concrete reconstructions, but they have lost the techniques for building temples from wood. That's where we come in."

Work on the site started in 2001 with surveys and careful archaeological excavations, and by late 2007, it was complete; in a spot where, for decades, there had been nothing but grass and weeds between the crumbling ruins of stone monuments, there now stands a fine compound of eight main buildings, rising from a clearing in the forest with the peaks of the Diamond Mountains towering behind. The opening ceremonies were held in October 2007, attended by a delegation of more than three hundred South Korean Buddhists. Thirty representatives from the North Korean Buddhist Federation, including North Korean Buddhist priests in striking red and black robes, were also on hand to take part in the recitation of sutras, the presentation of offerings, and the bestowing of blessings.

"There are North Korean priests in regular attendance at Singye-Sa now," says Mr. Park, "but few people attend the temple. Ordinary North Koreans can't go there at all. Some of the South Korean employees from the tourist resort used to visit the temple to pray, but now that tourism's stopped there are hardly any South Koreans at the resort any more."

All of this, of course, raises the obvious question, which I try to phrase as tactfully as I can. "I know this is a sensitive issue, but in North Korea, the official ideology is the Juche Thought of Kim Il-Sung and the "Army First" policy of Kim Jong-Il, and the Buddhist Federation is an arm of the state. So just how far do you think of your North Korean colleagues as actually being Buddhist?"

Mr. Park and Mr. Han laugh. This is, they agree, indeed a very difficult question indeed.

"There's no single answer to that," says Mr. Park.

Some people have one answer and some people have another. But as for me . . . well, you know, for a long time North and South had no contact with one another, so we had no chance to get to know the situation in the North. Obviously things are completely different there. The North Korean Buddhist Federation is a government agency, so it's difficult to say how far they're really Buddhist. Some people would argue that they're not Buddhist at all. But as far as we're concerned, we treat them as a religious organization.

"It was quite difficult to begin with," adds Mr. Han. "When we started off, we didn't even know what to call one another. In North Korea they don't really have the same word for addressing Buddhist priests as we do, and the terms they used sounded really weird to us, but in the end we settled on the word *seunim* (master), which sounded okay to both sides."

The next stage of the dream is a pilgrimage, a great pilgrimage of thousands of South Koreans to the restored Singye-Sa. They hope to be able to set off on this pilgrimage sometime soon, but the political tensions have put their plans on hold. The South Korean government is wary and has yet to give permission.

"Do you think North and South will be reunited one day?" I ask the two Buddhists as we get up to leave. I think I know the answer that I'm going to hear, one that I've heard many times before, which expresses a deep abstract longing for reunification but then goes on to add that, in practice, it is a long way off.

But Mr. Park and Mr. Han catch me by surprise. "There are two sides to reunification," says Mr. Park, "the form and the content. The form is a matter for governments. But the content is a matter for us people, and we are reuniting already."

Mr. Han nods and goes one step further, "Reunification has already happened," he says. "In our hearts, we are already reunited."

Two Birds

I am still thinking about this unexpected vision of reunification as we emerge from the basement office into the Seoul afternoon. The Jogye Temple, to which the office is attached, stands at the heart of one my favorite areas of

Seoul, Insa-Dong. Though a little too smart and touristy these days, Insadong still manages to preserve fragments of the atmosphere of the old walled city of Seoul, alongside the creative exuberance that makes South Korea such a delight.

Dark shops selling giant brushes for ink painting and thick traditional Korean paper stand alongside fashionable art galleries. Tranquil teahouses serve plum, date, or quince tea in courtyards surrounded with shops selling handcrafted noodles and fair-trade coffee. The companion who has accompanied me to the interview with the Buddhists works here, in a tiny museum dedicated to peace, tucked away in an alley so narrow that visitors must reach its entrance single file. The air of Insadong vibrates with the possibility of unexpected discoveries.

On my way back through its laneways to my hotel I have another visit to make, to see the work of an artist named Lim Moo-sang. I find him at the top of a steep and narrow flight of stairs in a little house on one of the main streets of Insadong. He is a man in late middle age, with a rather rugged and expressive face crowned by a mop of wavy black hair. He seems slightly shy, and his wife promptly offers us some of her homemade toffee, which is delicious but adds to difficulties of conversation.

All around, the walls are covered with Lim's paintings: bold lines and plains of color painted in natural hues of gray, deep blue, and pale purple, which come from the minerals of the Korean soil itself. All the pictures are of the same subject: for the past several years, he has been endlessly painting the Diamond Mountains.

His paintings are part of a long tradition. As early as the fifth century CE, the Chinese awe of sacred mountains was finding expression in *shan shui*—brush paintings of landscapes featuring mountains and water, an art that later spread to Korea and Japan. Early Korean landscape painters favored imaginative scenes that drew on Chinese themes, but from the late seventeenth century, the mountains of Korea themselves became the subject of some of the greatest Korean art. Greatest of all were the brush paintings of Jeong Seon, whose astonishing images of the Diamond Mountains are painted with strong dark strokes, quite different from the fine lines of Chinese landscapes. By the twentieth century, Japanese landscape painters had also discovered the Diamond Mountains, much as European romantic artists had discovered the Swiss Alps a century earlier.[19] Western artists were soon following in their footsteps. American printmaker Lilian Miller trained in Japan but used her Japanese techniques to create semi-impressionist prints of the mountains in all their changing seasonal colors; British artist and writer Elizabeth Keith produced vivid woodblock prints of waterfalls and temples in the Diamond Mountains.[20]

Lim Moo-sang is the latest in this line of artists, his inspiration drawn from the work of the Joseon Dynasty. As he has painted, his representations of the mountains have shifted little by little, from a style reminiscent of Jeong Seon's ink paintings to increasingly abstract explosions of peaks surmounted by red suns and distant white moons.

For the past year, travel to the mountains from South Korea has been impossible, but Lim goes on painting undeterred. It is, he says, the curves of the rocks that intrigue him: the timeless perfect arcs that have inspired and shaped Korean art for centuries—not angularly pointed but slightly softened by time and weather, countless but each distinct. Lim's description of the three-day trip he made across the border to the mountains a few years ago speaks of his intense response to the beauty of the place but also of the sadness evoked by its landscape and by the loss and decay of its Buddhist art.[21]

In one of his paintings, the faintly sketched images of two small birds chase each other across the mountain landscape. "North and South," he says.

Notes

1. E. G. Kemp, *Face of Manchuria, Korea and Russian Turkestan* (New York: Duffield and Co., 1911), 93.

2. Kemp, *Face of Manchuria, Korea and Russian Turkestan*, 95–96.

3. On King Gojong, see James Palais, *Politics and Policy in Traditional Korea* (Cambridge, Mass.: Harvard University Asia Center, 1991).

4. Louise Jordan Miln, *Quaint Korea* (London: Osgood, McIlvaine and Co., 1895), 102.

5. Miln, *Quaint Korea*, 103.

6. Kemp, *Face of Manchuria, Korea and Russian Turkestan*, 95.

7. On the construction of the Government General Building, see Hong-Key Yoon, *The Culture of Fengshui in Korea: An Exploration of East Asian Geomancy* (Lanham, Md.: Lexington Books, 2006), 289–94.

8. Quoted in Yoon, *The Culture of Fengshui in Korea*, 292.

9. On the iconography of the "five mountains screens," see Yi Sŏng-Mi, "*Euigwe* and the Documentation of Joseon Court Ritual Life," *Archives of Asian Art* 58 (2008): 113–33.

10. Kemp, *Face of Manchuria, Korea and Russian Turkestan*, 105–6.

11. Kemp, *Face of Manchuria, Korea and Russian Turkestan*, 107.

12. Kemp, *Face of Manchuria, Korea and Russian Turkestan*, 106–7.

13. For example, the temple of Yujom-Sa contained images of the Buddha that were said to have been brought there ten centuries earlier from Tokharistan; see Tokuda Tomijirō, *Kongōsan Shashinchō* (Wonsan, North Korea: Tokuda Shashinkan, 1918).

14. J. B. Pratt, *The Pilgrimage of Buddhism and a Buddhist Pilgrimage* (New York: Macmillan, 1928), 431–42.

15. Helen Foster Snow, *My China Years* (London: Harrap, 1984), 186.

16. Bertha Lum, *Gangplanks to the East* (New York: Henkle-Yewdale House, 1936), 110–11.

17. George Curzon, *Problems of the Far East* (London: Longmans Green, 1894), 104.

18. U.S. Congress, Senate Committee on Armed Services, *Worldwide Threat to the United States* (Washington, D.C.: Government Printing Office, 1995), 92.

19. See, for example, Ōmachi Keigetsu, *Mansen Yuki* (1919), in *Taishō Chūgoku Kenbunroku Shūsei*, vol. 8 (Tokyo: Yumani Shobō, 1999).

20. See Kendall H. Brown, *Between Two Worlds: The Life and Art of Lilian May Miller* (Pasadena, Calif.: Pacific Asia Museum, 1998); and Richard Miles, *Elizabeth Keith: The Printed Works* (Pasadena, Calif.: Pacific Asia Museum, 1991).

21. See Lim Moo-sang, *Geumgangsan* (Seoul: Dawoo Munhwa, 2008).

CHAPTER TEN

Islands in the Bay
To Busan

Street Theater

On the day I leave for Busan, a theater group is performing in the square outside my Seoul hotel. The drama is played out in traditional Korean style, with the acrobatic movements of the cast accompanied by a musician who heralds the climaxes of the story with rousing drumbeats. In the center of the makeshift stage, a motherly peasant woman in baggy pants and jacket is shaking her leathery forefinger as she harangues a group of young men with bandanas round their heads. Every now and again she turns to exchange sly asides with the audience, and the small but enthusiastic band of onlookers applauds, laughs, and responds with cheerful repartee.

It is almost like a dance in which audience and performers are partners. Their bodies sway back and forth to the rhythms of the narrative, and their voices swirl together in the gusts of wind that blow through the square. Sometimes passersby—the business people of central Seoul with their charcoal-gray designer suits and briefcases—stop for a moment to listen. The lighthearted mood belies the story being told: the performers are commemorating the anniversary of the most violent turning point in South Korea's long road from dictatorship to democracy—the Gwangju Uprising.

One of the tragedies of divided countries is that division creates enemies within—both real and imagined. Under the authoritarian governments that controlled South Korea until the 1980s, political opposition was readily labeled "communist subversion," just as anyone who falls foul of the authorities in North Korea today risks being labeled a "South Korean spy."

159

In May 1980, half a year after the assassination of Park Chung-hee, who had ruled South Korea with economic acumen and an iron fist for almost two decades, students in the southwestern city of Gwangju demonstrated in protest against the suppression of democracy by the new president Chun Doo-hwan. Instantly suspecting communist insurrection, the government responded by sending in two special force brigades who attempted to crush the protests with extreme, random, and gratuitous violence. The action served only to turn a peaceful demonstration into a miniature civil war.

Furious at the troops' behavior, some of the citizens of Gwangju began to seize whatever weapons they could and fought back. Remarkably, the military were forced into a temporary retreat from the city before returning again in greater force to crush the uprising. Even today, the death toll from the Gwangju Uprising is not known with certainty, although it is estimated at over two hundred.[1] President Chun Doo-hwan was later sentenced to death for crimes including his role in the massacre, but the sentence was commuted and he was released from prison in 1997.

On this sunlit morning, one side of the square is lined with a makeshift exhibit of photos: smudgy black-and-white images of demonstrators being beaten by troops, bloodied bodies lying in the street, and women weeping over coffins. It all seems improbably remote from today's South Korea, with its street theater and its vibrant online media, its ubiquitous giant video screens advertising everything from rock concerts to investment banks, and its young, who seem more interested in their fashion accessories and digital multimedia cell phones than in the political passions of yesterday.

South Korea's political transformation is one of Asia's most remarkable examples of democratization from within. Unlike North Korea, where the combination of utopianism and extreme repression succeeded in obliterating all visible signs of political opposition, in the South resistance to the regime survived even the darkest years, and once the weight of oppression was lifted, a tide of political passion, energy, and creativity surged to the surface.

Yet, inevitably, troubled undercurrents of memory and tension still flow. Most of the students and most of the soldiers involved in the Gwangju Massacre are still alive. Though protest blossoms freely on the streets of Seoul today, an elderly man watching the theater performance tells me, in fractured English and hand gestures but with real anger, that the present government is trying to ban political protests from this central square, reserving it for officially approved cultural events. The tide of democratization has faltered; some fear that it is receding.

The banners that flutter by the road as part of the Gwangju commemoration convey a double-edged message. They depict a black fist raised in defiance, but the fist is holding a flower.

The Iron Silk Road

The gap between North and South Korea is perfectly embodied in the central railway stations of the two capital cities. Pyongyang station is a vast and (from the outside) imposing building constructed sometime in the late 1950s. But within there is nothing but echoing gloom—a single hall spanned by a dimly visible high roof, empty of everything except the throngs of passengers who gather as a train arrives, and then disperse, bent double under their burdens of boxes and sacks. Seoul station has an equally imposing exterior—a colonial structure with postmodern additions. Inside is a consumer paradise of shining gray marble, its shops tempting travelers with arrays of Paris baguettes and organic ice cream.

A poster on one wall advertises the "UN New Silk Road Mayors' Congress" being held in a city on the line between Seoul and Busan. The Silk Road theme is echoed in the publicity produced by the South Korean railroad company Korail, which runs the Korean Train Express (KTX), the high-speed rail link from Seoul to Busan. With a curious interweaving of nostalgia, utopianism, and MBA speak, this proclaims,

> Our business ideal is based on client-oriented, value-creating and trustable management, and our vision is "Power Korail 2010" to open up the age of "Iron Silk-Road." . . . As we have overcome the pain of being the only divided country, the dream of Korail is to link the railroad of South and North Korea, and furthermore to become the motive power of "Iron Silk-Road" through China, Siberia and Europe.

The dream that inspired the architects of the Great Siberian Railway and the empire builders of the South Manchurian Railway lives again, after all the vicissitudes of the intervening decades. I wonder whether "client-oriented, value-creating and trustable management" will sound as foreign to the ears of future generations as "Long Live General Kim Jong-Il, the Sun of the Twenty-First Century."

For some reason, it took Emily Kemp twenty hours to travel from Seoul to Busan. She must have selected a particularly slow train, for even in 1910 the journey could generally be completed in around ten. Certainly her journey was an uncomfortable one, on narrow seats in an "American-style" carriage:

> It taxed the ingenuity even of the small and supple Japanese officers who were our fellow-travellers, to make themselves comfortable in the first class carriage. The attendant brought slippers all round, and when the officers had divested themselves of their boots and unrolled their blankets and eiderdowns, it became an interesting sight to see them try to accommodate their forms to the small seats for two.[2]

Today, courtesy of the KTX, the same journey takes just over two and a half hours, the green plush seats are comfortable, and passengers are greeted by the gentle piped music of a *gayageum* (Korean zither) performing the Beatles' "Let It Be." The man across the way from me removes his shoes, stretches out his feet on the neighboring seat, and snores rhythmically until just before Busan, when he suddenly awakes and buys a coffee from a passing snack cart, filling the carriage with the sweet scent of hazelnut syrup.

Seoul goes on for a very long time. The capital cannot expand further northward—North Korea stands in the way. So it extends southward in suburb after endless suburb. The mass of little red brick two-story buildings that once covered the hillsides of Seoul are disappearing, giving way to the peaks and canyons of pastel-colored apartment blocks. These are interspersed with a quite astonishing number of church spires surmounted by neon crosses, sprouting in the most unlikely places—from the top of department stores, office blocks, or supermarkets. South Korea is said to have more churches per head than any other country in the world.

Kemp described the journey from Seoul to Busan in poetic tones: "As we traveled southward the land gradually became greener and the fruit-trees showed their delicate blossoms. Over the willows there was a delicate film of green, and the pink azaleas on the hill-sides glowed in the evening light."[3] The gradual transformation of the landscape that she saw as she traveled down the Korean Peninsula has now become a binary divide: the contours of the hills, the colors of the fields, and even nature itself (it seems) is sharply bisected at the 38th parallel. Everywhere I see this southern scenery in counterpoint to the North Korean landscape through which I have just traveled—so much the same but so utterly different.

Here in the South the wide rice paddies, rippled like silk by the wind on this spring morning, are interspersed by lush forested hills, patches of industrial development, and the ubiquitous cream-and-apricot-colored high-rise apartment blocks that spring suddenly out of the landscape like growths of spindly fungus. As we head south, the mountains close in, and (as Kemp noted) the rice fields give way to fruit orchards. The blossoms and azaleas that she admired are past their best, replaced by white acacia, like patches of light snow in the dense green of the forests, and by the buds of a mass of dark red rambler roses that have been planted along the southern stretches of the line. But beyond the city of Daejeon we pass just one or two villages of houses that she might recognize—little one-story brick buildings shaped like those in the villages of North Korea, their tiled roof ridges curving delicately upward at either end.

As the train approaches Busan, the line runs along the side of a broad meandering river dotted with little bushy islands. Here farmers are out tilling the soil. One squats amongst his vegetable fields, taking a rest from his labors and watching the fishermen cast their lines in the river. The water is deep blue-green, very different from the gray-brown of the Sungari on whose bank I began this journey. The KTX skims through the landscape at alarming speed, on the ground yet utterly detached from it, repeatedly plunging into neon-lit tunnels or enclosed in antinoise barriers. Outside, the farmer admires the green shoots of his vegetables and the fishermen smoke as they wait for a nibble on their line; within our carriage, lions rip the leg off a dying antelope in the South African wildlife documentary that loops repeatedly across the video screens suspended above our heads.

Dragon Head Mountain

Busan has a fine new metro with a high-tech automatic ticket vending system that taxes the skills not just of aliens like me but also of elderly local citizens, who mutter, curse, and enter into a lengthy debate amongst themselves as the machine defiantly spits out their money without issuing a ticket. Two stops along the metro line, I alight at the foot of Yongdusan—Dragon Head Mountain—rising sheer behind Busan harbor.

Kemp and Mary MacDougall had not intended to stop in Busan. Their plan was to immediately board the ferry that would take them up the east coast of Korea to the port of Wonsan—the starting point for their trek to the Diamond Mountains. But the ferry was delayed, giving them time to explore this peak. Kemp describes it as "a beautifully wooded hill which has been laid out by the Japanese with great taste. Long flights of handsome stone steps lead directly upward under the shade of overhanging pine-trees, and winding paths lead more gently to the summit, offering alluring seats from which to admire the bay. There is a succession of Shinto shrines which seem to be much frequented."

Shinto, the amalgam of local Japanese folk beliefs molded into a state religion, was later to be imposed by the colonizers on the Korean population—a policy that evoked deep and lasting resentment. But in 1910, this cultural assimilation was barely beginning, and the worshippers who thronged Busan's Shinto shrines were visitors from Japan or inhabitants of the large Japanese settlement that occupied the center of the city.

"Some passers-by," wrote Kemp, "paid no more attention to the shrines than to bow and remove their hats, but on the whole they elicited a fair amount of worship, and it is clear that the Japanese are more attached to their religion than some people give them credit for."[4]

Before following her footsteps up Dragon Head Mountain, I take a detour into a narrow paved side street where a restaurant offers *samgyetang*, one of the best culinary inventions known to humankind—chicken soup made from a whole small chicken stuffed with sticky rice, ginseng, Chinese dates, and gingko nuts. Since this is Busan, I order *jeonbok samgyetang* with a big fresh abalone (for which the city is famous) added to the mix.

It occurs to me as I eat that Kemp says remarkably little about food in her travel accounts. In this, she differs from many other Western travelers of her day. Isabella Bird, during her journey through the Diamond Mountains in the 1890s, described how she adjusted to the diet of the monasteries by living on "tea, rice, honey water, edible pine nuts and a most satisfying combination of pine nuts and honey."[5] Elsewhere, though, Bird recoiled in disgust from the local diet. Korean butchery practices, which were designed to retain as much blood as possible in the meat, were, she wrote, "enough to make any one a vegetarian"; and she was also unimpressed by Japanese tofu—a "tasteless white curd made from beans," which she attempted to improve with a topping of condensed milk.[6]

Kemp, on the other hand, tells us nothing about the meals she consumed on her travels, though she does describe how, when they stopped at inns on the way to the Diamond Mountains, the guides accompanying her "each had a little round table, about four inches in diameter, on which were a large brass bowl of rice, another of water, and two or three small earthenware dishes of vegetables, or fish, and other condiments. These little tables are very neat, and the food attractively served."[7]

The steep stone steps up the face of Dragon Head Mountain have been replaced by a series of escalators, and the summit today is surmounted, not by a Shinto shrine but by Busan Tower, one of those unsightly concrete landmarks crowned by an observation deck and café, much favored by the urban planners and tourism promoters of the 1960s and 1970s. After the smog of

Seoul, the air of Busan is fresh and smells of the sea. A strong wind is blowing over the summit of Yongdusan. Far below, Busan's harbor curves around islands and between the indented contours of green mountains. Small boats embroider the surface of its deep blue waters with their shining wakes, and beyond, a long line of tankers and cargo ships waits in the offing.

The city is in the middle of celebrating the fourth centenary of its opening as a port, and the lower floors of the tower are filled with old maps, drawings, and photographs proclaiming Busan's history as Korea's "gateway to the world." There is both pride and pain in this history. Though Korea officially became a Japanese colony in the year of Kemp's visit, in reality a gradual process of colonization had begun thirty-four years earlier, when an energetically modernizing Japan followed the expansionist example of the Western powers by forcing Korea to sign a treaty opening its doors to foreign trade.

A woman who lives near the foot of Yongdusan is serving as a volunteer attendant at the exhibition. She speaks fluent English and is eager to tell visitors her city's history. "You know, Busan was the first very Korean port to be opened," she says. "We had an old Japanese trading post here already, but after the opening of the port it suddenly grew into a whole city of Japanese settlers."

The early settlers were a motley assortment—many of them poor farmers and former samurai displaced by the waves of social change sweeping Japan itself. It was the frontier lawlessness of port settlements like Busan and Wonsan that gave rise to dire warnings to travelers of dangerous Japanese "vagrants" and "ruffians" in Korea. But by 1910, the Japanese settlement already had its own local administration and police, order of a sort had been restored, and the colonizers were busy developing Busan's docks.

Old maps and sepia photos on the wall show the transformed landscape of the bay. The grand modern port designed by the colonizers allowed ferry passengers from Japan to transfer straight onto the train that could take them to Seoul, Pyongyang, Changchun, Harbin, and the Great Siberian Railway beyond. But, in the remorseless unfolding of history, it was also to serve another purpose as the empire disintegrated.

"This is how things were after Liberation," says the attendant, leading me in the direction of another row of photos on the wall. "My parents can remember those days. Just look at all those lines of people on the docks!"

Photos from the time of chaos that followed Japan's defeat in the Pacific War shows the dock of Busan crammed with a great human tide of ejected Japanese colonizers desperately pushing their way onto the transport ships that would take them home. Three million Japanese civilians were repatriated from Korea, Taiwan, Manchukuo, and other parts of the lost empire at the end of the Pacific War, while a similar number of Koreans flooded back into the Korean Peninsula from Japan and China—another of those great and largely forgotten human tides that have shaped today's Northeast Asia.

Looking at these photos, I remember a haunting image that I first saw about a year ago. Captured fleetingly on film by a visiting Western camera-man on the docks of Busan early in 1946, this image shows a small Japanese boy of about ten or eleven, who seems to have become separated from his family. The boy has an injured leg, roughly wrapped in bandages, and he supports himself on a makeshift crutch. Dressed in the tattered remains of a military jacket, he hobbles slowly along the quay toward a waiting ship, still managing a wan and tentative smile for the camera as he passes it on his way home. Just thirty-five years after the annexation of Korea, the power and glory, the visions, and violence of colonialism had disappeared overnight, leaving nothing but this figure of raw and suffering humanity, limping into an uncertain future.

House Mountain

"House Mountain," proclaims the sign on another floor of Busan Tower. Intrigued, I peer through the door and find an exhibition of a different kind. Here the walls are covered with paintings, drawings, and engravings, all filled with jumbles of tiny geometrical shapes piled one upon another up the slopes of hillsides. They seem like impossible, fantasy landscapes: the creation of some wild school of cubists with overheated imaginations. It is only when I reach the top of the tower and look out across the city that I recognize their realism for, indeed, on every side above the port rise the house mountains of Busan: astonishing mosaics of small square buildings—pink, white, terra-cotta, and jade green—patterned with the smaller black squares of windows and extending up precipitous slopes toward the forested summits of the hills. Between them run narrow alleyways or, in places where the hillside is too steep for vehicles, stone stairways.

Busan's house mountains are silent testimony to another watershed in the city's history—June to August 1950, when North Korean forces crossed the 38th parallel and swept down the Korean Peninsula occupying everything except for a 160-square-kilometer enclave within a line known as the Busan Perimeter. Ahead of the advancing North Korean forces came a massive influx of refugees, more than doubling the size of Busan's population in a matter of weeks. With the shifting tides of war, some of the refugees returned home, but many had no homes left to return to.

Ten years after the outbreak of the Korean War, the displaced people of Busan were still living in "hovels of sacking and petrol drums and flattened fruit tins, the insides lined with wrapping paper or magazines to keep out the wind."[8] The shanty towns they built sprawled up the hillsides toward the sky-line, but growing prosperity gradually transformed the buildings from make-shift shelters into little brick houses and then into the squares of concrete, plaster, and paint that now form the mosaics of the house mountains, while the valley below gradually filled with the gleaming towers of new apartment and office blocks.

Coming out of the exit from Busan Tower, I am confronted by a scene that seems like a celebration of the city's triumph over adversity. It is also a scene that would not have looked out of place in the Korea of 1910. A group of young musicians in traditional dress is playing drums and cymbals in an open-air arena overlooking the harbor. The concert is another of the free public cultural events that flourish everywhere in South Korea. The audi-ence wanders in and out of the tiers of stone seating, some watching intently, others pausing only briefly before moving on.

A gap-toothed man in a nylon waistcoat and cloth cap, surely old enough to have vivid memories of the Korean War, is offering a comically dispar-aging commentary to his neighbor: "These kids—they pick up a drum and think they can play it just like that! Look at this one here—he's got about as much rhythm as a jellyfish!"

The recent history of Korea is written in the bodies of its people. The family on the row of seats in front of me includes an old woman with her hair tied in a bun and her body bent double by years of farm labor. But the youngsters who sit beside her, intent on opening their packets of caramels—her grandchildren or maybe even great-grandchildren, I guess—are growing up long limbed and strong, and a full head taller than North Korean children of the same age.

Nearby, volunteers have set up the traditional entertainments of old Korea, and teenagers more used to computer games are tentatively trying out the pastimes of their ancestors. There are hoops and wheelbarrows and, most popular of all, the seesaws [neol], which many nineteenth- and early twentieth-century foreign visitors to Korea described as one of the delights of Korean culture. A pastime for girls and young women, the seesaw was a display of grace and energy: "In their upward flight each girl is thrown two or three feet into the air. Frequent rests are necessary, but the sport is the occasion of much glee."[9]

The grace and energy come, not from the seesaw itself, but from the skill of the person who rides it. To fly through the air and rebound on the heavy and inflexible board requires balance, timing, and considerable muscular strength. The seesaws reconstructed on Dragon Head Mountain attract young and old, including men in business suits, who try their turns with unembarrassed enthusiasm and as much glee as ever, most slithering off ignominiously after a few bounds, to choruses of laughter. Parents hold the hands of small children as they attempt ineffectual little jumps on one end of the board. One young girl, though, persists, gradually soaring higher and higher to the applause of the crowd that has gathered round her. She seems oblivious to the audience, lost in her own world. Her arms, and the cell phone and Hello Kitty ornament strapped to her belt, swing upward like wings as she reaches joyously toward the sky.

Nearby, tradition blurs into multicultural present. A group of Busan residents in colorful saris are presenting Bollywood dance on a stage bedecked with red and gold Chinese lanterns, their performance interspersed with earnest speeches of welcome from local dignitaries. In this age of international mobility, South Korea is home to more than a million foreign residents, many of them women from China, Southeast Asia, or beyond who have married into farm families in areas where brides are in short supply. Ethnic Koreans from Northeast China form an important part of the mix. I wonder if the daughter of the family we met in the village near Harbin is somewhere among the crowd.

Multiculturalism is a new and unfamiliar concept in South Korea, debated with much enthusiasm and a certain edge of unease. It also forms yet another divide between North and South: on the northern side of the Demilitarized Zone, official ideology clings grimly to ethnonationalism and myths of racial purity.

Geoje Island

Around five o'clock on the afternoon of April 12, 1910, Kemp, MacDougall, and their Chinese interpreter Mr. Chiao boarded a cargo and passenger ship "heavily laden with timber and petroleum" for the voyage up the Korean coast from Busan to the northern port of Wonsan—a journey that would take them a day and half. "A more lovely sight than the bay as we steamed out of it past the four sentinel rocks at the entrance in the level rays of the setting sun would be hard to imagine," wrote Kemp.[10]

I am unable to follow their voyage: the waters between South and North Korea are still frozen by the Cold War, and no ferry has made the journey between Busan and Wonsan for over sixty years. Instead, I take a boat trip across the bay, to see the view that Kemp admired and sketched as she departed from Busan. The sky has clouded over, and rays of sunlight slant diagonally across the darkening waters of the bay. The boat moves among a multitude of rocky islets, with a squall of seabirds following in its wake.

It is heading toward Geoje Island—the large island that shelters the entrance to the bay and at whose northern tip stand the four sentinel rocks that Kemp and MacDougall passed on their voyage. On either side the coast unfolds like a scroll, revealing a landscape of astonishing contrast. One moment, there is nothing to be seen but waves crashing against cliffs surmounted by a solitary lighthouse, the next, we round a headland that reveals massive dockyards or throngs of tall white apartment blocks, like bizarre rock formations, filling every available inch of the narrow valleys that run down to the sea.

The little island port where the ferry makes landfall is a typical seaside town with its cluster of windblown hotels and restaurants with faded awnings. But the main tourist attraction, which lies on top of a hill in the center of Geoje Island, is rather unusual. Its entrance is surrounded by barbed-wire fencing and is adorned with the flags of the United Nations and the sixteen countries that participated on the southern side in the Korean War. An archway inscribed in Korean and English welcomes visitors to the Historic Park of Geoje POW Camp. For between 1950 and 1953, Geoje (also spelled "Koje") was home to one of the biggest prisoner of war camps the world has ever seen.

The original camp covered the entire hillside as far as the sea, and at the peak of its expansion, contained 140,000 prisoners. Today's tourist park, constructed in the 1980s, covers only a fraction of the original area and consists mostly of reconstructed tents and Nissen huts. The few crumbling sections of masonry from the original camp look like the ruins of some prehistoric settlement, rather than the remains of buildings constructed within living memory.

Most of the visitors who throng the camp are South Korean families. They wander through its theme-park environment eating ice creams as they watch the miniature hologram images of North Korean prisoners of war appear and disappear like ghosts in the carefully constructed dioramas. There is a "Dark Ride Show" where you can experience the lawless terrors of the prisoner of war camp at night and a very popular panorama complete with head-sized circular holes, which allows the visitor to be photographed in the guise of a prisoner behind barbed wire, a momentary fantasy crossing of the border to the side of the enemy. A placard nearby explains, "The prisoners in the camp were gradually organized into the pro-communist group and the anti-communist one, causing the bitter ideological confrontation inside, and the poignant feud and hatred between them started swaying the camp."

In fact, Geoje camp was plagued by overcrowding, poor sanitation, water shortages, and lack of supervision, ultimately leading to violence between inmates, riots, and clashes between prisoners and guards. Suspected anticommunists were murdered by communists and vice versa. In the most spectacular incident, North Korean prisoners of war captured the camp's American commandant and subjected him to trial by "people's court" before their insurrection was put down. During the life of Geoje camp, over two hundred of its inmates were killed by guards or by their fellow prisoners.

"See you again," reads the cheery message on the POW camp gate as you leave.

Nearby, a father has stopped to photograph his young son, a little boy of about five in sandals, shorts, and stripy T-shirt. Ignoring the sign that warns against climbing on the ruins, the boy has perched himself on the broken remains of a crumbling concrete archway that once formed the entrance to one of the camp's barracks. He is far too young to understand the story of the war, but it is his generation that will live to see the story's end, and that will face the task of unraveling the decades of feud, hatred, and social and political divide as this last Cold War conflict reaches its impending, but still uncertain, final chapter.

Meanwhile, he is simply a child enjoying an afternoon's outing in a particularly exciting adventure playground. With nervous mother and proud father looking on, he balances precariously on the ruins with a cheeky grin on his face, and the fingers of one hand raised in a peace sign.

Notes

1. See Choi Jungwoon, *The Gwangju Uprising: The Pivotal Democratic Movement That Changed the History of Modern Korea*, trans. Yu Young-Nan (Paramus, N.J.: Homa and Sekey Books, 2005); Henry Scott Stokes and Lee Jae Eui, eds., *The*

Gwangju Uprising: Eyewitness Press Accounts of Korea's Tienanmen (Armonk, N.Y.: M. E. Sharpe, 2000).

2. E. G. Kemp, *Face of Manchuria, Korea and Russian Turkestan* (New York: Duffield, 1911), 107.

3. Kemp, *Face of Manchuria, Korea and Russian Turkestan*, 107.

4. Kemp, *Face of Manchuria, Korea and Russian Turkestan*, 110–11.

5. Isabella Bird Bishop, *Korea and Her Neighbours* (New York: Fleming H. Revell, 1898), 139–40.

6. See Bird Bishop, *Korea and Her Neighbours*, 294; and Isabella Bird, *Unbeaten Tracks in Japan* (New York: G. P. Putnam's Sons, 1881), 293.

7. Kemp, *Face of Manchuria, Korea and Russian Turkestan*, 116–17.

8. Trevor Philpott, "The Refugees: A World Survey," *Rotarian* (December 1960): 16–28, 26.

9. Daniel L. Gifford, *Everyday Life in Korea: A Collection of Studies and Stories* (New York: Fleming H. Revell, 1898), 65.

10. Kemp, *Face of Manchuria, Korea and Russian Turkestan*, 111–12.

CHAPTER ELEVEN

The Road to the Mountains
South from Wonsan

The Empty Harbor

I can never hope to convince you of the beauty of Wonsan. And, with my usual good fortune, the house where I am staying has what must be one of the loveliest views from any civilized dwelling in the whole world. . . . We are not far from the Diamond Mountains here, and looking in one direction there are billows upon billows of mountains.[1]

So wrote the British printmaker Elizabeth Keith, in a letter sent to her family in the 1920s.

Wonsan's broad bay is still beautiful. A few grime-streaked apartment blocks dot the hillside, but most of the city is built on a more modest and human scale than Pyongyang. Its wide streets are lined with white, gray, and faded blue buildings decorated with pillars, plaster moldings, and stone facings. Despite the massive bombing of the city during the Korean War, some of these even date back to colonial times. Parts of the Benedictine monastery where the monk and scholar Norbert Weber once lived still stand on a local university campus, though the monks themselves were rounded up and imprisoned, and several were executed by communist forces soon after the division of Korea.

In our hotel's huge dining room overlooking the bay, we are the only guests apart from a group of Russians who are here to negotiate a salmon farming project. Glass chandeliers hang from the vaulted ceilings and a video of a Russian army choir plays on a screen in one corner. The ornate stucco cornices of the restaurant are patterned with the papery nests of wasps, which haunt its upper reaches unmolested. Beyond the wide windows stretches the expanse of the harbor, with a small causeway surmounted by a miniature white lighthouse, running out into its calm ultramarine depths.

I ask one of the Russians how long they are staying and receive, in reply, a rueful and resigned smile. "That all depends on our Korean friends," he says.

When Emily Kemp arrived here by ship from Busan, around dawn on the morning of April 14, 1910, the two port cities of Busan and Wonsan were like twins, conjoined by the lines of the freighters and ferries that regularly plied the coastal waters between them. Opened to trade with Japan in 1879, Wonsan also had a large Japanese settlement, constructed on the western side of the bay in a marshy area where the air was dank and disease rife.[2] But Wonsan was a much more Korean town than Busan; even before its opening to the outside world, it was one of the country's main trading centers with a population of around ten thousand.[3]

By the time Kemp and Mary MacDougall arrived, the town also had a sizeable Western missionary community, for Wonsan had been at the heart of the wave of Christian conversions that swept northern parts of Korea between 1903 and 1907.[4] Here, as elsewhere, Kemp and MacDougall were met by missionary friends "with whom we walked through a good part of the modern town. It is well laid out, and has wide roads leading to the quarters where the American missionaries live on the slopes of hills overlooking the sea and embowered in trees."[5]

The twin ports of Busan and Wonsan are now sundered by the division of the Korean Peninsula, and while Busan's bay is full of vast container ships, looming out of the hazy horizon like low-lying islands, Wonsan's harbor is empty. The one ship in port is the Mangyongbong 92—the ferry that once sailed between Wonsan and the Japanese port of Niigata and that has been lying idle ever since Japan imposed sanctions on North Korea following the 2006 nuclear test. Outside our hotel, a thickly wooded park extends to the water's edge. The only movement on the mirrorlike surface of the bay comes from a group of small boys with tin cans suspended from pieces of string, who splash and ripple the waters as they hunt for shellfish below the sea wall.

The Persimmon Farm

In 1910, the journey from Wonsan to the Diamond Mountains was still an uncertain adventure. After the annexation of Korea, the colonial government became eager to open up the mountains and their hidden treasures, and by the early 1920s visitors were offered a choice of tour routes including trips by car from Seoul, courtesy of the ubiquitous South Manchurian Railway Company, or by a steamer from Wonsan, which made the return journey six times a month.

In 1925, work began on the Kongo-San Electric Railway, which was to offer passengers a spectacular journey over precipitous mountain passes to a station near Changan-Sa—the Temple of Eternal Peace.[6] Meanwhile, blithely dismissing generations of Korean poets, artists, and pilgrims, the colonial government advertised the region to foreign tourists as having been "lost to the rest of the world" and "wrapped in a shroud of mystery" from the fifteenth century until "rediscovered by Mrs. Isabella [Bird] Bishop who, in the face of many hardships and obstacles, explored it, making its superb, unrivalled scenic beauty known to the world."[7] The Japanese government even had plans to make the Diamond Mountains into one of its empire's first national parks.[8]

Kemp and MacDougall left Wonsan for the mountains before these innovations had smoothed the route, at a time when the hardships and obstacles of exploration still remained. Their only means of transport were foot and pack pony; tigers still roamed the peaks, and there were no guide books other than the travel accounts left by earlier visitors. With their Chinese interpreter and German map, and with Kemp suffering from a severe cold, they set off accompanied by four ponies and three Korean guides who had been hired for them by their local missionary friends. The ponies had no saddles, so Kemp, MacDougall, and Mr. Chiao used their bedding as substitutes, while the fourth pony carried their baskets of stores and two cots that they had been lent for the occasion. They had lost their umbrellas en route and bought Korean waterproof paper coats as a replacement.[9]

Only belatedly did Kemp discover that none of the Korean guides had ever traveled any part of the route before.

The first obstacle they encountered was the river, unnamed in Kemp's account but readily recognizable from her description as the Namdae Stream, a broad shallow river that flows into the sea southeast of Wonsan. There was no bridge across the river, only a ferry attached to a rope, enabling travelers to pull themselves across its amber waters from one side to the other. When Kemp and her party arrived at the river, the ferry was on the wrong side. After a long wait, a Korean woman appeared on the far bank of the river and slowly boarded the ferry. She sat there silently, making no attempt to move the boat, despite shouts of encouragement from Kemp's guides. The shouts turned to impatience and rising anger before the woman began to pull on the rope, and the boat slowly moved across the stream. "It was only when we saw her close at hand that we discovered she was blind, so probably that had made her afraid of crossing alone."[10]

By now, the travelers were already falling behind their tightly scheduled itinerary and were unable to reach their intended destination for the day, stopping instead at a farm cottage three miles short of their goal. As was still common practice when foreign travelers or Korean dignitaries arrived, after some discussions over payment, the inhabitants of the cottage were unceremoniously turned out of their sleeping quarters to make way for the uninvited guests. "All Korean houses," Kemp observed,

> have a small platform outside them, either planking or made of dried mud, on which the shoes are left before any one enters. The floors are heated from be-low and covered with matting, so that chairs are considered unnecessary, and the Koreans enjoy the heat which penetrates through the bedding on which they lie at nights. We found it distinctly trying, despite having the doors open and cots to sleep on; but we were delighted to find the houses so much cleaner than we expected.[11]

The uncertainties of today's journey to the mountains are of a different order. Like Kemp, we are in the hands of our guides. In our case, the guides know the route perfectly well; the one question is where they will choose to take us. When I arranged our visit to North Korea, I asked for it to include the northern fringes of the Diamond Mountains—the only part currently acces-sible to foreign visitors approaching the region from the northern side of the 38th parallel. But our guides have their own plans and are liable to alter the route on the spur of the moment in response to mysterious communications from headquarters in Pyongyang. Before heading across the lower reaches of Namdae Stream, we must first make a required visit to a collective farm.

The grounds of our hotel are being renovated, and when our driver Mr. Kim attempts to negotiate the driveway, he finds his path blocked by a large truck from which stones are being shoveled onto the drive with agonizing slowness. The workers ignore Mr. Kim's hooting and crescendo of curses and continue stoically with their work. A woman with a small child is among the group of workers sitting by the road. The child is staring blankly into space while the mother, her face powdered with glittery gray grit, concentrates on the grim task of pounding the stones into gravel.

In Wonsan, there are even fewer cars than in Pyongyang. Here and there an oxcart creaks along the uneven pavements. Down one side street we catch a glimpse of people huddled around what seem to be a couple of makeshift market stalls.

Much of the life of North Korea takes place along the roadways. Outside the city, the dirt roads are full of people: walking, riding bicycles or oxcarts, pushing handcarts, or squatting by the road as they wait to hitch a lift on a passing truck. Some read books as they wait; some chat to companions; and others simply wait. The women walking along the road often carry bundles wrapped in cloth on their heads. At one point we pass a man on a bicycle, with his wife riding sidesaddle behind him and the baby strapped to the wife's back, like unstacked Russian dolls. Farmers are plowing the red earth of the fields with spindly oxen. It is a warm day, and boys shriek as they leap into the murky water of fishponds.

Here and there, rather to my surprise, we pass stalls by the road selling ice pops, with little clusters of customers gathered around them. But these, it turns out, are strictly socialist popsicles. "Each local government unit is allotted its set number of ice pops, and then five people per unit are given the job of selling them," explains Ms. Ri.

The model collective farm lies down an earthen track marked by a red flag and radiates a palpable aura of unreality. Immaculate white farmhouses stand in a row beside the ploughed fields and surrounding the village fishpond. The walls of the central square are decorated with tastefully painted murals proclaiming, "Let us all participate in the 150-Day Campaign!" On the other side of the square stand the village bathhouse and the community hall cum cinema, which displays a poster advertising a feature film about heroic ace fighter pilots. The insidious North-South divide extends even to notions of beauty: today's South Korean movies feature ethereal and soulful male stars, while the North favors chunky males with robust complexions, much in the style of the youthful John Wayne.

The streets of the village are deserted, giving the place itself the feel of a movie set—presumably the villagers are all in the fields playing their part in the 150-Day Campaign. But one of the residents, a middle-aged woman with the demeanor of a rural Women's Institute volunteer, is on hand to guide the foreigners who regularly visit the farm.

"The Great Leader came here in 1959," she says, "and when he saw this spot, it reminded him of his own birthplace, Mangyongdae. He was deeply moved, and he told the villagers that they should plant persimmon trees. Now our persimmons are famous all over the country."

"The Great Leader taught the farmers to grow things in the scientific way and the chemical way so that the farmers can be workers," adds Mr. Ryu.

"Look at this tree," says our village guide as we pass a particularly fine specimen. She pulls down one of its branches, its spring leaves still sparkling with dew. "Guess how many fruit this tree produces at harvest time?"

We hazard a variety of guesses, all far short of the correct answer, which appears to be two thousand—but perhaps an extra zero has slipped into the translation.

The problem with chemical farming is that you need chemicals, and the problem with chemicals is that you need electricity to produce them. North Korea today has neither electricity nor the foreign currency to import chemicals, and the highly fertilizer-dependent strains of rice, fruit, and vegetables, which the farmers were encouraged to plant, fail to thrive. Hence the large number of heavy sacks on the backs of train passengers and of pedestrians by the roadside. Fertilizer is gold, and people will go to enormous lengths to obtain it.

A primary school lies beyond the persimmon orchard, and as we arrive the children are in the middle of a sports competition, running relay races with miniature red flags as batons. As soon as we appear, two of the smallest children rush toward us to grab our hands and draw us into the midst of the race. I find myself clutching a little boy's hand, hard and scabby—a hand that has pulled up many weeds and endured many winter chilblains. The children urge one another on with shouts and chants. Their faces are burnt deep brown by the sun; their clothes are an assortment of ill-matched tracksuit tops and pants, and their footwear ranges from decaying sports shoes to Wellington boots. They have learnt the ritual of greeting strangers with clockwork precision, but their expressions are uncomprehending—intent on getting through the ritual without slipups. I wonder how, as adults, they will look back on this childhood performance. I wonder, too, what sort of world, as adults, they will inhabit.

Our village guide takes us to her house, a cottage by the side of the fishpond. The surface of the pond is covered with drifting fluff from the surrounding willow trees. Outside the cottage is a path neatly paved with cockle shells. The garden is planted with persimmon trees under which cabbages and spring onions are set out in rows, and a stack of homemade coal-dust briquettes (the normal fuel for North Korean home heating) is drying outside the front door. The cottage is similar in size and shape to those Kemp drew as she passed through this district in 1910 but is made of concrete rather than wood and lacks the raised platform described by Kemp. It is also the same, in size and shape, as almost all farm cottages in North Korea. If we use our imaginations to strip away the embellishments from this dream home, we can capture a fleeting image of the cottages whose interiors we will never see.

This cottage has two tiny rooms on either side of the entrance, their floors covered with lino, their walls whitewashed or decorated with striped wallpaper. There is very little furniture, but the house is spotless and the living room is adorned with pictures, including the obligatory portraits of the leaders Kim Il-Sung and Kim Jong-Il. Our host proudly shows us the methane gas cooker in the kitchen and brings out her accordion to sing us a song of welcome, which she performs with gusto and completely off key, under the approving gaze of her mother-in-law, a woman with iron gray hair and a weathered but serene and beautiful face.

Ordinary village houses in North Korea will have the same two rooms, the same portraits on the walls. But a methane gas cooker is an unheard of luxury. Coal briquettes and firewood gathered from remaining straggly patches of woodland are the normal sources of power for cooking and heating. Built in the growth years of the 1960s and 1970s, many cottages are now in disrepair, ill-fitting window frames and broken panes letting in the bitter winter cold, roofs patched and walls repaired with the infinite ingenuity that North Korean people bring to the task of struggling though everyday life.

Sokwang-Sa

We drive on, further inland into the foothills that rise above the coastal plain. The unpaved road becomes narrower and more deeply rutted, and on either side, the rice fields give way to potato patches. A few kilometers up the road we come to a gate, and Mr. Kim stops the car at the edge of the mountain river that runs over pebbles alongside the road, while our guides enter into intense negotiations with the man who guards this roadblock. Eventually, matters are resolved to their satisfaction and we drive through into the forest beyond: the thickest and healthiest forest I have seen in North Korea so far. Here, the cause of the delay becomes evident—a large group of children, teachers, and parents are enjoying a school outing in the forest, and unlike the schoolchildren at the collective farm, this group has not been prepared and rehearsed to meet foreigners.

South of the dividing line, Korean children generally respond to the presence of a Western-looking face by enthusiastically shouting whatever phrase of English comes to mind; at the South Korean temple of Bulguk-Sa, I was once accosted by a little boy of about five who rushed up to me and breathlessly declared, "I love you."

North Korean children, except those specially groomed for the task, seldom see a foreign-looking face, and at first these children give us nervous, oblique glances. But once we utter a few greetings in Korean, the sullen expressions dissolve into smiles. The teachers have set a portable tape recorder at the foot of one of the towering pine trees, and adults and children are dancing. The adults move with grace and beauty to the rhythm of the music; the children jiggle up and down, playfully bumping into one another or breaking away from the group to play hide-and-seek amongst the trees.

Realizing that our guides are not going to prohibit interaction, the schoolteachers prove eager to practice their English on us. One points out a giant zelkova tree—"a thousand years old," he says—which stands by the track that leads up the hillside toward a line of carved and gray-roofed gateways.

"Come here, come here," he calls, spreading his arms around part of the elephantine trunk. "You must put your arms round the tree. If you can hug tree, you will grow young. The more you hug, younger you grow."

The teacher, a youngish man in a shiny and threadbare black suit, proceeds to grasp our hands so that we can hug the tree together. It takes the three of us to encircle its vast trunk. I press my face against its flaking acrid bark. One of the many legends of the Diamond Mountains tells how an old man gathering wood discovers a spring and drinking its waters finds his youth and strength magically restored. The avaricious local mayor hears of this spring and drinks with such greed that he is transformed into a mewling baby.

This vast tree has somehow survived dynasties, invasions, colonization, the Korean War, and sixty years of the Democratic People's Republic. The tree-hugging experience makes no noticeable impact on Sandy's wrinkles or mine, but folk beliefs survive, deep rooted, as untouched by the bitter light of experience as they are by the passing storms of scientific farming and the Juche Idea. But by now our guides are becoming a little nervous, and to the visible disappointment of the teachers, they hurry us up the slope to the buildings above.

This place is the site of Sokwang-Sa, the Buddhist monastery whose abbots' influence extended over the temples of the Wonsan region and as far south as the Diamond Mountains. Isabella Bird visited Sokwang-Sa in the 1890s and describes a scene that in some ways has barely changed: a bridle track running along a "clear mountain stream," the "heavy foliage of an avenue of noble pines," and the magnificent zelkova trees.[12]

The great complex of temples that stood here at that time was built in the fourteenth century on the orders of the founder of the Joseon Dynasty. One of its series of halls displayed an array of five hundred miniature stone figurines with faces representing every human type—Asian and Caucasian faces from oases along the length of Silk Road and beyond, faces expressing humor, greed, folly, malice, and piety.[13]

Today, all that remains of Sokwang-Sa are a few fragments of the foundation stones—"destroyed during the Victorious Fatherland Liberation War," we are told.

But the temple's gatehouses still stand on the steep hillside, resplendently painted with many hued lotus flowers, dragons, and demons—no doubt with help from the Buddhist friends in Seoul. As we crane our necks to admire the intricate carvings, a farmer comes striding down from the mountains, whistling quietly to himself, with a staff in one hand and wild produce gathered from the higher slopes tied in a great bundle on his back.

"The local government has decided to rebuild this temple," our guide tells us, "and the ministry in Pyongyang has approved. Soon construction will start. Then the monks will be able to come back and live here."

"Monks? Which monks?" I ask.

"The ones who live in the town at the moment," says the guide, with the air of someone stating the obvious.

"How many of these monks are there?"

The guide gives a vague shrug. "Oh, a few. When you come back next time, you can see a temple standing here, and the monks living in it."

That, we agree, would indeed be a sight worth seeing.

The Fishermen of Sijung

A fine concrete bridge now spans the river that caused Kemp and her party such delay. An inscription picked out in red on one side proclaims it as

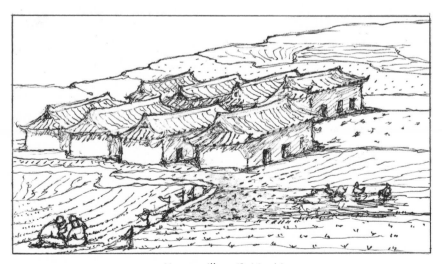

Korean village (S. Morris)

having been opened on April 15, 1989, Kim Il-Sung's seventy-seventh birthday. (The North Korean state likes to lay foundation stones and cut ribbons on such auspicious days.) The road runs parallel to a railway line, but on the slow drive south we see only one train: a very long goods train piled high with sacks, on top of which a few intrepid travelers are perilously perched, hitching rides.

On the second day of the journey from Wonsan to the Diamond Mountains, Kemp was determined to make up for the previous day's delay, "but at such a suggestion our men looked black and greatly demurred. They said thirty-seven miles was too long a journey."[14] The road they traveled ran parallel to the seashore, though strangely Kemp's account fails to mention the route's most obvious feature—the breathtaking views that it offers of the coast south of Wonsan. She noted, though, the wildflowers—the hepatica and heartsease, the crocuses and anemones, and looking at the villages they passed on that sunlit day, she "received an impression of universal content and comfort. The people looked for the most part respectably dressed and housed, and 'every prospect pleased.'"[15]

Conscious of the long journey ahead and the need to return to Seoul in time to catch their transport back toward Siberia, Kemp kept up a relentless pace. They traveled for thirteen and a half hours on their second day, pressing on, despite the protests of the Korean guides, past an attractive village overshadowed by tall pine trees, where there was "even a police officer standing near the invariable notice board which adorns every village in Korea since the Japanese occupation."[16]

By the third day of their journey, the weather was closing in and the sky was heavy with cloud. Continuing along the coast, they passed through a series of fishing villages and peered into the baskets of the village women to look at the strange assortment of sea creatures that made up the catch. Fish in the markets of Seoul, Kemp noted, was much more expensive than in London "owing to the Japanese monopoly," but these remote villages were still almost untouched by Japanese influence. She saw no further sign of the colonizers until, rounding a bend in the road, they suddenly "came into an exquisite little landlocked harbour, evidently a naval base, and completely concealed from the sea." Here, there was a colonial post office and "a Japanese woman was trotting along with a baby on her back."[17] Beyond the town, they plodded through sand dunes for some distance before turning inland.

Now, at last, they were at the doorstep of the Diamond Mountains.

They were also rapidly losing their way. Kemp identifies the little harbor as a town labeled on her German map "Tschagu-Tschiendogu," a name that bears no discernable resemblance to the names of any of the towns in the district. It is clear that the Korean guides had no idea where they were and were already chafing at the unreasonable demands on their stamina imposed by this eccentric Englishwoman.

As we come over the brow of the hill, the sea stretches out below us, wide and calm, its horizon softened by a faint spring haze. The coast beyond is rugged and indented, with small rocky islets breaking the sea surface and, between them, the dark specks of fishing boats.

On a long stretch of sandy beach where we stop for a rest, a couple of boats are pulled up on the shore. The day is clear and warm. The waveless sea is cloudy turquoise in the shallows, deep blue further out toward the horizon. It seems an inviting day for a swim, and Mr. Kim the driver quickly strips down to his boxer shorts and plunges into the water. Sandy and I follow more cautiously. The shallows are filled with the soft fronds of many forms of seaweed, and the water is breathtakingly cold.

Sandy takes out her sketch pad and walks down the beach to draw one of the fishing boats. Beyond, we can just see small olive-brown shapes that appear and vanish on the surface of the waters like giant bladders of seaweed— divers are out searching for shellfish in their baggy suits that serve as floatation devices as well as providing some measure of protection against the cold.

A fisherman who is loading his boat with nets comes over to look at Sandy's sketchbook. Wherever we go, her drawings attract much interest and comment but no noticeable hostility. Cameras are viewed with suspicion in North Korea, as having the power to steal secrets if not souls, but drawing is seen as a harmless eccentricity. With our guides translating, the fisherman is gradually drawn into conversation, a little shyly at first, but then gathering confidence, a warm smile illuminating his young, wind-darkened face.

He shows us the net attached to two planks of heavy wood like skis, which he drags along the seabed to gather shellfish. "I go diving sometimes as well," he says. "It can be terribly cold, but it's beautiful under the water."

"Do women dive too?" I ask, thinking of the South Korean island of Jeju, famous for its women divers, but the fisherman shakes his head.

"It's nearly all men. Fishing too. It's too dangerous for women."

Sometimes in summer he takes visitors out for rides on his boat around the bay: "important people from Pyongyang," he says, who come here for holidays.

"Could you take us, too?" we ask.

But the shyness returns. He can't take foreigners.

His boat is the simplest vessel imaginable, made of heavy wood and barely big enough to fit three people. It has a minute propeller, with a chunk of wood as an oar to add further momentum. The fisherman drags the boat down the beach, he and a companion step agilely aboard and give a brief wave as they set off toward deep water.

There is a café behind the beach and even a little kiosk selling bottles of German sun lotion and tacky souvenir animals made from shells, but the building is completely deserted apart from four men in Kim Jong-Il–style suits, who suddenly appear in their black Toyota four-wheel drive as we are about to leave. They have hard, unsmiling faces, and for the first time since our arrival I feel reluctant to attempt a greeting.

"Important people from Pyongyang," I think.

Our guesthouse, just a little inland from the beach, must be about halfway between the two villages where Kemp and MacDougall spent the night on their journey down the coast. It is a simple building made of gray stone and concrete with tile murals of the Diamond Mountains on the outside walls. It looks out across the glassy waters of Lake Sijung, whose black mud is known for its healing properties. Notices in the lobby advertise assorted mud treatments, said to be particularly good for women. The notices are written in English as well as Korean, but although there are a few elderly Koreans staying in the guesthouse, we are the only foreigners. Our room has traditional Korean under-floor heating and, like Kemp, we find the heat stifling, so early in the morning we slip out for a walk in the cool fresh air of the guesthouse grounds, which extend along the shores of the lake.

The water is clear but darkened by the mud beneath. Big fish dart though the shallows, leaving clouds of turbulence in their wake. Beyond the lake, the mountains pile in row upon row, dark gray fading to pale blue as they recede into the distance.

There is a small stone gatehouse where the drive joins the main road, but it is deserted. We stand by the gatehouse watching the villagers cycling by to work along the coast road. Everything is very still—just the calling of birds in the trees and the occasional barking of a dog in the distance. Then a couple of fishermen appear, striding down the drive, one of them pulling a handcart behind him. I follow and watch them unload a tangled heap of brown fishing net onto the paving stones outside the guesthouse. As soon as they have left, three young women who work here come out, spread the net across the paving, and begin carefully to twist and pick at it. They are dressed in black jeans and colorful tracksuit tops, with pink plastic slippers on their feet and their hair tied back with decorative hairpins.

There is something very peaceful about the scene—the easy rhythms of the women's voices as they chat and the way they move with the practiced grace of people used to working with one another. At first I assume they are mending the net, but looking more closely, I realize they are gleaning the last fragments of the fishermen's harvest. The tiny glistening silver fish that have remained trapped in the knots of the net as it was emptied are carefully prized loose, one by one, and popped into a plastic bucket. The task is meticulous and time consuming. No fragment of food is too small to be treasured.

Like Kemp, we have reached the threshold of the Diamond Mountains, the place where the dreams and hopes, the conflicts, and sufferings of this divided region are concentrated.

While we were planning the journey and while we have traveled its route, the endless circumvolution of North Korea's negotiations with its neighbors has been continuing. Sometimes a breakthrough seems near, and the borders seem about to reopen. But then again talks break down, and the chorus of mutual recriminations suddenly grows shrill. The border remains closed; tensions between North and South remain high. The North Korean leadership clings grimly to power by whatever means it deems necessary; the South Korean government has lost its grand visions for the peninsula's future and seems content to wait for the North to fall apart of its own accord. Meanwhile, China is growing increasingly impatient at the unending instability on its eastern frontier; the United States is absorbed with crises on the other side of the globe; Japan recoils in horror from the "rogue state" next door; and the rest of the world looks on with sardonic distaste at the bizarre spectacle of the last Stalinist state.

Sardonic distaste is a good excuse for indifference—an effective defense against the need to think seriously about the future or to care about its human implications. What will happen to the stone breakers and the persimmon farmers and the fishermen of Sijung, as aid continues to dry up, borders remain closed, and the regime sinks deeper into crisis? What will happen to them if the system implodes? How will Northeast Asia overcome the challenge of reintegrating this bubble of desperate poverty in the midst of material abundance—a challenge it will surely face very soon?

No one has any answers to these questions. The neighboring powers and the United States certainly have plans for military emergencies. Their governments have prepared detailed and secret strategies in case a crumbling North Korean state should launch an invasion, explode a nuclear weapon, or collapse into a civil war that threatens to spill over its borders. But the outside world, it seems, has closed its mind to the social and cultural life of this place.

There are no plans to respond to a future—a very imaginable future—when even the fish retrieved from the knots in fishing nets are no longer enough to stave off another mass famine, or an equally imaginable future when borders become more porous and throngs of North Koreans set off in search of a better life in Dandong and Shenyang, Seoul and Busan, and Tokyo and Osaka—just as more than a million East Germans left that country after the Berlin Wall came down. Neither governments nor international organizations are seriously planning how this land might be helped to overcome the environmental ravages of decades of Juche economics, or thinking of the hope for the future that lies in the quiet and shrewd ingenuity of the North Korean people. Just a few small underfunded nongovernmental groups struggle to keep the lines of communication open.

The Diamond Mountains have many faces, appearing and disappearing as the light changes. Sometimes the mountains are a meeting place; sometimes, a place of pilgrimage. At this moment, as we stand by Lake Sijung, gazing at the foothills reflected in its surface, they have become again, as in the conflicts of centuries past, a precipitous rocky barrier.

But nowhere else on earth are predictions more perilous. Tomorrow the light may change; tomorrow the landscape may be transformed.

Notes

1. Elizabeth Keith, *Eastern Windows: An Artist's Notes of Travel in Japan, Hokkaido, Korea, China and the Philippines* (Boston: Houghton Mifflin, 1928), 22.

2. "Dispatch from H.M. Minister in Japan, Forwarding a Report on Corea," 1883, in House of Commons Parliamentary Papers Online, ProQuest Information and Learning Co. 2005 (accessed via the National Library of Australia), 4.

3. "Dispatch from H.M. Minister in Japan," 3.

4. On the Japanese population of Wonsan, see Yokota Tomajirō, *Gensan no Hitobito* (Wonsan, North Korea: Higashi Chōsen Tsūshnsha, 1927). ("Gensan" is the Japanese pronunciation of the place-name "Wonsan"). On Christian conversions, see George T. B. Davis, *Korea for Christ* (New York: Fleming H. Revell Co., 1910), 62–68.

5. E. G. Kemp, *Face of Manchuria, Korea and Russian Turkestan* (New York: Duffield, 1911), 112.

6. Kongō-San Denki Tetsudō Kabushiki Kaisha, *Kongō-San Denki Tetsudō Kabushiki Kaisha 20-nen Shi* (Tokyo: Author, 1939).

7. Department of Railways, Japan, *An Official Guide to East Asia, Vol. 1: Chosen and Manchuria* (Tokyo: Department of Railways, 1920), 88.

8. See Kongō-San Denki Tetsudō Kabushiki Kaisha, *Kongō-San Denki Tetsudō Kabushiki Kaisha 20-nen Shi*, 165–66.

9. Kemp, *Face of Manchuria, Korea and Russian Turkestan*, 114.

10. Kemp, *Face of Manchuria, Korea and Russian Turkestan*, 114.

11. Kemp, *Face of Manchuria, Korea and Russian Turkestan*, 115.

12. Isabella Bird Bishop, *Korea and Her Neighbours* (New York: Fleming H. Revell, 1898), 169.

13. Bird Bishop, *Korea and Her Neighbours*, 171.

14. Kemp, *Face of Manchuria, Korea and Russian Turkestan*, 118.

15. Kemp, *Face of Manchuria, Korea and Russian Turkestan*, 116.

16. Kemp, *Face of Manchuria, Korea and Russian Turkestan*, 118.

17. Kemp, *Face of Manchuria, Korea and Russian Turkestan*, 119–20.

CHAPTER TWELVE

Traveling Hopefully

Lost

South of Sijung, we round a bend in the road and suddenly come upon a small port town clustered around a beautiful harbor that, approached from the north, appears almost landlocked. Rowing boats and divers are at work on its tranquil waters, and some of the divers are sorting their hauls of shellfish on the narrow strip of beach. This is the town of Tongchon, and it looks so exactly like Emily Kemp's description that it is tempting to think this is her "Tschagu-Tschiendogu."

If it was, then she and her companions were seriously off course and would have ended up on the fringes of the mountains, far from the temples they were trying to reach. Perhaps, however, "Tschagu-Tschiendogu" was the next port down the coast, Changjon (now called Kosong), for although neither town at that time had a significant naval base, Changjon did have a small whaling station, run by a Russian entrepreneur named Kaiserling.[1] From "Tschagu-Tschiendogu," Kemp and her party planned to walk inland to a secluded monastery to spend the night. Their goal was almost certainly Singye-Sa, the northernmost and nearest of the major monasteries—the monastery now lovingly reconstructed with the help of the South Korean Buddhists.

Finally, Kemp and Mary MacDougall were entering the landscape they had traveled so long and hard to see. As they walked the winding path away from the shoreline and into the mountains, "the rocks stood out like

mammoth beasts in all sorts of strange shapes," looking "black and forbidding in the gloom." After a while, they entered a beautiful valley "with cliffs
towering steeply upwards to a considerable height, and showing the jagged
outlines that have given the Diamond Mountains their name."[2] Here, they
suddenly encountered a group of monks out for an evening stroll, and after
some negotiations conducted by the interpreter Mr. Chiao using Chinese
characters scratched in the ground, the travelers were led to a monastery.
It was "situated up a short path at right angles to the road" and was "by no
means impressive," but here at least they had a bed for the night.

Singye-Sa, which was the first of the major temples they should have
encountered, was then in a state of some dilapidation. But even so, it con-
sisted of a substantial compound of buildings with an impressive ancient
stone pagoda standing at the top of a broad flight of steps. The reconstructed
temple—whose design is based on archaeological excavations and on photographs taken around the time of Kemp's visit—has eight main buildings
including a Hall of Blessings, a Hall of Buddha's Disciples, an inner sanctum,
and monks' dormitories, all built with walls of apricot-colored plaster and
wide, gray roofs whose eaves are ornately carved and decorated.[3] Singye-Sa
is also only a mile from the village of Onjong-ri, which in 1910 contained a
Japanese inn.

None of this fits Kemp's description of the small and isolated place where
they found lodging, and whose monks seemed utterly unaccustomed to foreigners and both prurient and slightly hostile toward their visitors.

As Kemp and her companions cooked and ate a meal, their hosts watched
unrelentingly, one of them scratching a note to Mr. Chiao to ask if they were
"Jesus missionaries." Kemp and MacDougall felt uncomfortable under this
intrusive male gaze and slept with Mr. Chiao lying on the verandah outside
as a guard, their dreams intermittently broken by the unfamiliar sounds of
frogs croaking in the forest and the repeated beatings of the fish gong that
called the monks to prayer. Further discussion conducted in Chinese script
yielded the information that they were forty miles away from the temple they
particularly hoped to visit—which must surely have been the region's most
famous building, the Temple of Eternal Peace. So, abandoning their original
plans, early the following morning they retraced their steps down the valley
and headed up a precipitous ravine that, they hoped, would take them in the
direction of the main road to Seoul.

Either the monks were playing a malicious practical joke or the travelers
were a long way off course indeed. Forty miles from the Temple of Eternal
Peace would place them among the very northernmost of the mountains, far
from the area described in such luminous terms by earlier visitors like Isabella

Bird, and forty miles were too much even for the indefatigable Emily Kemp. Ships, trains, and further travel plans awaited them. Abandoning efforts to see the region's Buddhist treasures, they had to be content with exploring the natural splendors of the Diamond Mountains.

Kemp was not one to be disheartened by such minor setbacks. As they toiled up the rugged ravine in gathering cloud, she admired the "fascinating flowers"—the glades filled with irises, cyclamens, saxifrage, and white crocuses; the green frogs, pheasants, and chipmunks that appeared fleetingly among the foliage; and the brief glimpses of breathtaking views to be caught now and then when they glanced back toward the sea behind them. Unknown birds called from the depths of the forest, and "the treasures of the woods seemed limitless."[4] Fronds of fern were unfurling beside the rocky path. "A babbling brook kept us in constant temptation as our path crossed and re-crossed it, and before we reached the top we passed through more than one drift of snow."[5] Occasionally, shafts of sunlight would break through the cloud, illuminating the pinnacles of rock impossibly high above.

She and her companions marched for seven hours before stopping, by which time squalls of rain were blowing across the mountains as a storm gathered on the horizon. They were many miles from any other human beings, on an uncertain track through a landscape of cliffs and chasms, without reliable guides or map. Perhaps it was their Korean companions' sense of direction or perhaps it was just sheer luck that finally brought them without serious accident to the far side of the mountain range and to a village at the foot of a valley, where they found an encampment of Japanese officers occupying the best inn. They arrived just before the storm broke.

A Place of Meditation

The next day, the soldiers gave Kemp's party directions to an "execrable road" that took them over further mountain ridges westward and southward, in the direction of the Seoul highroad. Along the way they glimpsed multitudes of butterflies and glorious views, and passed a series of little water mills set by streams that gushed down the slopes. But now they were heading away from the heartland of the mountain range without having seen the most ancient and beautiful of its monasteries. They trudged on until it grew dark and the moon appeared, and suddenly out of the darkness a couple of men strode past, silently carrying between them the white bundle of a corpse wrapped in a winding sheet.

"Our own party had fallen silent," wrote Kemp, "for we were tired and disappointed; the gloom prevented us from seeing the steepness of some of the descents, but we clung desperately to our steeds, for we were too weary to walk."[6]

In this uncharacteristically subdued mood, Kemp and her companions finally reached the road to Seoul. From that city they would catch a steamer to the Manchurian port of Dalian, to pick up the Iron Silk Road for the journey back to Europe via Russian Turkestan.

Yet, despite the hardships and the narrowly missed opportunities, at the end of her journey, in the travel account that she dedicated to her three surviving sisters, Kemp recalled it all in a positive light. Although they had not found the people they met on route particularly friendly, they had encountered none of the brigands and "Japanese vagrants" that she had been warned of and instead experienced a "general air of comfort."[7] She was, after all, one of the pioneers of travel by westerners to the Diamond Mountains, having charted a path and ridden through stretches of the range that perhaps no other European had seen before, and as a pioneer she was able to offer advice to those who would follow in her footsteps. She recommended the travelers of the future to visit the mountains in May or autumn and above all to go with reliable Korean guides who knew the route. In defense of the long-suffering Mr. Chiao, however, she added that his presence had been invaluable in lending prestige to their traveling party, "for the Koreans hold the Chinese in great respect."[8]

Kemp never visited Korea again, though she made several more journeys through China. During the First World War she worked in military hospitals in Paris,[9] and once the war was over, she returned to travel and writing, observing Japan's growing domination over northeastern China and the massive social changes that were transforming the face of China itself. "If Japan and China became friends and had a just settlement of their mutual claims," she wrote in the early 1920s, "there would be an unexampled area of prosperity before both countries."[10]

Kemp continued to publish well into her seventies and "kept up, down to her last days, the liveliest interest in China's life and destiny. She seemed to know and be in touch with not only all the important Chinese people who came to England, but every humblest Chinese student."[11] The substantial wealth she had inherited from the family textile mills was used to support charities and to buy an art collection bequeathed, after her death on Christmas Day 1939, to the Ashmolean Museum in Oxford.[12] This includes a number of rare and precious works, including Italian and Flemish paintings, as well as a fine portrait of Kemp by her friend and teacher, the French engraver Alphonse Legros. But perhaps the most striking piece in the collection is another work by Legros: an ink drawing on the theme of "death and the maiden." It shows a full-figured and slightly languid young woman locked in the disturbingly erotic embrace of a grinning skeleton.[13] I wonder with what emotions Kemp hung this on her wall and wonder, too, how much I really know about our ghostly traveling companion after all.

Kemp's most generous and ambitious gift, though, was the building of a chapel in the grounds of her old college at Oxford University, for which she paid anonymously. The present was a somewhat contentious one. The college authorities seemed uncertain what to do with the chapel—afraid of stirring up religious passions in an Oxford where sectarianism was rife. The controversy, as one historian has recently observed, enhanced the college's reputation as a place of "independent women who had no fear of voicing their opinions."[14]

The chapel still stands today, and it is an appropriate memorial: a plain stone structure with white arched interior. It is attached to no particular denomination, has no attendant clergymen, and serves, as Kemp intended, simply as a place for "meditation, prayer and other spiritual exercises." Its focus on simple religious fundamentals is something that Kemp (according to one of those who knew her) had learnt through her "contacts with the peoples of the Far East, both the Christian converts and the spiritual men and women of other religions, Buddhist, Taoist and the rest."[15]

The inscription, which Kemp asked to be placed over the door of the chapel, reads, "Mine House shall be Called a House of Prayer for all Peoples."[16] The college dean recorded, after Kemp's death, that she had planned the chapel as a symbol of "universal brotherhood"[17]: Remembering Kemp's life, we might add "and sisterhood."

A Short Walk in the Diamond Mountains

Beyond Tongchon, our road curves inland, passing little rows of cottages whose white plaster exteriors are decorated with friezes of apples and persimmons painted above their doorways. Driving parallel to the coast, we cross a wide plain where reeds and grasses grow tall and tangled in the sandy soil. To the south, the jagged peaks of the Diamond Mountains rise against the spring sky. The road starts to climb, and Mr. Kim swings the Toyota with practiced ease round a series of hairpin bends. Now and again we plunge into long tunnels. Like all North Korean tunnels, these are utterly unlit, but our headlights pick out the occasional shapes of pedestrians, moving like ghosts through their darkness. It is miles since we last passed a house, and yet the figures still appear: a woman in trim pleated skirt and brocade jacket, pushing her bicycle up the mountain road, and a couple with a tiny baby cradled in a crimson velvet baby carrier. Where have they come from? Where are they going?

We stop on a high pass where the mountains slope away on one side in the direction of the sea, and on the other, a small footpath climbs toward a peak. At the bottom of the path stand two plaster statues of deer: North Korean cousins of Walt Disney's Bambi. Nearby, workmen in their olive-brown outfits are eating a picnic lunch. Mr. Kim has done this trip many times before and stays behind to watch the car. Ms. Ri is wearing elegant pearl-pink high-heeled shoes, entirely unsuitable for mountain walks. So Mr. Ryu, Sandy, and I alone set off up the path to the mountains.

The pathway is steep and paved with rough blocks of granite. The only sounds are birds and the constant murmur of the little stream that cascades through rocks nearby. The waters of streams and rivers of this region are crystalline and, perhaps because of some element in the earth, tinged with a pale glassy green. We hear a cuckoo and then, far away, the harsh cry of a pheasant. This mountain slope is not forested but covered with the soft green of small saplings. A few dark pines stand sentinel on the ridges above. Between them rise spires of bare rock.

Near the top of the path we come upon a pool of gray-green water, suspended in a hollow below the summit of the mountain, with a sheer cliff rising behind. The granite of the rock-face is crevassed and folded by eons of wind and rain, and flowering white saxifrage clings to its cracks like drifts of snow. Seen at close hand, the color of the rock is extraordinary, merging from ashen blue to deep coppery gold. I remember the eighth-century Chinese monk Chengguan: "Although it is not wholly made of gold, up, down, all around, and when you go into the mountain's precincts it is all gold in the midsts of the sands of the flowing waters." The sand along the edge of the pool is scattered with shells—remnants of picnics that visitors from the fishing villages far below have brought with them on walks through the mountains.

We climb to the summit. It is only a short walk. Having come this far, we long to go further—to walk for hours and days through the mountains and ravines that stretch out before us—but our guides are in control. To the east, brown deforested mountain slopes descend toward the hazily shining sea. To the west and south, the mesmeric mountain range draws the gaze deeper and deeper amongst its pinnacles and into its labyrinth of gorges.

The great Korean artist Jeong Seon captured this landscape three hundred years ago in a style that came to be known as "true-view" painting. But Jeong Seon's paintings, although meticulously accurate and filled with atmosphere, show a landscape that no human eye has ever seen—the mountains as contemplated from a celestial vantage point. Jeong Seon's eye spreads out the entire range to human gaze—each peak, each valley and waterfall, and each monastery and hermitage half concealed behind cliffs and overhanging trees.

Looking out over the landscape before us, I can almost imagine that I am seeing it from Jeong Seon's transcendent perspective. The mountains are intricately folded and scored by water courses and ravines. In places they are thick with forest. Elsewhere, the bare rock rises in menhirs, obelisks, and cairns. The longer you gaze, the more shapes emerge: rocks like human faces, like gargoyles, like gaping mouths.

Yet here, too, as always (it seems) in the story of this divided land, the real goal remains tantalizingly close but just out of reach.

That ridge on the pale horizon of our vision must surely be the range over which Kemp and her companions struggled on their slow and stumbling pack ponies. In the valley beyond, just out of sight, Singye-Sa rises reborn and glowing with its freshly painted colors, and to the east stands the South Korean tourist resort behind its green plastic fencing: its four-star hotel, Familymart, souvenir shops, and concrete circus dome now abandoned, empty, and blown by the wind of the mountains. Further south—further still beyond our gaze—a line of stones marks the site of the vanished Temple of Eternal Peace. Somewhere amongst the invisible folds of hills, the three giant Buddhas still gaze impassively from the rock-face at the passing of ages, the breeze still sways the gong that hangs outside the surviving temple of Pyohun-Sa, and the crumbling tiny Podok Hermitage clings tenaciously to its cliff, as it has done for centuries.

We sit down on a patch of worn rock just below the peak to catch our breaths.

Sandy is a keen recorder player and carries a descant recorder with her wherever she goes. To Mr. Ryu's astonishment, she now extracts the recorder from her backpack and plays the bittersweet lilt of a Scottish highland song.

We are beginning to worry about Ms. Ri and Mr. Kim, waiting patiently at the bottom of the path, but Mr. Ryu smiles calmly. "They can wait a little longer," he says.

In the peace of the mountains, away from the presence of his colleagues, he begins to reminisce about his mother, the mother whose family was

Mountain pool, Diamond Mountains (S. Morris)

shattered by the Korean War, whose adulthood was ruled by the rigors of dedication to the Juche dream and who is growing old in the society through which we have just traveled.

"My mother," Mr. Ryu explains, "always says, 'you only ever have one piece of good luck in life. The important thing is to know your good luck when it happens. Most people let luck just come and go, never even see it.' That's what my mother tells me. And then she always says, 'my one good luck was to meet your father.'"

Mr. Ryu's good luck, it seems, was to meet his wife.

He was a soldier in the People's Army when the matchmaker first introduced them, but, he says, "when my wife saw me at first meeting, she thought I looked too thin and weak, not a proper soldier at all." Mr. Ryu laughs ruefully, shifting his thin frame into a more comfortable position on the rock. "But the matchmaker didn't tell me that there was this problem," he continues,

> so then we have one more meeting, but when I want to meet her a third time, she didn't come. I go to her house to look for her, and her sister comes to the door and says, "she doesn't want to see you." I was angry, very angry. But then,

suddenly the next day, my wife (well, she wasn't my wife then, of course), she telephones me. I scold her, but then she starts to talk and talk. She tells me how her parents are ill and how she is looking after her mother every day. And suddenly we understand each other, and . . .

Here Mr. Ryu pauses, rummaging though his mental store of English phrases in search of the correct expression, "and then," he says, "I lose my heart."

Mr. Ryu falls silent. We sit for a while, listening to the frogs croak in the shallows of the pool. To the south, where these mountains end, the barbed wire still stretches along the world's most militarized frontier. In the land beneath these mountains, the war has never ended. North Korea and Northeast Asia stand uneasily on the brink of epochal transformations. Below, the black Toyota four-wheel drive is waiting to take us back to Pyongyang. But for now it can wait.

We sit and watch the ripples chase each other across the waters, as the wind from the sea silently continues its endless shaping of the Diamond Mountains.

Notes

1. See Tokuda Tomojirō, *Tenka no Zekkei—Kongō-San* (Wonsan, North Korea: Tokuda Shashinkan, 1915); see also Kan'ichi Asakawa, *The Russo-Japanese Conflict: Its Causes and Issues* (New York: Houghton Mifflin, 1904), 46.

2. E. G. Kemp, *Face of Manchuria, Korea and Russian Turkestan* (New York: Duffield, 1911), 120.

3. Daehan Bulgyo Jogyejong Chongmuwon Sahwibu-Munhwabu, ed., *Geumgangsan Singyesa Bukwon Bulsa Baekseo* (Seoul: Daehan Bulgyo Jogyejong Chongmuwon, 2009).

4. Kemp, *Face of Manchuria, Korea and Russian Turkestan*, 123.

5. Kemp, *Face of Manchuria, Korea and Russian Turkestan*, 123.

6. Kemp, *Face of Manchuria, Korea and Russian Turkestan*, 126.

7. Kemp, *Face of Manchuria, Korea and Russian Turkestan*, 132.

8. Kemp, *Face of Manchuria, Korea and Russian Turkestan*, 133.

9. E. G. Kemp, *Reminiscences of a Sister: S. Florence Edwards, of Taiyuanfu* (London: Carey Press, 1919), 93.

10. E. G. Kemp, *Chinese Mettle* (London: Hodder and Stoughton, 1921), 220.

11. Helen Darbishire, "In Memoriam: Emily Georgiana Kemp," in *Somerville College Chapel Addresses and Other Papers*, 10–13 (London: Headley Brothers, 1962), 11.

12. See Darbishire, "In Memoriam: Emily Georgiana Kemp."

13. Alphonse Legros (1837–1911), "Death Embracing a Maiden," graphite with pen and pale brown ink, held in the Ashmolean Museum, Oxford.

14. Judy G. Batson, *Her Oxford* (Nashville: Vanderbilt University Press, 2008), 212.

15. Darbishire, "In Memoriam: Emily Georgiana Kemp," 12.

16. See Darbishire, "In Memoriam: Emily Georgiana Kemp," 12.

17. Vera Brittain, *The Women at Oxford: A Fragment of History* (London: Macmillan, 1960), 186–87.

Selected Bibliography

Armstrong, Charles K. *The Koreans*. London: Routledge, 2007.

Austin, Alvyn. *China's Millions: The China Inland Mission and Late Qing Society, 1832–1905*. Grand Rapids, Mich.: Eerdmans, 2007.

Bird Bishop, Isabella. *Korea and Her Neighbours*. New York: Fleming H. Revell, 1898.

Curzon, George. *Problems of the Far East*. London: Longmans Green, 1894.

Duus, Peter. *The Abacus and the Sword: The Japanese Penetration of Korea 1895–1910*. Berkeley: University of California Press, 1995.

Grayson, James Huntley. *Korea: A Religious History*. Rev. ed. London: Routledge Curzon, 2002.

Kemp, E. G. *Chinese Mettle*. London: Hodder and Stoughton, 1921.

———. *The Face of China: Travels in East, North, Central and Western China*. London: Chatto and Windus, 1909.

———. *The Face of Manchuria, Korea and Russian Turkestan*. New York: Duffield, 1911.

———. *Reminiscences of a Sister: S. Florence Edwards, of Taiyuanfu*. London: Carey Press, 1919.

———. *Wanderings in Chinese Turkestan*. London: Wightman, 1914.

Palais, James. *Politics and Policy in Traditional Korea*. Cambridge, Mass.: Harvard University Asia Center, 1991.

Park, Chris C. *Sacred Worlds: An Introduction to Geography and Religion*. London: Routledge, 1994.

Pratt, J. B. *The Pilgrimage of Buddhism and a Buddhist Pilgrimage*. New York: Macmillan, 1928.

Pratt, Keith. *Everlasting Flower: A History of Korea*. London: Reaktion Books, 2007.

Robinson, Jane. *Wayward Women: A Guide to Women Travelers.* Oxford: Oxford University Press, 1994.

Springer, Chris. *Pyongyang: The Hidden History of the North Korean Capital.* Budapest: Entente, 2003.

Uden, Martin, ed. *Times Past in Korea: An Illustrated Collection of Encounters, Events, Customs and Daily Life Recorded by Foreign Visitors.* London: Korea Library, 2003.

Weber, Norbert. *In den Diamantbergen Koreas.* Oberbayern, Germany: Missionverlag St. Ottilen, 1927.

Yamamuro, Shin'ichi. *Manchuria under Japanese Dominion.* Translated by Ezra Fogel. Philadelphia: University of Pennsylvania Press, 2006.

Yosano, Akiko. *Travels in Manchuria and Mongolia.* Translated by Joshua A. Fogel. New York: Columbia University Press, 2001.

About the Author

Tessa Morris-Suzuki was born in England and lived and worked in Japan before emigrating to Australia in 1981. She is currently professor of Japanese history in the College of Asia and the Pacific at the Australian National University, where her research focuses on Japan's frontiers and minority communities and on questions of historical memory in East Asia. Her previous books include *Re-Inventing Japan: Time, Space, Nation* (1998), *Exodus to North Korea: Shadows from Japan's Cold War* (2007), and *Borderline Japan: Foreigners and Frontier Controls in the Postwar Era* (2010).